INVIOLABLE VOICE:
HISTORY AND TWENTIETH-CENTURY POETRY

STAN SMITH

INVIOLABLE VOICE

HISTORY AND TWENTIETH-CENTURY POETRY

GILL AND MACMILLAN
HUMANITIES PRESS

First published 1982 by
Gill and Macmillan Ltd
Goldenbridge
Dublin 8
with associated companies in
London, New York, Delhi, Hong Kong,
Johannesburg, Lagos, Melbourne,
Singapore, Tokyo

7171 1200 4

Published in 1982 in USA and Canada by
Humanities Press Inc.
Atlantic Highlands, New Jersey 07716
ISBN 0–391–02580–5

Origination by A.D.C., 56 Pembroke Road, Ballsbridge, Dublin 4.
Printed and bound in Great Britain by
Biddles Ltd., Guildford and King's Lynn

130215

For Carol, Philip and Stephen
Et O ces voix d'enfants, chantant dans la coupole!

Contents

Acknowledgments

I have discussed the ideas in this book with many people over the years. But I should like to give especial thanks here to Peter Widdowson, that indefatigable entrepreneur, who first suggested the book, and to Gill and Macmillan for encouraging me to write it. Moira Anthony was an invaluable help in typing two lengthy chapters, when energy flagged and time pressed. Earlier versions of parts of some chapters have appeared in *Critical Quarterly, Literature and History, The Literary Review,* and *New Blackfriars,* and I should like to thank the editors of those journals; as, too, the University of Dundee for assistance in pursuing the research of which this is the fruit.

Two people who have read the whole text, and made highly practical and intelligent contributions to its final shape, but are in no way responsible for its inevitable mistakes or partisan tone, are R. J. C. Watt and Jennifer Birkett. The latter has my especial thanks, for patience beyond the call of any duty. To them I say, 'Jug jug'.

Finally, author and publishers thank the following for their permission to quote copyright material:
George Allen & Unwin for extracts from poems by Brian Patten from his *The Irrelevant Song* and *Grave Gossip;* the Executors of the Estate of C. Day Lewis, Jonathan Cape Ltd and the Hogarth Press for an excerpt from C. Day Lewis, 'In me Two Worlds', *Collected Poems 1954;* The Society of Authors as the literary representative of the Estate of A. E. Housman, and Jonathan Cape Ltd, publishers of A. E. Housman's *Collected Poems,* for an excerpt from 'Tell me not here, it needs not saying'; Carcanet Press Ltd for an excerpt from John Cornford 'Full Moon at Tierz', *Understand the Weapon, Understand the Wound;* Chatto & Windus Ltd for excerpts from poems by D. J. Enright from his *Daughters of Earth, Unlawful Assembly, Some Men are Brothers* and *Sad Ires;* Andre Deutsch Ltd for an excerpt from Geoffrey Hill, *King Log.* Reprinted by

1

Inviolable Voice: The Poem in History

Above the antique mantel was displayed
As though a window gave upon the sylvan scene
The change of Philomel, by the barbarous king
So rudely forced; yet there the nightingale
Filled all the desert with inviolable voice
And still she cried, and still the world pursues,
'Jug Jug' to dirty ears. (T. S. Eliot, *The Waste Land*)

Most poetry seems to function at a level remote from history, where a dissociated mind confronts a landscape innocent of social meaning. This illusion is one of the most powerful enchantments poetry weaves. But there is no such thing as an 'innocent' poem. All poetry, at its deepest levels, is structured by the precise historical experience from which it emerged, those conjunctures in which its author was formed, came to consciousness, and found a voice. A writer is always the creature of circumstance: a particular set of social relations, of class, family, sex and generation, offer their own cultural, ideological and emotional forms, which he or she acquires even before it has become a matter of personal choice, of acceptance or rejection. Language itself is the siren voice that tempts us into identity, makes us this or that particular person. And language embeds everywhere the history which we come to acknowledge as our own, for good or ill. The language and literary conventions the poet inherits likewise carry with them prejudices and pre-emptions, a history infolded in every intricacy and turn of style.

Some of the finest poetry written in this century has come out of the struggle against such determining forces, out of the stubborn resistance of the self to that which its experience has made it. For Sylvia Plath, for example, identity itself is the primary historical datum: the self is a secretion of history, and therefore not initially 'my' self at all, but the voice of its antecedents, its progenitors, a 'mouthpiece of the dead'. But even when identity is not so radically called into question, there is no denying the enormity of this insight, in the twentieth century. We are all inventions of history, whether the marionettes of Hardy's 'Immanent Will', or the dancing bear, the chattering ape of Eliot's 'Portrait of a Lady', unable to break out of the spirit's sweaty prison. For if the poem is the creature of a moment – that moment of its inception which may last a week, a year, or a lifetime – the life from which it arises is itself a historical creation, a being *inscribed* – and the writing metaphor is a deliberate and recurrent one in this book – by all the events that make it man, or woman.

At times, such historical predisposing of the text is no more than a rumour, a stray breeze of nuance, a whiff of larger events that take place offstage, precisely where the poem isn't. Sometimes, like the messenger in a Greek tragedy, a brief flurry of interruption can remind us what is going on out there, in that less articulately ordered world. The words arrange, re-arrange, and in so doing dissemble, the ragged incoherence of a history that is being lived in all its open-ended, unpredictable bluster *somewhere else*. A man may be digging a hole, to bury, for some symbolic and unspecified reason, two clay pipes in the earth: a harmless, pastoral activity. But it is 1915; the fields of Flanders are riddled with trenches, in a war which has already killed hundreds of thousands of the men who dug them. The man who writes is himself to die, within two years, in that ravaged No-Man's-Land. The poem is called 'Digging', the poet Edward Thomas:

> What matter makes my spade for tears or mirth,
> Letting down two clay pipes into the earth?
> The one I smoked, the other a soldier
> Of Blenheim, Ramillies, and Malplaquet
> Perhaps. The dead man's immortality
> Lies represented lightly with my own,
> A yard or two nearer the living air
> Than bones of ancients who, amazed to see

Almighty God erect the mastodon,
Once laughed, or wept, in this same light of day.

Opening and closing lines of the poem seal off history within the circular, self-enclosing movement of the poem. And yet that history remains open to the future. The last line looks back to a past, the first line to a future generation, who may be linked in 'tears or mirth' by these relics of two men themselves two centuries apart. The light of day is the same for all, the days different. The landscape is the same, and yet subtly altered. The difference lies in that 'yard or two' of subsequent earth which contains the bones of mastodon, ancients, and eighteenth-century soldier, and is shortly to hold Thomas's own. The concern with 'immortality' takes on a more urgent and immediate power. 'Represented lightly' by the two clay pipes, it seems to collapse two centuries of English history into co-presence, linking the current war with the continental campaigns of the Duke of Marlborough (on whom Thomas published a monograph in 1915). So the poem too is a 'representation' of this complex overlaying of histories. Three sentences which can be read in half a minute compact within their brief space millennia of human time. As T. S. Eliot wrote in 'Tradition and the Individual Talent' four years later, if the dead are remote from us because we know so much more than they did, 'they are that which we know'.

When a man or woman confronts a landscape, or considers an individual's death in battle, this is not an encounter with unchanging metaphysical categories, 'Nature', 'War', etc., but a response, in a particular cultural and historical nexus, to an experience shaped and transformed by the network of social relationships of which it is the centre. 'War' was a different concept to the man who fell at Troy, at Blenheim, or at Arras, though his death was as absolute. 'Nature' meant something different to those ancients and to Thomas, who can note, shrewdly enough, elsewhere that in a capitalist economy 'nature' means 'land' and 'land' means 'money': 'A mile of it is worth a guinea', says the country girl in his 'Up in the Wind'. Thomas's nature has been redefined by the birth of Darwinism and the death of God, transformed by the developing capacity of man to desecrate or remould it, by war or labour or sheer caprice. It is also – and it's a note which will recur throughout this book – transfigured with meanings, meanings which change as the historic experience of men changes.

A similar historical precision informs the poem which opens Seamus Heaney's first volume, *Death of a Naturalist* (1966), which in a deliberate nod of acknowledgment to Thomas, is also called 'Digging'. Heaney's poem in part celebrates a personal history, reaching back, in a regressive movement, from his father digging potatoes outside the window, to his grandfather, cutting turf on Toner's bog, and, by implication, beyond this, to the anonymous generations of his ancestors. But it also looks forward, into the poet's own future, as if making some covenant which binds together all these many moments. The physical act of digging, in presence and in memory, cuts through other, 'living roots', in the poet's head. As he was to make clear in subsequent poems, these are not merely the roots of a historic, Northern Irish culture, but the roots of language itself, etymological and grammatical roots. The poem concludes in what, like Thomas's poem, seems to be a return to its opening, with the realisation that there is both disjunction and continuity in the poet's relation with his past, his native tradition:

> But I've no spade to follow men like them.
> Between my finger and my thumb
> The squat pen rests.
> I'll dig with it.

This, however, is not simply a rounding in closure which takes us back to the beginning. For in omitting a significant and highly charged image from the opening lines, the conclusion suppresses certain negative possibilities which have lain dormant throughout the poem, which also relate to the particular, and bloody, history of this Northern Irish countryside. The poet is not just a creator, any more than his peasant progenitors. He is also a destroyer, an uprooter, and destruction, as in Thomas's poem with its undertones of war, may be something he not only predicts but in some way invokes, as part of his cultural mission. The poem actually begins:

> Between my finger and my thumb
> The squat pen rests; snug as a gun.

Written before the resurgence of the troubles in Ulster in the late sixties, the poem nevertheless inscribes in its very ambivalences a premonition of that irruption, a possibility reiterated in all its language of sharp, cutting edges slicing into soggy peat. For Heaney, in fact, in a volume such as *North* (1975), the relationship of poetry with its historic culture is essentially one of *complicity*.

Heaney's poem evokes Thomas's as part of its *literary* ancestry. The literary tradition cannot simply be dissolved back into the circumstantial details of each poem's individual genesis, so that every poem stands, naked and original, before the brute facts of the historical context which gave it birth. Nevertheless, there are real and pressing reasons why, using the pastoral mode to handle the contradictions of his own political situation, Heaney should turn to the precedent offered by Thomas's work. As I shall argue in chapter three, Thomas's poetry stands at a watershed in English culture, and defines the terms within which subsequent crises within that historical experience came to be grasped. The particular reworking of the literary tradition effected by every text, its variations of language, allusion, theme, can be understood only if that text is seen, not as a timeless, seamless unity, but as the recombination of different and often contradictory discourses, in a moment of real time which is the overall determining context of their coming together. Thomas's shadowed tranquillity, with all its rumours of war, its tense and threatened sensitivity, made it an appropriate precedent for poets as diverse as Auden and Heaney, for it offered a convenient model, suitably generalised, for a crisis that was to recur at the heart of British culture through several subsequent decades.

The most famous and authoritative statement of the relationship between text and context, the synchronic moment of the poem and the diachronic momentum of a cultural tradition, is that first set out by T. S. Eliot in a two-part essay in *The Egoist* in 1919. Written in the after-echo of that war to end all wars in which so many poets died and the European inheritance was so profoundly questioned, 'Tradition and the Individual Talent' shows few direct signs of the history which immediately precedes it. Rather it is in its omissions, and in the insistent urgency with which it devalues the very concept of history, that the strains of its age are disclosed.

Eliot speaks of poetry as 'not the expression of personality, but an escape from personality', in which the poem becomes 'an expression of *significant* emotion, emotion which has its life in the poem and not in the history of the poet'. 'Significant' here means primarily 'signifying', composed of signs – words, images, rhythms – which stimulate a response in the reader. To achieve this significant form, the poet must have the 'historical sense', which

> involves a perception, not only of the pastness of the past, but of its presence; the historical sense compels a man to write not merely with his own generation in his bones, but with a feeling that the whole of literature from Homer and within it the whole of the literature of his own country has a simultaneous existence and composes a simultaneous order. The historical sense, which is a sense of the timeless as well as of the temporal and of the timeless and of the temporal together, is what makes a writer traditional. And it is at the same time what makes a writer most acutely conscious of his place in time, of his contemporaneity.

It is a classic formulation, but in its very lucidity it is not so much an assertion of the importance of history, as of its cancellation. Neither the 'pastness' of tradition nor its 'contemporaneity' is what really concerns Eliot. 'Tradition' in fact is a substitute for the concept of 'history', for the interpenetration of past and present of which Eliot speaks takes place in a *timeless* moment, in a cerebral, *aesthetic* space which is ultimately not answerable to history at all. Thus a new poet can only be valued when 'set . . . , for contrast and comparison, among the dead'; and this is 'a principle of aesthetic, not merely historical criticism'. (The force of that 'merely' should be felt.) When a new work of art is created it simultaneously changes all the works of art which preceded it, because, as he suggests later, they do not *really* precede it: 'poetry [is] a living whole of all the poetry that has ever been written.' Eliot's formulation of this simultaneity, this *synchronicity,* of tradition, is clear and emphatic:

> The existing monuments form an ideal order among themselves, which is modified by the introduction of the new (the really new) work of art among them. The existing order is complete before the new work arrives; for order to persist after the supervention of novelty, the *whole* existing order must be, if ever so slightly, altered; and so the relations, proportions, values of each work of art toward the whole are readjusted; and this is conformity between the old and the new.

Anyone who has approved 'this idea of order', he says, will see that the past can be altered by the present as much as the present is 'directed' by the past. This co-presence takes place, not just in the mind of the individual talent, but in 'the mind of Europe – the mind of his own country – a mind which he learns in time to be much more important than his own private mind'. The individual talent has access to it only by 'a continual self-sacrifice, a continual extinction of personality' which separates completely 'the man who suffers and the mind which creates'.

There are certain insistences in this account of the relation of poetry to history, concentrated in that word 'order'. 'Order' is not a simple and unitary concept, but can be dissolved into social, political and aesthetic moments. It is a word which recurs in Eliot's thought, as in that of Ezra Pound and Wallace Stevens, and usually with this triple aspect. What is most striking about Eliot's account here, though, is its moderation, its caution. All the emphasis is on the *slightness* of the alterations effected in 'the existing order'. In a review of Harriet Monroe's anthology, *The New Poetry,* in *The Egoist* two years earlier, he had indeed spoken ironically of a generational revolt against rhetoric, led 'to wonder whether a whole generation can arise together and insurrect' in a 'spontaneous revolution'. In July 1919, just two months before the first part of 'Tradition and the Individual Talent' appeared, he

returned to the theme in *The Egoist,* speaking of that change in
a poet's work that comes from encounter with the dead and
leaves him 'changed, metamorphosed almost, within a few
weeks even, from a bundle of secondhand sentiments into a
person'. This, he says, is not a matter of passive influence or
borrowing: 'we have not borrowed, we have been quickened,
and we become bearers of a tradition'. Contemporary poetry
is 'deficient in tradition': 'No dead voices speak through the
living voice; no reincarnation, no re-creation'.

What happens to the concept of the individual talent in
Eliot's theory is very curious. On the one hand, the poet is
virtually abolished as a separate being, becoming merely a
'bearer of tradition'. On the other hand, once 'the mind which
creates' is separated off from 'the man who suffers' – the real,
living person – that mind expands to become the absolute
circumference within which 'tradition' is realised. When Eliot
speaks, famously, of the poet's mind as no more than a
'catalyst', 'inert, neutral and unchanged' in the
transformations it effects, the subjective side of the equation
seems to have disappeared almost entirely into the objective,
taken over by the dead voices of tradition which speak through
it. The poet deals with both 'emotions' and 'feelings'; but,
though both of these seem to be equally subjective, on analysis
they break down into *objective* phenomena. 'Emotions', Eliot
says, are 'evident in the situation', they derive from a pre-
existent subject-matter. 'Feelings', likewise, are already
contained in a pre-existent language, 'inhering for the writer
in particular words or images'. The poet's mind is no more
than a 'receptacle' for these feelings and emotions, seizing and
storing them up until the elements which can form a new
compound are together.

It is then that Eliot's volte-face occurs. For the 'intensity' of
a work derives not from the emotions inherent in the subject-
matter, or from the feelings inherent in words, but from 'the
intensity of the artistic process, the pressure . . . under which
the fusion takes place'. The mind of the poet, summarily
dismissed as no more than an inert catalyst, is equally
summarily restored, but as a new thing, a process of
production, which transforms both language and subject-
matter into a new, aesthetic whole. In that essay of 1921, 'The

Metaphysical Poets', Eliot elucidates this process further. The 'chaotic, irregular, fragmentary' experience of the ordinary man – falling in love, reading Spinoza, the noise of the typewriter, the smell of cooking – form new *wholes* in the *poet's* mind. This mind is no more than 'a more finely perfected medium in which special, or very varied, feelings are at liberty to enter into new combinations'. Including among the 'raw materials' of poetry the printed words of Spinoza and the sound of the typewriter which prints, Eliot collapses the gulf between the raw material of production, the process of production itself, and the finished product. It is a revealing telescoping of ideas.

Lurking within Eliot's formulae, and disclosed by this apparently casual set of examples, is a central problem for understanding the way a poem relates to history. A poem is produced at the intersection of two histories: the history of the formal possibilities available to the poet – conventions, themes, language – and the history of the individual as a particular expressive 'medium', a product of his own time and place. In standard terms, this intersection is seen as one in which determinate raw materials – the poet's experience, memories, ideas – are worked upon by determinate means – literary forms and conventions – to make the finished product, a poem. But there is not on the one hand raw material and on the other hand the means of production. The so-called 'raw material' is itself historically worked. It is not a chaotic jumble, but an articulated and coherent field. At the centre of it, in fact, lies that highly organised phenomenon, language. But language is also at the centre of the other half of the equation, the poetic *means* of production. Equally importantly, the poetic forms and linguistic possibilities the poet inherits are themselves not just pre-existing 'means' of production. They are also raw materials, which have to be worked in certain ways, to achieve this end-product.

Thus, what seems from one point of view to be 'raw materials' reveals itself from another point of view to be 'means of production', and vice versa. And language, as both producer and produced, lies at the heart of both, giving the lie to any aesthetics that assumes a division of 'form' and 'content'. Yet this division does correspond to something, and if we look at Eliot's poetry we can see what. For what traditional theory sees as the opposition of form and content, structuring language and unstructured 'experience', is really the opposition between a pre-existing and transcendent *subject* and the *content* of that subject's experience, the *object-world* of things and events which the subject appears to confront. It appears that the subject, the self, may take or leave this world, and in Eliot's poetry it is always on the point of renouncing, quitting or dismissing a world felt to be 'chaotic, irregular, fragmentary'. But the self never does make that final renunciation, because it cannot. The world it regards as in some ways exterior and alien to itself is in fact the most basic datum of its being: the self is made up of what it sees and experiences. For Eliot, this can only mean that the self is a passive victim of history, of its own imbrication in the material world. Unless, that is, the self can transcend this world by transforming it, into the new, *mental* construct, of the poem, religious faith or a 'tradition' which is beyond real, contingent history. But having made this separation of viewing frame and viewed world, in a desperate last-ditch attempt to rescue the self from history, he can only bridge the gulf between them by means of a magical, intuitive and inexplicable communion which takes place in those timeless moments, those intersections 'in and out of time', where the individual talent celebrates its possession by the dead voices of tradition. In this process, it might be noted, 'tradition' and the 'individual talent' become fused, one and the same thing on the same side of the equation. And what is set against them, as object to their subject, is *history,* the contingent and given world, capable of being extinguished and redeemed in 'the mind of Europe', the 'mind' of tradition.

Eliot's most famous pronouncement on the way in which the everyday world of history is transformed by the elite consciousness of the artist into a new, mental construct, is the essay on 'Ulysses, Order and Myth' in *The Dial* in November 1923. Joyce, he says, has been seen as as 'a prophet of chaos', releasing a 'flood of Dadaism' on the world. *Ulysses,* published the previous year, has been seen as 'an invitation to chaos, and an expression of feelings which are are perverse, partial, and a distortion of reality'. 'Classicism', set against 'chaos', does not mean 'selecting only mummified stuff from a museum', however. It involves an active reworking of experience, 'doing the best one can with the material at hand'. The term 'classicism' is misunderstood because it is applied both to literature and to 'the whole complex of interests and modes of behaviour and society of which literature is a part'. (It is a confusion, therefore, in the terms I have already employed, between the 'raw material' of art and the artistic transformation, or reworking, of that material.) This material includes 'the emotions and the feelings of the writer himself, which, for that writer, are simply material which he must accept'. *Ulysses* is not a traditional novel, because the age it expresses is too formless to allow for realism, and requires a 'stricter' formal principle. This Eliot identifies as 'the mythical method', a discipline Joyce imposes on the quotidian chaos by the use of a structuring analogy with the *Odyssey:*

> In using the myth, in manipulating a continuous parallel between contemporaneity and antiquity, Mr. Joyce is pursuing a method which others must pursue after him . . . . It is simply a way of controlling, of ordering, of giving a shape and a significance to the immense panorama of futility and anarchy which is contemporary history. Instead of narrative method, we may now use the mythical method. It is, I seriously believe, a step toward making the modern world possible for art, toward that order and form which Mr. Aldington so earnestly desires. And only those who have won their own discipline in secret and without aid, in a world which offers very little assistance to that end, can be of any use in furthering this advance.

It is in the context, then, of disdain for a history felt to be disorderly, meaningless and polluting (a history in which one's own 'emotions and feelings' are shamefully implicated) that Eliot's formal pronouncements must be read. The word 'order' here has more than literary reverberations. The author imposes 'significance' upon chaotic material, as the authoritarian and elite consciousness of the leader imposes order upon the 'anarchy' of society. Only a few years later, Eliot was to write thus of Machiavelli, in *For Lancelot Andrewes* (1928):

. . . . if you have to govern an alien and inferior people – a people inferior in the art of government – then you must use every means to make them contented and to persuade them that your government is to their interest. Liberty is good; but more important is order; and the maintenance of order justifies every means.

The 'mythical method' has an application in politics as well as aesthetics (Eliot's argument here is for the advantages of an established national church). Although Eliot never carried his concern for 'order' as far as his friend Pound, he did 'confess to a preference for fascism in practice' in *The Criterion* in July 1929, because 'the fascist form of unreason is less remote from my own than is that of the communists'. But, even in preferring his own Maurrasian position as 'a more reasonable form of unreason', the phrasing makes clear the correlation he assumes between political and and aesthetic concepts of order.

Ezra Pound, interestingly, saw Joyce's use of the analogy with the *Odyssey* as no more than an aspect of Joyce's 'medievalism'. For Eliot, it is fundamental, and provides a model for the construction of both a poem and a self. Most of the time, in reading *Ulysses,* one is not in fact aware of the analogy, or is merely distracted by it. Joyce's world is not an 'immense panorama of futility and anarchy', but a complex and highly organised civilisation, structured by all the systems of exchange – money, work, personal and public intercourse – which go to make up the modern city. The public institutions through which its characters pass are products of collaborative human effort – schools, libraries, museums, newspaper offices, hospitals, even pubs and brothels – which are the loci of continuing human intercourse. And there are other, less palpable but equally material institutions which shape these lives – of ritual, custom, religion, politics, all of which for Joyce are profoundly enmeshed in the omnipresent, engulfing, fecund element of language. No doubt such organising principles do not appeal to Eliot's fastidious aesthetic eye, but they are are nonetheless real and, what is more, they are not imposed by an exterior vision, but inhere in the 'content' of experience.

It is because they are part of the 'content' of Joyce's realism that they are also formally organising principles. The plot of the novel is determined by the street-plan of Dublin; encounters occur because two roads meet, because men of like disposition and employment converge on particular pubs or offices. Bloom and Dedalus are themselves introduced by the generic roles (of father and son) they struggle to fulfil or escape. There is, in Joyce's Dublin, no pre-existent 'anarchy' which the privileged consciousness of the artist organises into 'significance'. This world does not need to be made 'possible for art'. The order is *there,* in reality, and the artist's achievement is to render its surface multiplicity and variousness while suggesting its unity and interrelatedness. When there is a short in the electric circuit, trams come to a halt all over Joyce's Dublin. When Leopold Bloom turns on the tap, water flows all the way from Roundwood Reservoir.

Insisting that the real 'anarchy' of 'contemporary history' is ordered by 'the mythical method', Eliot is resisting the democratic openness and vitality of Joyce's world. For him, it remains essentially that despised 'lower middle-class society' he was to characterise with such distaste in *The Idea of a Christian Society* (1939): 'one in which the standard man legislated for and catered for, the man whose passions must be manipulated, whose prejudices must be humoured, whose tastes must be gratified, will be the lower middle-class man'. In Eliot's work, as so frequently in the English tradition, the self stands outside, over against, social reality, which is seen as a reified, exterior history. In Joyce, the scion of an oppressed nation, on the other hand, the self is inescapably involved in history. It may be a nightmare from which he is trying to awake; he may take refuge in silence, exile, cunning; but in flight he carries that history with him. As Stephen Dedalus says, tapping his brow with theatrical emphasis, 'in here it is I must kill the priest and the king'. Self and history are not antithetical poles. For Eliot in *The Waste Land,* however, setting his lands in order means stepping out of the bustle of history altogether, into some aristocratically disengaged position at the still centre of the turning world, in 'the heart of light, the silence'.

And yet there is, in that poem, the hint of a rather different relation between self, history and poetry, contained in that allusion to the story of Philomel, in 'A Game of Chess', which provides the epigraph to this chapter. There is a curious conjunction of references in 'Tradition and the Individual Talent' which helps to supply the connection. Insisting that 'the difference between art and the event is always absolute', Eliot there goes on to refer to Aeschylus' account of Agamemnon's murder, Dante's account of the last voyage of Ulysses, and Keats's 'nightingale' Ode. All three allusions recur, in one or another combination, in the 'Sweeney' poems and in *The Waste Land*. The two Greeks, of course, are encountered in literature as inextricably caught up in a bitter history of war, massacre and rapine, voyagers from and towards violence, both agents and victims of aggression. Keats's nightingale, on the other hand, sings apparently aloof from that world of contingent violence, a traditional figure of the innocence of poetry.

The note in *The Waste Land* which refers us to Ovid's story of Philomel is a salutary reminder of the real roots of the myth. Tereus, the Thracian warrior-king, wins Procne in marriage. Carrying her sister Philomel by sea from Athens, he ravishes her, imprisons her in a dark wood, and tears out her tongue to prevent her telling of her violation. Philomel sends her sister a tapestry which depicts the rape. Procne avenges her husband's crime by serving him their own dismembered son in a stew. Enraged by the discovery, Tereus pursues the sisters with his sword. By divine intervention they are all turned into birds: Philomel into the nightingale which ever after sings the name of her violator: 'Jug jug jug jug jug jug . . . . Tereu' *(Waste Land,* lines 204-6).

The Philomel theme always occurs in *The Waste Land* at moments of maximum linguistic disruption, where the order of the text is breaking down, before the onslaught of an anarchic reality, into fragmentary allusions, pub song, playground rhymes, and the spasmodic, ostensibly non-signifying noise of birds. Discursive speech, coherent syntax, repeatedly gives way to broken exclamatory utterances, where articulate human language degenerates towards the purely expressive iterations of the animal kingdom: '0000 that Shakespeherian rag', 'Ta ta. Goonight. Goonight', the 'Twit twit twit' of the swallow (Procne), 'Jug jug' of the nightingale, the 'Coco rico' of the cock, the 'Drip drop drip drop drop drop drop' of the hermit-thrush, the indeterminately animal or human 'Weialala leia' of 'The Fire Sermon', and the Sanskrit sacred chant which concludes the poem, 'Shantih shantih shantih'.

What makes the Philomel story central to all these moments, and to the larger pattern of the poem, is the process of metamorphosis itself. The pattern is produced in the lines which immediately follow the inset of Philomel in 'A Game of Chess':

> And other withered stumps of time
> Were told upon the walls; staring forms
> Leaned out, leaning, hushing the room enclosed.
> Footsteps shuffled on the stair.
> Under the firelight, under the brush, her hair
> Spread out in fiery points
> Glowed into words, then would be savagely still.

There are three moments to the Philomel story: violation, repression and translation: each occurs twice. Philomel is doubly violated, in that she is raped, and then prevented from telling of that rape by a brutal, silencing mutilation. Only when the story is translated into another medium – tapestry – can it be told. But this process is then repeated, in the dismembering of Tereus' son and its violent aftermath, the divine intervention which puts an end to the pursuit, and the further translation, in which the atrocities of history are transformed into the consequence-less utterances of song. In the passage above, a similar process occurs. The 'withered stumps' of a shrivelled history are translated into tales, 'told' silently on the walls. The threatening 'forms' which stare out 'hush' the rooms to a deeper silence. Most powerfully, the ferocious physical activity of the hair-brushing 'Glowed into words' – an odd metamorphosis – before lapsing into a savage stillness which is the cessation of both activity and speech; 'savagely' taking us back to the 'barbarous king' and forward to the 'rudely forc'd' virgin.

What is figured here is a complex relationship between history and its telling, between the material order of events and the equally material order of signs which translates into a new form and medium a repeated pattern of violation and transcendence. Experience, as Eliot was to say in *Four Quartets,* is reborn in another pattern, and the motif of resurrection which runs through *The Waste Land* is partly an image of this *aesthetic* rebirth. Inviolable, the voice of poetry everywhere speaks of the violation and repression in which it is founded. The tapestry enchants as it horrifies, the song returns, in its purity, to a pursuing world which retranslates it, back into the cruder, corrupter expectations of 'dirty ears'. Whether propaganda (the tapestry) or pure expression (the song), art retains this essential duplicity. It is in the very moment of rupture and violation, that moment in which history thrusts its barbarous attentions upon the subject, that the voice breaks into song. This perhaps explains why the original version of 'These fragments I have shored against my ruins' was 'These fragments I have spelt into my ruins'. Like the Sibyl's leaves and the Tarot pack, the work of art is not complete until the 'hypocrite lecteur' has brought his own mind to bear upon it, reading out the secret history contained within the inviolable voice. Only one privy to the enormity spoken of in that song could guess its secret. Understanding *The Waste Land,* understanding any work of art, Eliot's use of the Philomel myth suggests, becomes a confirmation of our own vicarious complicity in the tale it tells, a vindication of its representative power. *Complicity* is the guilty secret inscribed in the very heart of every poem.

In an interview in 1964, the modern poet Christopher Middleton spoke discontentedly of the state of contemporary poetry:

> English poetry right now is suffering from this very dangerous cleavage of poetry from history. There are very few English poets who seem to have any sense of history as something happening in me and you and all around us all the time; they've steered off into a parochial corner of the universe, and have lost the historical sense.

For Middleton, this 'historical sense', 'a sense of being involved in a social crisis', is intimately linked with 'an interest in the radical remaking of techniques'. The heritage of Modernism, for all its obscurantist tendencies, implicitly carries with its revolutionising of the forms of language a critical, tense engagement with the realities of contemporary history, even when, as in Eliot's work, it seems unequivocally committed to a flight from history. What Middleton diagnoses as a recent condition, the divorce of the everyday, the personal, from a larger, public 'history', is a recurrent pattern in English poetry in this century, for what are ultimately historical reasons, to do with the nature of the two great imperial powers which share that language. Even the poets of the thirties conform to Middleton's model. Indeed one of them, Stephen Spender, expressed it even more forcibly in his 1935 study of modern literature which took its cue from *The Waste Land, The Destructive Element:*

> In violent times the moral acts of the individual seem quite unrelated to the immense social changes going on all round him. He looks at civilisation and does not see his own quiet image reflected there at all, but the face of something fierce and threatening, that may destroy him. It may seem foreign and yet resemble his own face. He knows that if he is not to be destroyed, he must somehow connect his life again with this political life and influence it.

Spender catches the doubleness of this complicity and disengagement. The face in the mirror of civilisation is simultaneously foreign and like one's own face. The struggle to reconnect is simultaneously a struggle to overcome the disastrous consequences of a connection which *already exists,* 'that may destroy him'.

Significantly, for the English poets who toyed with revolutionary politics, the gap between self and history remained an absolute one. The gulf is a product, not of terror, but of relative security. Distance is inscribed in all those poems of the thirties which proclaimed their fierce commitment. Even John Cornford, who died in the Spanish Civil War, can only connect his individual life, in 'Full Moon at Tierz', with that larger movement through the intervention of an abstract and hortatory rhetoric. This is not to question the seriousness of commitment or the authenticity of response in the English poets of the thirties. Rather it is to acknowledge a pattern of experience which they share with their predecessors and successors, and which has its origins in the objective conditions in which the English intelligentsia came to consciousness, at the centre of an Empire, as George Orwell noted, still protected by the Royal Navy, and cushioned from global crisis by layers of imperial fat.

In *History and Class Consciousness* (1922), Georg Lukács spoke of bourgeois thought as a process which 'always, if not always consciously' acts as 'an apologia for the existing order of things or at least a proof of their immutability'. He cites Marx's comment on the ideological function of economic orthodoxy: 'Thus there has been history, but there is no longer any'. It is precisely this translation of the temporal and conjunctural into the timeless and absolute that a writer such as Eliot attempts in his poetry and in his aesthetic theory, a redaction acknowledged in the Introduction to *The Sacred Wood* (1920):

> It is part of the business of the critic to preserve tradition – where a good tradition exists. It is part of his business to see literature steadily and to see it whole; and this is eminently to see it *not* as consecrated by time, but to see it beyond time; to see the best work of our time and the best work of twenty-five hundred years ago with the same eyes.

Matthew Arnold, the *éminence grise* of this discussion, he suggests, tainted his criticism by too keen an interest in the passing and transitory world 'outside the literary preserve altogether, much of it political game untouched and inviolable by ideas'. In the Preface to the 1928 edition of the book, Eliot returned to the theme, mischievously asserting that poetry may be a 'superior amusement' but is certainly not 'the inculcation of morals, or the direction of politics' or an 'equivalent of religion', and is 'something quite different from a collection of psychological data about the minds of poets, or about the history of an epoch', though it certainly has something to do with these: 'we cannot say what'.

Lukács's own analyses of the ideology of literary production have given us some indication of what more can be said about the relations between poetry and history, aesthetics and politics. His analysis of the ways in which reality is characteristically perceived in modern literature provides us with terms which apply to all the writers considered here. At the centre of bourgeois ideology, Lukács argues, is that separation out of subject and object in which an hypostatised individual confronts a reified history, a social reality endowed with all the intractability and inertia of an object. The perception of reality, of history, as a changing ensemble of human activities is something which has to be fought for again and again, against the grain of such an ideology. That struggle mars, deforms, constrains, but also gives energy and vitality to the work of many of the poets I discuss in this book: it is the violation that provokes silence into articulate voice. In the distorted ideology imposed by bourgeois social relations, Lukács says:

> The objects of history appear as the objects of immutable, eternal laws of nature. History becomes fossilised in a *formalism* incapable of comprehending that the real nature of socio-historical institutions is that they consist of *relations between men*. On the contrary, men become estranged from this, . . . and cut off from it by an unbridgeable gulf. As Marx points out, people fail to realise 'that these definite social relations are just as much the products of men as linen, flax, etc.'
>
> In the second case, history is transformed into the irrational rule of blind forces which is embodied at best in the 'spirit of the people' or in 'great men'. It can therefore only be described pragmatically but it cannot be rationally understood. Its only possible organisation would be aesthetic, as if it were a work of art. Or else, as in the philosophy of history of the Kantians, it must be seen as the instrument, senseless in itself, by means of which timeless, suprahistorical, ethical principals are realised.

The outline here of the differing ways in which the historical process can be perceived is almost a programme for this study. There is, on the one hand, a tendency in American poetry to reduce history to an aesthetic construct, active or passive: Eliot's 'tradition', Pound's 'paideuma', Wallace Stevens's 'supreme fiction'. This collapses the gulf between subject and object by making all subjective: 'tradition' *becomes* the individual talent, the 'mind of Europe' Eliot's mind. Such a tendency is epitomised, at its extreme, in Robert Penn Warren's Preface to his narrative poem, *Brother to Dragons: A Tale in Verse and Voices* (1953), a vision of history as an active, subjective myth-making which, in its brash confidence in man's self-creative power, expresses the assurance of American imperialism at its high water mark: 'Historical sense and poetic sense should not, in the end, be contradictory, for if poetry is the little myth we make, history is the big myth we live, and in our living, constantly remake'.

The American tendency has been on the whole an optimistic one, imputing an active, fiction-making role to human endeavour, like that celebrated in Stevens's 'Idea of Order at Key West'. But that has always been a precarious optimism, taking enormous moral and formal risks, as the poetic and psychic breakdowns recorded in the work of Pound, of Hart Crane, of Theodore Roethke, Sylvia Plath and Robert Lowell all reveal. Eliot's sensibility, in its stasis and melancholy, its metaphysical pathos, seems from the start to have predisposed him to that English tradition which he adopted finally in 1927 by a double declaration of allegiance, taking out British citizenship and entering the Church of England in the same year. This is no incidental conversion, but a translation, or metamorphosis, which throws light on both the poetic traditions considered here. Standing at the intersection of these two cultural moments, Eliot's teasing equivocations in that 1928 Preface add an important qualification to Lukács's confident assertions.

For poetry is never merely an 'apologia for the existing order of things'. Rather it is the complex record of a struggle, both within and against that order, where the aesthetic impulse and the poetic voice wrestle with the very historical forces which give them birth, occasion and pretext. The English tendency, most movingly exemplified in the work of Thomas Hardy, has been to see history as a fossilised and alien force, bodied over against the self across an unbridgeable gulf, and yet strangely influential in denying, thwarting, suppressing all the self's movements to freedom and fulfilment. Certainly, such a perception seems to have appealed to Eliot, and to have offered even consolation and refuge. But, as the work of Hardy reveals, there has always been, in the English tradition, a struggle against these reified social relations – a struggle which has issued in tragedy, disillusion, despair, but which has nevertheless been renewed again and again. The pessimism of the Engish tradition is in one sense a testimony to its realism, and to the reality of the obstacles it confronts. This struggle has been, very often, a struggle to recover an idea of history, whether, as in the case of Hardy, to close the dark space between the moments of his youth and his old age, or, as with Edward Thomas, to invent an English radical tradition which reconciled massive social change with continuity, or, as with the marxisant poets of the thirties, in the words of Spender, to get 'on the side of History', to establish some rapport with a fetishised exterior 'History' in which all will be resolved, and guilt overcome. All these are struggles in which failure is an honourable outcome, and indeed an inevitable one.

Against Eliot's conception of culture as an 'ideal order' composed of the monuments of the past, one might set Walter Benjamin's account, in his *Theses on the Philosophy of History* (1940), of the actual processes by which a tradition is forged. Benjamin speaks in quite different terms of the relation between culture and barbarism, voice and violation – terms closer to those of *The Waste Land* than of *The Sacred Wood*. The creation of a cultural tradition is not a matter of an easy and unproblematic reshuffling of items in an imaginary museum; it involves profound struggle. It is, in fact, the site of a *class struggle,* in which the individual components of a culture are continually traversed by contending powers. (The division I've suggested between Eliot's poetic and critical accounts of the creative process is itself one sign of this struggle.) A 'tradition', once established, records both victories and, in its silences, defeats. It affirms, but it also excludes, and what is excluded is dictated, not just by aesthetic, but by political and social criteria. The traditional advice to those who wish to relive an era, says Benjamin, is to blot out everything they know about the later course of history:

There is no better way of characterising the method with which historical materialism has broken. It is a process of empathy whose origin is the indolence of the heart, *acedia*, which despairs of grasping and holding the general historical image as it flares up briefly . . . . The nature of this sadness stands out more clearly if one asks with whom [they] actually empathise. The answer is inevitable: with the victor . . . . Whoever has emerged victorious participates to this day in the triumphal procession in which the present rulers step over those who are lying prostrate. According to traditional practice, the spoils are carried along in the procession. They are called cultural treasures, and a historical materialist views them with cautious detachment. For without exception the cultural treasures he surveys have an origin which he cannot contemplate without horror. They owe their existence not only to the efforts of the great minds and talents who have created them, but also the anonymous toil of their contemporaries. There is no document of civilisation which is not at the same time a document of barbarism. And just as such a document is not free of barbarism, barbarism taints also the manner in which it was transmitted from one owner to another. A historical materialist therefore dissociates himself from it as far as possible. He regards it as his task to brush history against the grain.

This is not a unitary statement: there is all the difference in the world between viewing these cultural treasures with 'cautious detachment' and with 'horror'. Benjamin was writing in extreme circumstances: a Jew, a Marxist, on the run from the Nazis, shortly to commit suicide rather than fall into their hands. In such a situation, the dismissal of the whole cultural heritage he loved and spoke of so scrupulously in his criticism as mere 'spoils' of war is an understandable excess. But he is right to stress the *duplicity* of every work of art: it is at once an inviolable voice, proclaiming 'beauty is truth, truth, beauty', and a testament to the violations and barbarities of a class society, recording silently those 'hungry generations' against whose dark anonymous labours it stands out as against a foil. The argument of this book is that the struggle of which Benjamin speaks crosses and recrosses the terrain of twentieth-century poetry; that every text is inscribed with its traces, and that the duty of the critic is to decipher these obscure, these hidden testimonies.

2

Thomas Hardy and the Figures of Time

The dates are significant. The earliest poems in Hardy's first volume, *Wessex Poems,* are dated between 1865 and 1867, though the collection wasn't published until 1898, after his last novel, *Jude the Obscure* (1896). Many of the poems in subsequent volumes are revisions of work which dates back to the mid-sixties, when Hardy was around twenty-five. Though his finest sustained body of work undoubtedly lies in those sudden, strange elegies of 1912-13, for a recently dead wife from whom he'd been estranged, in all but fact, for many years, the characteristic mood of his poetry had been formed in those early years – momentous years in the formation of the modern sensibility. But this mood had then been subtilised and complicated by subsequent experience, to produce a poetry which is a complex overlaying of psychological times.

The ideological side of the assault on Victorian values in that period, and its importance for Hardy, are well known: the quickening of the debate about evolution in the fifties and early sixties, the gradual dispersal of the Victorian heyday in the darkening economic and social climate after 1870. But such a disenchanting of reality, coincident with Hardy's own passage from youth to maturity, and intertwining with it, could not have had the impact it did without some larger context of displacement, on which it set the seal.

The title *Wessex Poems* indicates what this larger context might be. In his Preface to the *Selected Poems of William Barnes,* in 1908, Hardy took the opportunity, in praising this Dorset dialect poet, to regret 'the silent and inevitable effacements reducing the speech of this country to uniformity, and obliterating every year many a fine old local word'. Hardy's own poems are sprinkled with a fair share of such usages, as if in a resistance determined to preserve in print what would soon pass from parlance. The fictive recreation of this world, as 'Wessex', is a similar attempt at reclamation.

The processes of homogenisation included, most immediately, a system of national schooling instituted by the 1870 Education Act which, with one side of his nature at least, Hardy would have wholeheartedly endorsed. But the larger context is a more equivocal one, manifest everywhere in the writings of the period. Hardy himself, in his verse drama *The Dynasts* (1903-08), instinctively returned to the moment which lay at their originating point, for his own native Dorset: the Napoleonic Wars, and the final defeat of Bonaparte at Waterloo in 1815, which, in assuring the global ascendancy of British maritime power, also marked the beginning of the end for old-style English agriculture, by opening up the prospect of competition from cheaper colonial granaries and, later, from the large-scale sheep and cattle farming of the Americas, Australia and New Zealand. The pattern of economic change in Hardy's 'Wessex' is clear to see in his novels, figured forth evasively, as a product of mere malevolent chance, in that accident in *Far from the Madding Crowd* (1874) which reduces Gabriel Oak from small farmer to journeyman labourer. Faced by competition from cheap foreign produce, English agriculture responded with a process of mechanisation, centralisation and the creation of a class of landless and often unemployable rural labourers, in an economy which, increasingly subordinate to the London market, became more efficient and cost-effective as it dispensed with the need for a large pool of agricultural reserve labour. Jude Fawley, moving from an already declining village to the urban centre of Christminster, an artisan following work, is in many senses a representative figure of this process. But so, too, is Hardy's career, with its undoubted rise in the world. The poems of 1865-67 were in fact written in London, where Hardy was apprenticed to an architect. The centralisation and concentration of the economy was in turn reinforced by the institutional transformations in education, the domestic and imperial civil service, and the cultural establishment from which the modern experience and sensibility were to emerge.

If Hardy's poems echo with the tales of supplantings,

deserted and deserting lovers, former beauties and 'lamps long extinguished', of 'levelled churchyards' and names erased from gravestones, and so on, what these figure forth is the extent of that transformation in which communities rose and fell, not in any timeless natural rhythm, but according to the dictates of what 'The Two Men' calls 'the Market's sordid war', which was shaping a new and radically different England from the demographic shifts of which his characters are the living, walking embodiments. A poem such as 'Memory and I' indicates why that endless *recherche* for a lost time is so central to Hardy's poetry. The being sought, back in the 1860s, is not simply a youth, joy, hope, faith, love taken away by time; it is also a world lost with them, a world which survives now only as 'a crumbled cot / Beneath a tottering tree', in 'gaunt gardens' or a 'ravaged aisle' where a 'phantom lingers'. As 'In the Mind's Eye' says, 'Change dissolves the landscapes'; only the ghost, the 'phantom / Borne within my brain' survives, to record, that once such things occurred, such places 'throbbed' (a favourite word) with life.

Far from the Madding Crowd had been serialised in *The Cornhill Magazine*. In 'The Jubilee of a Magazine' Hardy makes, out of the parallel between the journal's updated format and logo and the actual transformations of the rural economy, an ironic commentary on the gulf between pastoral and reality. If the two are seen to be mutually sustaining, the magazine is nevertheless not too sternly taken to task. Its 'gentle aim' has been a decent one. But its readership, self-styled 'sleepy squires' in a torpid idyll, for whom, like Rip Van Winkle, fifty years is a brief space, had never intended to draw such conclusions. Throughout the poem there is a sustained overlaying of two perspectives, effected through that continuous punning which sees the magazine as 'flower-fresh', 'bright leaves' and, finally, with that play on 'engrained', an imaginary harvest:

> Yes; your up-dated modern page –
> All flower-fresh, as it appears –
> Can claim a time-tried lineage,
>
> That reaches backward fifty years

(Which, if but short for sleepy squires,
Is much in magazines' careers).

– Here, on your cover, never tires
The sower, reaper, thresher, while
As through the seasons of our sires

Each wills to work in ancient style
With seedlip, sickle, share and flail,
Though modes have since moved many a mile!

The steel-roped plough now rips the vale,
With cog and tooth the sheaves are won,
Wired wheels drum out the wheat like hail;

But if we ask, what has been done
To unify the mortal lot
Since your bright leaves first saw the sun,

Beyond mechanic furtherance – what
Advance can rightness, candour, claim?
Truth bends abashed, and answers not.

Despite your volumes' gentle aim
To straighten visions wry and wrong,
Events jar onward much the same!

– Had custom tended to prolong,
As on your golden page engrained,
Old processes of blade and prong,

And best invention been retained
For high crusades to lessen tears
Throughout the race, the world had gained! . . .
But too much, this, for fifty years.

The page is 'up-dated', 'modern', yet the image of rural labour it propagates is obsolete. The image 'never tires' (which in itself suggests its distance from any actuality). The 'ancient style' is ostensibly that of the labour, but in fact that of the magazine, for all its modern format still moving 'through the seasons of our sires'. The terza rima carries the momentum of change forward, underlining, with the heavy extra stresses of stanza five, the abrasive violation of the new ways. Through the gap between image and reality slips, not a lost Eden for which the poet nostalgically laments, however, but a series of lost opportunities for human betterment, which might have combined 'custom' and 'invention'. Equivocally, the poem suppresses many of its possibilities: anger at a literary ruralism, at sacrificed human energies, lives. In the end, with its plangent diminuendo, after the crescendo to the exclamation mark, and its trailing dots, it succumbs almost to a benign head-shaking.

Hardy's juxtaposition of the moving world of history and the fixed, static, mechanically reproduced, endlessly repeated images of the printing press, forms part of a larger pattern of imagery in his poems. 'Engrained' simultaneously calls attention to the coarse, uneven texture of the page, as paper, made from wood-pulp, and evokes the smoothly eliding language of pastoral, in a literary tradition which reaches back to Virgil. It represents, in miniature, an ambivalence which pervades Hardy's work.

A poem such as 'In Front of the Landscape' sums up this double vision. On the one hand it sees the actual, turbulent movements of the self in history as a 'Plunging and labouring on in a tide of visions', pushing forward 'amid waste waters', where 'the customed landscape' is 'Blotted to feeble mist', and the language, in its troubled turgidity, reproduces this sense of a dragging, obstructive material world. On the other hand, in the final stanzas the observing self seems to withdraw from this eddying, besetting turmoil, into spectatorial abstraction, 'the intenser / Stare of the mind', where these 'lost revisiting manifestations' undergo as ghostly memories, 'a fuller translation than rested upon them / As living kind'. And this 'translation' allows the poem to settle into a kind of repose in the final lines, where, though he 'perambulates' still, the poet seems to place himself 'in front of the landscape', at a remove. Such an abstracting movement, to become pathological in the line of poetry which claims descent from Hardy, is usually complemented in his work by a movement back, a struggle to re-establish rapport with the tangible material world, figured most poignantly in the great elegies by that search for a lost wife whose presence will restore meaning to the landscape. Its genesis is hinted at in that return to origins in 'Childhood Among the Ferns', which employs the same gauche, slightly comic verb. Recalling his childhood, the poet evokes a figure simultaneously absorbed in the moment and already distancing himself from it in querying expectation, asking:

> Why should I have to grow to man's estate
> And this afar-noised World perambulate?

Speech itself here articulates the gap between immediate self and 'afar-noised World', calling it into being in the very act of questioning. Hardy's equivocal stance is repeatedly that spelt out in 'Self-Unconscious'. The self walks through the world, surrounded by a subjective halo in which he watches 'shapes that reveries limn', and only seldom grasps the reality of 'The moment that encompassed him', 'While himself he did not see at all'. Such a seeing of the self can come only in retrospect, which intrudes distance into the actual, and brings not 'vision' but 'derision' (a word attributed to Time in 'After a Journey'). 'Could he then have stood / At a clear-eyed distance, and conned the whole', he might have avoided such derision. The passage of time dispossesses, but it also brings insight into that which is lost, creating an ironic gulf between subject and object in the very act of memory itself. In a poem such as 'The Self-Unseeing', the memory of a former time is ambiguously charged by the realisation that, in that past time, it was the future, in expectation, which robbed the moment of its full joy; and yet the poem salvages a real advantage from this compounded loss:

> Childlike, I danced in a dream;
> Blessings emblazoned that day;
> Everything glowed with a gleam;
> Yet we were looking away!

This is the very figure of time in Hardy's poetry. Such a double movement, of being both involved in and detached from an external changing scene, is most powerfully evinced in those poems of 1912-13 in which his dead wife Emma becomes in her own sad duplicity – as an internal and subjective memory who may be an objective, external ghost, as a dead person more alive than the living, as a figure of the past who is also vibrantly present – the epitome of such contradictions. The movement of these poems is a struggle, at the level of personal life, against the enforced separation of subject and object, in which the attempt to reclaim the past is also a struggle to re-win the present, to restore, in Lukács's terms, a 'fossilised' history to its 'real nature' as 'relations between men'.

In these poems, the spatial gap between subject and object, 'here' and 'there', 'I' and 'you', is also a temporal one – that gap of forty years between the 1870s, when he first courted Emma Gifford, and the desolate present in which, revisiting their 'olden haunts', he seeks once again to recover her. The uncertain nature of this other he pursues – whether an imaginary 'voiceless ghost' or a real 'woman calling' – indicates the strain, in consciousness itself, to impute any reality to 'history'. All we know is the present moment, with its short views and collapsed perspectives. Yet if we are to be more than frail transients, ghostly visitants 'flitting' through the solid, material landscapes where 'The waked birds preen and the seals flop lazily' with a heavy, corporeal presence, some credence and reality must be given to these vanished and vanishing moments. These poems, for all their insistence on the continuity of a *personal* time and place, attempt in Benjamin's words 'to brush history against the grain', to refuse 'empathy with the victor', with that 'Time' which, here, is a metaphysical mask for 'history'.

'The Shadow on the Stone', not included in the 'Poems of 1912-13', though clearly cognate, indicates the Orphic nature of the quest in all these poems. He imagines that the shadow cast from over his shoulder is Emma's; but, unlike Orpheus, though he 'wanted to look and see / That nobody stood at the back of me', he resists the temptation. Looking would not, as for Orpheus, be an expression of yearning, but of doubt: 'to keep down grief / I would not turn my head to discover / That there was nothing in my belief'. And he 'went on softly from the glade', like the poet returning from the underworld, 'My head unturned lest my dream should fade'. The fragility of this mood is guarantee of its power. The poem takes every precaution to insist on the improbability of any supernatural visiting, to stress the likely ordinariness of these phenomena (the only sound in 'sad response' to his query is 'the fall of a leaf'). Nevertheless, in resisting that urge to final denial, it keeps open a larger faith.

In the Apology to *Late Lyrics and Earlier* (1922), Hardy speaks of those 'obstinate questionings' which are often 'alleged to be "pessimism"'' but are really '"questionings" in the exploration of reality, ... the first step towards the soul's betterment, and the body's also'. That double emphasis indicates what lies at the back of all his poems: the struggle to reconcile mind and matter, fact and value. From 'a series of fugitive impressions' he seeks to 'divine without half a whisper', with an 'intuitiveness ... proof against all the accidents of inconsequence', a significance and coherence in events, to make them 'the visible signs of mental and emotional life' which 'must like all other things keep moving, becoming'. In an 1887 diary entry, recorded by Florence Hardy in *The Life of Thomas Hardy,* he had written: 'It is the on-going – i.e. the "becoming" – of the world that produces its sadness. If the world stood still at a felicitous moment there would be no sadness in it.' But a poem such as 'At Castle Boterel' demonstrates that it is in the very struggle with that 'becoming', with that momentum at the heart of the moment, that transcendence, reclamation, redemption lie.

The poem opens with what seems like a failed Orphic quest, with the poet leaving a memoried site, never to return. Yet at this point of departure he chances, like Orpheus, to glance back, and it's as if this last hesitancy is what brings the hoped-for and unexpected reward. The poem in fact begins at the very last instant of opportunity for the revelation it then vouchsafes:

> As I drive to the junction of lane and highway,
>   And the drizzle bedrenches the waggonette,
>   I look behind at the fading byway,

And see on its slope, now glistening wet,
  Distinctly yet

Myself and a girlish form benighted
  In dry March weather. We climb the road
Beside a chaise. We had just alighted
  To ease the sturdy pony's load
    When he sighed and slowed.

What we did as we climbed, and what we talked of
  Matters not much, nor to what it led, –
Something that life will not be balked of
  Without rude reason till hope is dead,
    And feeling fled.

It filled but a minute. But was there ever
  A time of such quality, since or before,
In that hill's story? To one mind never,
  Though it has been climbed, foot-swift, foot-sore,
    By thousands more.

Primeval rocks form the road's steep border,
  And much have they faced there, first and last,
Of the transitory in Earth's long order;
  But what they record in colour and cast
    Is – that we two passed.

It's a characteristic moment in Hardy's poetry: against the
stony permenance of the material world are set the transitory
forms of men and women, moving like phantoms about the
enduring landscape. Yet here the memory insists upon its
corporeality, upon the *effort* of that earlier climb, the *weight* of
the two who make it, alighting to ease the load of what is
nevertheless a *sturdy* pony. And this links them to those other,
physical travellers, 'foot-swift, foot-sore' in an imagined
community of effort. That word 'form', always charged with
complexity in Hardy's verse, is carried over from the girl to the
rocks, which 'form the road's steep border'. These rocks
embody a contradiction central to the poem, between brute
materiality and the ephemeral world of human feelings,

memory, the heart's affections. They belong to the beginning
and the end of things; they abide. Earth's long order is a
procession of transitory beings. That is the objective fact. But
the subjective perception is quite different. The landscape is
still inhabited by its ghosts. Its image is so deeply imprinted
on his mind that he cannot look at the scene without evoking
that lost time. It is recorded in the hillside as absolutely as
'earth's testimonies' – the fossil record – tell of earlier and now
vanished forms of life in 'Before Life and After'. As many feet
have worn tracks on its surface, though each individual
passage is insignificant, so too many other minds have
transformed by their perceptions the ostensibly intractable
world of matter. The landscape is not primeval, untouched: it
has a 'story'; it belongs in our records:

> And to me, though Time's unflinching rigour,
> In mindless rote, has ruled from sight
> The substance now, one phantom figure
> Remains on the slope, as when that night
> Saw us alight.
>
> I look and I see it there, shrinking, shrinking,
> I look back at it amid the rain
> For the very last time; for my sand is sinking,
> And I shall traverse old love's domain
> Never again.

The human stands to the natural as phantom to substance,
apparently. Yet the phantom 'Remains on the slope'. The
human may be fluid, running away like water, while the
material is solid unchanging rock; but that last image, of
'sinking' sand in an hourglass, gives us pause, translating solid
stone into the fluidity of spirit, in an image which stands at the
intersection of permanency and flux, as the poet stands at the
junction of personal and collective, byway and highway.
Though the hesitant questionings and the diffident replies all
insist on the subjectivity of his conviction, this is not dismissed
as mere illusion. Matter simply *is*. It is only endowed with
value by the mind that interprets its blankness, reads its
records. The objective can be quantified ('but a minute',

'ever', 'Primaeval', 'first and last', 'long order'); but only the subjective has *quality*.

In 'After a Journey' the same transvaluation of matter occurs. The whole first stanza is full of negatives which insist on the importance of consciousness, inserting absence into the world. The questionings with which the poem tentatively begins, apparently about something in the external world '(Whither, O whither will its whim now draw me?' 'What have you found to say of our past / Scanned across the dark space wherein I have lacked you?'), turn in the next stanzas into exclamations and then, in the last lines, to a joyous affirmation that nothing has changed, an appeal to

> Trust me, I mind not, though Life lours,
>   The bringing me here; nay, bring me here again!
>   I am just the same as when
> Our days were a joy, and our paths through flowers.

The dark space of lack is translated into total reclamation. Stanza three indicates how:

> I see what you are doing: you are leading me on
>   To the spots we knew when we haunted here together,
> The waterfall, above which the mist-bow shone
>   At the then fair hour in the then fair weather,
> And the cave just under, with a voice still so hollow
>   That it seems to call out to me from forty years ago,
>   When you were all aglow,
> And not the thin ghost that I now frailly follow!

The whole scene suddenly clicks, in a clinching correspondence of inner and outer. The 'voiceless ghost' of memory leads him on, but it is also the landscape which leads him, the 'unseen waters' ejaculations' which then become the 'voice still so hollow' of the cave, the paths which, in climbing a cliff-side, one must follow, now as then. Memory, that is, has its objective determinants in the external world. The images of the mist-bow in the waterfall and the echo in the cave embody this coincidence of subject and object. Consciousness is as fluid and changeable as water; yet the waterfall seems not to have changed at all between the 'then fair hour' and now. It describes the same trajectory in the air, has the same ephemeral iris hovering above it. It's not the same water, of course, or the same light; but the *form* is the same. In the midst of flux, there is permanence. The mist-bow is both a real pattern in nature, something out there formed by the play of sun on water, and something in here, in consciousness, only existing in the form it has through the action of the mind, as the voice of the cave is real vibrations in material air, turned into significance by the ear, giving us back our own words as externalised presence. The mind brings permanence to nature, telescoping two moments forty years apart into one fused time, as 'here' and 'there' are transformed into 'everywhere' in the first stanza. This fragile consciousness is really the power that binds time and space together into coherence and order. Time, which derides men in stanza two, is also their invention.

This is the significance of that play on the words 'form' and 'figure' in 'At Castle Boterel'. These are always complex words in Hardy's poetry, often occurring in conjunction. In 'Love the Monopolist', for example, as the train pulls out of the station, the lover watches 'An airy slim blue form there standing', staring 'with strained vision' as 'The figure turns round' before he is out of sight. Even the stress on vision as straining emphasises its corporeality, a 'figuring' after its object. A 'figure' is always, in Hardy's poetry, both a material, external thing, like the woman's body, and a subjective act, an interpretative reading of things, as, in 'The Phantom Horsewoman', the bereaved poet sees, 'Warm, real, and keen', 'A phantom of his own figuring' riding along the beach. The word itself hovers at the point where subjective and objective merge, in the working of the figuring mind. In 'The Figure in the Scene' the poet pencils the woman in to the landscape he is sketching, so that even now 'her rainy form is the Genius still of the spot'. In 'Sacred to the Memory' Hardy distinguishes between the actual inscription 'carven' on a headstone. 'In bare conventionality', and the real inscribing of her presence, on a landscape which now she can never quit:

> They know not and will never know
> That my full script is not confined

> To that stone space, but stands deep lined
> Upon the landscape high and low
> Wherein she made such worthy show.

And yet, as the words 'story' and 'record' indicate in 'At Castle Boterel', the inscription, to be realised, has to be deciphered. In 'A House with a History' the present occupants of the house

> . . . read not how
> Its prime had passed before
>
> Their raw equipments, scenes, and says
> Afflicted its memoried face . . . .
>
> To them that house's tale is theirs,
>   No former voices call
> Aloud therein . . .

The tracking and tracing of the past is a way of reconstituting an effaced tradition and community. But it has its dangers. In 'The Re-enactment', 'the weird witchery of the parlour's hidden tale / Which I, as the years passed, faintly / Learnt to trace' comes between the self and its immediate words and deeds, dimming them with its 'intenser drama'. The dead may stifle the living. In 'Life Laughs Onward' he seeks out an old abode only to find a new dwelling on its site, daisies concealing an old grave, and the noise of children on a terrace proving that 'The figure that had once sat there / Was missed by none'. Uncharacteristically, this is a positively chastening revelation:

> Life laughed and moved on unsubdued,
> I saw that Old succumbed to Young:
> 'Twas well. My too regretful mood
>   Died on my tongue.

'Heredity' suggests that the 'form' and 'figure' which survive the individual lives in which they are embodied are Darwinian versions of the Platonic 'Forms', locating, in biological and historical process, that relation between eternal and transitory, form and matter, which for Plato had been a question of ghostly paradigms:

> I am the family face;
> Flesh perishes, I live on,
> Projecting trait and trace
> Through times to times anon,
> And leaping from place to place
> Over oblivion.

> The years-heired feature that can
> In curve and voice and eye
> Despise the human span
> Of durance – that is I;
> The eternal thing in man,
> That heeds no call to die.

This is the significance, surely, of that oblique reference to their love-making ('Something that life will not be balked of') in 'Castle Boterel'. The abiding forms of the world are an inheritance transmitted from one generation to the next, perpetuated from instant to instant by that act which 'filled but a minute', but in which hope and feeling are renewed, 'quality' reaffirmed, in the primary encounter of man and woman, and of flesh and spirit.

For Hardy, the relationship between the self and history, like that between mind and landscape, is mediated through the imagery of represented 'figures', written and spoken 'forms'. Script seems to have had a powerful and ambiguous hold over him, retaining perhaps some of the magic with which it was invested for the autodidact Jude, but drawing also, as 'In a Waiting-Room' suggests, on a scriptural tradition. In a tawdry waiting-room, the poet reads on and on in the Gospel of St John, a text thronged with 'figures – additions, multiplications . . . with sundry emendations' scrawled absentmindedly by some travelling salesman as a reckoning of profit and loss. The use of the word 'figures' here, in an unusual sense for Hardy, should alert us to the transaction between God and Mammon in this interplay of texts. The poet wonders if there could have been

> Any particle of a soul
> In that poor man at all,
> To cypher rates of wage
> Upon that printed page.

The perdition of this 'morning sick as the day of doom' is compounded by the couple who stand over him and the 'scribbled book', a soldier and his wife who, a 'casual word' discloses, are parting, they believe for ever.

Three kinds of language jostle here, each one gloomier than the rest: the printed text of the gospel, the arithmetical scribbling of the traveller, and the sombre and laconic speech of the couple. Print, script and speech alike communicate an unremitting, apocalyptic gloom to the atmosphere. The last stanza is a deliberate, even contrived interruption of this despondency, thrusting the gospel of good news, 'Like the eastern flame / Of some high altar' into this 'drizzling gray', in the form of two children whose excited laughter redefines the whole squalid room with words which 'spread a glory through the gloom'. The poem is a little epiphany, in which the dead forms of language, fixed on the past, on profit and loss, separation and grief, are transfigured by a speech that moves into the future tense, pre-empting possibility: ' "When we get there it's most sure to be fine, / And the band will play, and the sun will shine!" '

The identification of script with fixity, denial, repression, the past, is a recurrent theme in Hardy. The most remarkable instance of this is 'The Inscription', a narrative sunk deep in medieval gloom. In the legend it recounts, a lady has a brass inscribed above the crypt where her newly deceased husband is buried, to 'fix his name / As a memory Time's fierce frost should never kill'. Foolishly, she also 'bonded her name with his own on the brazen page, / As if dead and interred there with him, and cold, and numb', with a plea for others to pray ' "Of their Charytie / For these twaine Soules" ', vowing to forgo heaven's bliss should she ever lie with another. As if to enforce his point, Hardy has the inscription printed in Gothic script, and repeats, superfluously, that it is 'Writ in quaint Church-text', where even now, 'the folk yet bow / Themselves in prayer'. The story takes its inevitable course: time brings another suitor, and the woman regrets her too hasty vows, and their enduring evidence. When her suitor persists, with importunate words, her response is the silent gesture of showing him the inscription, so that he reproaches her 'that one yet undeceased / Should bury her future – that future which none can spell'. (This last word brings together both language and conjuration, in a significant conjunction.) Seeking advice from the priest, the lady is told that 'To erase from the consecrate text her prayer as there prayed' would be a grievous sin, while she fears, too, the more immediate mortification of 'the jibe / That would rise at her back in the nave' should she remarry in front of the changeless brass. Even the 'words absolute' of her lover's letter cannot change her mind.

Oppressed by the forms of language, cancelling the possible future in the name of a dead and inscribed past, the lady is reduced once more to silence. She often stands silently 'Before the script', until one night she is found 'feeling the words with her finger, gibbering in fits'. Finally, she is seen 'Tracing words in the air with her finger', as if trying to restore to the intangibility of breath – the element of speech – that which is 'incised' unchanging in brass. Speech itself, throughout the poem equated with spontaneity, an openness toward the future, has degenerated in the meantime into mere gibberish, before the oppressive undertakings of script. At this point, the poem steps back from the narrative, identifying its own status as a tale ('And, as talebearers tell . . .') to recall us to our own time and place, in the unspelt future of the poem, telling us that we too 'may read even now / The quaint Church-text' 'where folk yet bow / Themselves in prayer'. By ending on this last antithesis, repeating two earlier moments in the poem, Hardy calls special attention to the poem's continuous counterpoint of material script and intangible speech, fixity and freedom, doom and grace, as models of the way in which the self relates to the opportunities of its particular history.

For Hardy, identity seems closely bound up with the idea of writing. 'His Heart: A Woman's Dream', has a bereaved woman speak of 'Perus[ing] the unguessed things found written' on her dead husband's heart, which is 'inscribed . . . / With quaint vermiculations close and clear – / His graving'. The pun on 'graving' suggests a subliminal link between identity, self-enclosure, fixity and death. The man can only be 'read' in 'His whole sincere symmetric history' when he is dead, and then only in auguring dream. These 'chronicled' and 'recorded' proofs of being cannot be revealed in ordinary discourse, and the macabre fantasy of extracting the heart adds a peculiar twist to the idea of failed communication. In 'The Masked Face' the poet finds himself 'in a great surging space', a 'giddying place, / With no firm-fixed floor' which the masked face tells him is Life. He asks how he came to be there, whether the place can be changed, made more wholesome, and the 'fast-locked' doors set wide. The reply is unequivocal, and it identifies the individual life with the act of writing itself:

> The mask put on a bleak smile then,
>   And said, 'O vassal-wright,
> There once complained a goosequill pen
>   To the scribe of the Infinite
>   Of the words it had to write
> Because they were past its ken.'

Script for Hardy always has this tendency to congeal, to change from its status as *signifying* text, a carrier of meaning, into an opaque and self-sufficient *sign,* independent of what it signifies, oppressing with its material presence. In 'The Pedigree', for example, scanning the 'hieroglyphs' of his lineage, he finds the 'tangles' of the family tree trouble him, seeming to twist into 'a seared and cynic face', tokening towards the window like a Mage, then becoming a mirror in which he could trace the long perspective of his progenitors, 'All with the kindred look, / Whose names had since been inked down in their place / On the recorder's book'. This in turn leads to a horrifying realisation: that he is in fact *written in advance* by his ancestors, that even the autonomy of his personal speech is inscribed already, waiting to be uttered:

> And then did I divine
> That every heave and coil and move I made
> Within my brain, and in my mood and speech,
> Was in this glass portrayed
> As long forestalled by their so making it . . .

Only an act of rebellious self-address can break the spell of
this enchantment, in which the 'line' of his pedigree becomes
also a line of writing. The dialogue creates a doubleness
within the self, an internal distance in which the spoken and
the unspoken contradict each other. This Hardy indicates by
a shift of printer's case, into italics:

> Said I then, sunk in tone,
> 'I am merest mimicker and counterfeit! –
> Though thinking, *I am I,*
> *And what I do I do myself alone.*'
> – The cynic twist of the page thereat unknit
> Back to its normal figure, having wrought its purport wry,
> The Mage's mirror left the window-square,
> And the stained moon and drift retook their places there.

The 'cynic twist' of a Mage-like exterior history can be
overcome only by an active struggle against the past, within
the self, which frees both it, the many individuals who
compose it, and the individual inheritor, from enslavement to
its alien, fossilised forms. The Mage is a Mephistophelian
tempter, urging a sullen despair upon the poet – a malign
version of that 'Immanent Will' which at other times Hardy
envisages as subject to some partial control.

The most explicit statement of his doctrine of 'evolutionary
meliorism' is contained in the Apology to *Late Lyrics and Earlier*.
Here Hardy makes it clear that he sees the human species not
simply as the *object* of historical forces – the mistake to which
the Mage tempts him in this poem – but also as, in part, the
maker of its destiny. The very act of commenting on 'the
barbarizing of taste in the younger minds by the dark madness
of the late war', the premonition that 'we seem threatened
with a new Dark Age', are not effusions of hopelessness, but
active *interventions* in the historical process, calls to arms.
Hardy is insistent on this point:

Happily there are some who feel . . . that comment on where the world stands is very much the reverse of needless in these disordered years of our prematurely afflicted century: that amendment and not madness lies that way. And looking down the future these few hold fast to the same: that whether the human and kindred animal races survive till the exhaustion or destruction of the globe, or whether these races perish and are succeeded by others before that conclusion comes, pain to all upon it, tongued or dumb, shall be kept down to a minimum by loving-kindness, operating through scientific knowledge, and actuated by the modicum of free will conjecturally possessed by organic life when the mighty necessitating forces – unconscious or other – that have 'the balancings of the clouds,' happen to be in equilibrium, which may or may not be often.

The carefully balanced assessment of the shifting ratios between 'free will' and 'the mighty necessitating forces' is salutary. If, in retrospect, Hardy sounds not despairing but over-optimistic, his stress on the duty and the necessity of 'amendment', acting *as if* something can be done, adds a deeper historical dimension to that apparently personal struggle with time, fate and necessity. A melancholy habit of the English tradition sets the elite consciousness of the poet at a contemplative, spectatorial distance from the great mass of men and women who are the objects of his gaze, underwriting a larger sense of social helplessness and passivity. There is much of this in Hardy; but there is too a resistance, a 'perambulating', often awkward engagement with things, a 'tracking' of lost connections through the years and dead scenes, in some determined quest to close the gap, keep faith with that world of forty years ago from which the isolate, egregious self emerged. In this, Hardy's verse, with its stubborn clinging to dialect and to the forms of popular experience, of ballad, song and folk anecdote, goes against the grain of the bourgeois culture in which he wrote, and records everywhere in its language the strain of that resistance.

At his most acute, he does not see historical process in terms of a simple opposition between 'continuity' and 'change'. As in 'The Pedigree', each new generation is not simply a reproduction or rejection of its predecessor, but a complicated reworking and transformation of its diverse elements. This is particularly apparent in his unexpected advocacy of 'an alliance between religion . . . and complete rationality, . . . by means of the interfusing effect of poetry' – a hope all the more striking for the intransigent religious scepticism of its holder. God, as he says in 'God's Funeral', is a 'man-projected Figure'. But in the process of this historic self-projection, man has endowed the divine with his own evolving morality. The poem, admitting to nostalgia for a lost 'blest assurance', when he could 'start the wheels of day with trustful prayer', 'struck speechless' by the cries of true believers, nevertheless discerns some 'small light' on the horizon, a light which the poem's uncertain tone, 'dazed and puzzled 'twixt the gleam and gloom', cannot be sure is there, so that it concludes with the poet 'mechanically' following those who do hope.

Nostalgia for a lost faith, seen at its most moving in the wry, wistful scepticism of 'The Oxen', leads again and again to a kind of poem which presupposes for its dramatic structure the imagery, framework and assumptions its argument ostensibly denies. Thus, in the imaginary dialogues of 'New Year's Eve' or 'God's Education', or in the image of 'The Spinner of the Years' in 'The Convergence of the Twain', Hardy calls up a personal God in the very process of denying or redefining his existence. In 'A Plaint to Man' an imaginary deity reproaches man for creating him, 'A form like your own – for praying to', speaking of himself as some Platonic lantern-slide, 'Shown forth in the dark upon some dim sheet', and envisaging, in his final demise, that man will eventually face 'The fact of life with dependence placed / On the human heart's resource alone, / In brotherhood bound close'. Hardy has in fact inverted the Platonic myth: the ideal is merely a fantasy of the material, the imaginary form in which men perceive their own mystified social relations. Similarly, in a series of failed allegories, such as 'The Weary Walker', a traditional motif – here, the pilgrimage to the holy city – is taken and subverted. The closing rhyme of each quatrain merely repeats the word it is supposed to rhyme with, reiterating through the whole poem the inescapable 'road' which leads to no destination, but is its own goal and purpose. The allegorical structure, and the subverted 'rhyme' pattern, raise expectations which the poem fails to fulfil, leaving us with a peculiarly harrowing, dull frustration. The 'supernatural', whether as the ambiguous ghost of a loved one, or the non-existent realm which underwrites our activities in this world, thus figures forth in Hardy's poetry a recurring dilemma. For it consistently occurs at that point where the mind struggles with a recalcitrant material world bodied over against it, and struggles to re-appropriate that world. The supernatural, that is, is a sign and a site of a desperate attempt to 'brush history against the grain'.

In all its counterpoint of traditional forms and subversive content, Hardy's verse grapples with that contradiction of objective and subjective which is explored, too, in the 'obstinate questionings' of his elegies and love poems. The clash of fluid and fixed, free and determined, realised in the recurring opposition of voice and script, is also represented in that 'Gothic art-principle' recorded by Florence Hardy in *The Later Years:* 'the principle of spontaneity, found in mouldings, tracery, and suchlike – resulting in the "unforeseen"... character of his metres and stanzas, that of stress rather than syllable, poetic texture rather than poetic veneer'. As convention is thus transformed in its reworking, so the historical process is itself a making new, a re-determining of the historical ensemble.

Hardy's poetry abounds in voices. Whether it is 'the woman calling' in 'The Voice', the 'one speech' of reproach in 'The Voice of the Thorn', 'Voices from Things Growing in a Churchyard', or the oscillating moods of 'The Voice of Things', where the same sea-waves at different moments in his life 'huzza', indulge in 'long ironic laughter' or 'supplicate' like a congregation murmuring confession, the poet always stands in front of a landscape whose many voices require his interpreting mind to fulfil their possibilities, even though, as in the last poem, he may stand as if 'outside, / Prayer denied'. The voice affirms possibility, energy, hope, against the petrified givenness of script. Prayer is an appropriate concept, not only because it carries with it associations of a superseded but still valued spirituality, but because it is a dialogue in which there is only one voice, a dialogue in which the answering silence can only be redeemed by faith and imagination. It therefore acts as a strikingly apt metaphor for that condition in which Hardy perennially finds himself: simultaneously estranged from the material world, the world of history, a world ostensibly without ratifying values, and yet caught up within its continuing discourses, striving to speak to and of it, to rescue some meaning from them. But *song* is an equally fitting and more frequent image, whether it is that of 'The Darkling Thrush', or 'The Something that Saved Him' in 'A closing-in blind alley' so that, in the last words of the poem: 'I upsprang, / And looked back at den, ditch and river, / And sang'.

In a world where voices 'chatter', 'babble', and 'shrill', where words have material weight, 'In all their intimate accents / Patter upon' the surface of things ('In the British Museum'), silence is always significant, usually ominous. He speaks in one poem of 'the stress of silence'; in another, of a 'Silence [which] cloaks like snow'. 'The Last Signal' begins: 'Silently I footed by an uphill road', to observe, across the darkened landscape, William Barnes's funeral procession. Even the dead find ways to break their silence: the coffin briefly catches the sun:

> Thus a farewell to me he signalled on his grave-way,
>   As with a wave of his hand.

The poem, like so many of Hardy's, in dealing with the motif of a one-way communication which nevertheless imputes a real communion, hovers on the brink of superstition, yet never succumbs. It does not suppose any actual intent on the part of the dead man; rather, it testifies to the solidarity and faith of the perceiver, projecting in such accidents a reflex of his own, sign-seeking concern.

In A. E. Housman's 'Tell me not here' (*Last Poems*, 1922) the motif of speech becomes the image of a larger dispossession, as a morbidly dissociated self moves spectrally, a stranger and afraid, about a world it never made. There is a peculiar poignancy to Housman's vision:

Tell me not here, it needs not saying,
    What tunes the enchantress plays
In aftermaths of soft September
    Or under blanching mays,
For she and I were long acquainted
    And I knew all her ways. . . .

For nature, heartless, witless nature,
    Will neither care nor know
What stranger's feet may find the meadow
    And trespass there and go,
Nor ask amid the dews of morning
    If they are mine or no.

Housman sees the stranger as a trespasser on territory which through long acquaintance the poet has privately 'possessed'. But then the last two lines acknowledge that nature recognises no such exclusive property rights. The human presences of poet and stranger, the significance each attributes to nature, are all equally a trespass, a transient and subjective invasion of the brute world of matter. The poet may have known all her ways, but nature does not reciprocate. The enchantress's tune is merely the dispossessing cuckoo that 'shouts all day at nothing'. Traveller's joy beguiles only hearts deprived of their own: the flower's 'joy' is merely a name, a verbal illusion, stuck on to nature. The epithets applied to nature are significantly ambiguous: Housman hovers continually between the objective fact and the subjective need. Nature's nescience precludes sympathy: it can 'neither care nor know'. But the habit of feeling pulls against the intellectual recognition of its speciousness: personified, she is 'heartless' as a cruel mistress is, 'witless' as a dumb blonde might be. And as nature does not ask, so he does not need to be told: 'It needs no saying'; for, in this world at once sentimentally anthropomorphised and tragically disenchanted, language is redundant.

This is radically distinct from Hardy's vision in 'During Wind and Rain'. The poem articulates many of the themes considered in this chapter, presenting an image of men and women in history which fuses the public and the domestic, the individual and social. At the same time it displaces into a temporality beyond the human, abstractly identified as the interruptive 'years', the key element in its view of history. The sudden switch of focus effected by the pivotal exclamation in each stanza balances the positive, creative activities of the human family against the omen-laden, violent world of natural entropy, condensed into a single febrile line:

> They sing their dearest songs –
> He, she, all of them – yea,
> Treble and tenor and bass,
>   And one to play;
> With the candles mooning each face . . .
>   Ah, no; the years O!
> How the sick leaves reel down in throngs!

The pattern is repeated in each stanza, balancing several mild verbs of constructive human labour against the single destructive kinesthetic verb of the last line. Though they 'clear the creeping moss / . . . Making the pathways neat / And the garden gay; / And they build a shady seat', that encroachment hinted at in the 'mooning' of the first stanza, with its funereal, changeable light, predominates in the final stanza. Despite the sense of possession and value ('their dearest songs', 'brightest things that are theirs'), there is no ultimate security of tenure. The seeming movement up in the world ('a high new house') is one moment of a larger degeneration ('They change'). Change is the essence of their lives, though each stanza seems to rest in a tranquil and everlasting stasis. And yet security, ambition, purpose are not devalued by this ultimate supersession. In a subtle variation on that opposition of voice and script which runs through his poetry, Hardy moves from the songs of the first stanza to the inscriptions of the last. The engraved names record a reduction to fixity of those lives which, though fleeting, seemed in each previous moment to have been living as if forever. But the verbs used, even to describe the erasing power of nature, are ones which insist upon human productive power, upon the analogy of language and labour. For the inscriptions to exist, community has had to continue: men

have carved these names, as men now plough the landscape
which has acquired these particular men and women. And
language (the names) and the possessive adjective both, it
seems, outlive death:

> They change to a high new house,
> He, she, all of them – aye,
> Clocks and carpets and chairs
>   On the lawn all day,
> And brightest things that are theirs. . . .
>   Ah, no; the years, the years;
> Down their carved names the raindrop ploughs.

The sustained ambivalence of Hardy's vision is beautifully
focused in this poem. The renewal implicit in that image of
destruction in the last line is something which depends, all the
time, upon the mind's stubborn impulse to begin again, to
reclaim, to track the lost ones 'Through the years, through the
dead scenes', to 'scan and trace / The forsaken place' ('Where
the Picnic Was') for those abiding signs, the burnt circle in the
grass, where the poet himself, 'Last relic of the band', may
keep faith with the past. It is the mind's duty to call back these
things, though it is always easy, in Hardy's verse, for the
balance to topple over, and allow the past to overwhelm the
present, as in 'Places':

> Nay: one there is to whom these things,
> That nobody else's mind calls back,
> Have a savour that scenes in being lack,
> And a presence more than the actual brings;
> To whom today is beneaped and stale,
>   And its urgent clack
>   But a vapid tale.

Hardy's whole poetic output is, in a sense, a wrestling with
the consequences of that lack, that split in the bourgeois soul
of which Lukács writes. This is a breach in being itself,
between an individual locked in a rigidly delineated
separateness, and the social process from which that
individual has congealed, a figure in front of a landscape,

figuring forth, for all his isolate being, the predetermined patterns of his ancestors. Traversing Hardy's poetry is a fluctuating sense of human agency in history which can leave us unsure whether the poet endorses the opinion of his character, Napoleon, in *The Dynasts:*

> By laws imposed on me inexorably!
> History makes use of me to weave her web.

In fact, the issue has to be negotiated anew from poem to poem, in the shifting encounters of an ever-weaving history and poetry's inviolable voice.

3

A Public House and not a Hermitage: Edward Thomas

Edward Thomas was the unwitting spokesman of a generation of intellectuals who had grown up in the expectation of plenty. Children of a parvenu professional class created by the expansion of an administered, centralised state and an imperial bureaucracy, they had seen their ambitions dashed by the recessions of the 1880s and '90s. Like many of his contemporaries, Thomas had anticipated a successful literary or academic career. By the time he graduated from Oxford in 1900, his future was already settled for him: genteel poverty, and a life of continuous hack journalism which was to bring him, by 1911, to breakdown and attempted suicide. Convinced of his marginality and dispossession, Thomas came increasingly to see himself and his contemporaries (in a phrase borrowed from Turgenev) as 'superfluous men'. A review of Ernest Dowson in the *Daily Chronicle* (26 May 1905) spells out the condition:

> To us he seems to have rediscovered regret and all the emotions which the inaccessible and irrecoverable arouse. . . . Deep within the dark background of them all is the comic, terrible cry of the superfluous man, . . . of self-pity, self-love, self-hate, of that regret and hunger for they know not what which are their only emotions that touched the sublime.

To probe the 'dark background' of Thomas's poetry is to discover that the mood defined here, valuably diagnosed by D. W. Harding as 'nostalgia', is not a merely metaphysical and private gloom but a situated response to a specific moment in the evolution of modern consciousness: the mood of an era. Thomas's poetry expressed the crisis of a liberal individualism faced with the prospect of its own redundancy, in an age when social hegemony seemed about to pass to another, more virile class. In an essay called 'Aurelius, The Superfluous Man' in *The Happy-Go-Lucky Morgans* (1913), Thomas could hint at the social aetiology of the mood: 'the superfluous are those who cannot find any society with which they are in some sort of harmony'; 'in a civilisation like ours', he continues, 'the superfluous abound and even flourish'; caught at the interface of the two major classes, 'they neither produce like the poor nor consume like the rich', and so lack a grip on established reality, experiencing that volatility spoken of by another superfluous man, in *The South Country* (1909). This man, a town-bred clerk of Welsh ancestry, cannot escape the 'terror that enrolled [him] as one of the helpless, superfluous ones of the earth'. Denied 'harmony' in atavistic return to the land (the chapter is itself called 'A Return to Nature'), he is forced forward into semi-revolutionary postures which find him, finally, in a march of the unemployed. He is scathing in his self-contempt:

'I belong to no class, or race, and have no traditions. We of the suburbs are a muddy, confused, hesitating mass, of small courage though much endurance. As for myself, I am world-conscious and hence suffer unutterable loneliness.'

Deracination, vacillation, vast ambition and a pervasive defeatism, an incommunicable sense of exclusion which yearns for the ratifying womb of class, race or tradition, these are the impulses behind Thomas's poetry, and account for his wider ambivalence of mood. Thomas sought, in a populist vision of the English people, its history, language and landscapes interfused in one collective subjectivity, that 'tradition' and 'home' which his age and social experience, as a member of an amorphous sub-class, denied him: a common repository of values at once ancient and yet open to the most revolutionary impulses for renewal and transformation. The inevitable destiny of such an ambiguous amalgam of radical and conservative sentiments was the muddy confusion of Flanders, where, between 1914 and 1918, a generation of superfluous men doused their discontent, and found, ironically, that resolution and commitment denied them

during the peace. There is a tragic doomed continuity which
leads from the secluded garden of the poem 'Old Man' to the
desolation of the trenches. His death in 1917 also marks the
end of a particular kind of radical populism, and a decisive
crisis in the continuities of the English cultural tradition.

Landscape and language are repeatedly linked in Thomas's
thought. The material world, he suggests in *Maurice
Maeterlinck* (1911), is a 'great myth', transfigured with
meanings that accrue from history. Folksongs, he says in one
review in the *Daily Chronicle* (23 January 1908), 'imbed the
history of men as abundantly as language itself', while, in
another (18 June 1907), he suggests that for those who sing
them, 'England is really old and as full of the past as language
is'. The antiquity of the language is cognate with the
ancientness of the land – both partake of the same mystery.
Thomas's writings are full of incidents in which a revelation is
half vouchsafed, and the final withholding only adds intensity
to the *frisson* of recognition. In 'I never saw that land before'
the self comes home, momentarily, to a reality it has known all
along, and yet from which it is expelled again almost at once:

> I never saw that land before,
> And now can never see it again;
> Yet, as if by acquaintance hoar
> Endeared, by gladness and by pain,
> Great was the affection that I bore
>
> To the valley and the river small,
> The cattle, the grass, the bare ash trees,
> The chickens from the farmsteads, all
> Elm-hidden, and the tributaries
> Descending at equal interval;
>
> The blackthorns down along the brook
> With wounds as yellow as crocuses
> Where yesterday the labourer's hook
> Had sliced them cleanly; and the breeze
> That hinted all and nothing spoke.

I neither expected anything
Nor yet remembered; but some goal
I touched then; and if I could sing
What would not even whisper my soul
As I went on my journeying,

I should use, as the trees and birds did,
A language not to be betrayed;
And what was hid should still be hid
Excepting from those like me made
Who answer when such whispers bid.

The hinted meaning is focused there, in that central stanza where a man establishes some actual, tangible relation with the landscape, marking it with his presence yet also wounding it, demonstrating its subordination to a continuing community of work from which the poet is excluded. There is an interesting counterpoint in the tension between the clean slice of the labourer's hook – its forthright utterance – and the breeze's obliquity; as there is, too, in that between the apparent openness of the landscape to the traveller's gaze and the *hiddenness* of the farmsteads. The moment of communion is cut off from past and future, memory and expectation, as the self, like the breeze, journeys with similar reticence through a landscape whose mystery it shares. Yet each finds its mystery made familiar, 'endeared', by that symbol in which a goal is – significantly – 'touched'. The disclosure of the last lines is available only when a language is shared, discreetly, when the bidding and response is conducted in whispers. Everything else would be betrayal, of language, landscape, and the deepest identity of this apparently estranged self.

Thomas's most famous poem, 'Old Man', is an exploration of this subtle language of the sense, in which a deeper estrangement and intimacy are ambiguously inscribed. The self's exposure before an enigmatic reality is felt to be at once an intensely solitary experience and yet, in some unexplained way, universally significant.

The poem catches a symbolic moment in the social transmission of meanings, in which the present is irradiated with a significance beyond it, in the very process of communication. But the transmission is fraught with dangers, opening up a gulf in which meaning may be lost in the very attempt to fix it.

> Old Man, or Lad's-love, – in the name there's nothing
> To one that knows not Lad's-love, or Old Man,
> The hoar-green feathery herb, almost a tree,
> Growing with rosemary and lavender.
> Even to one that knows it well, the names
> Half decorate, half perplex, the thing it is:
> At least, what that is clings not to the names
> In spite of time. And yet I like the names.

The contradictory associations of the alternatives stress the arbitrariness of language, a mere perfume of meaning hovering over an intractable materiality. Not only are they decorations, but they confuse its identity. Yet this perplexity is part of the 'meaning' of the plant – perhaps this is why the poem speaks of the names perplexing 'the thing it is', and not the observer. Through the words alone, nothing is communicated – a 'nothing' which attains more ominous resonances by the end of the poem. To know both names and thing fully they must be apprehended in their mysterious intersection. But this takes place in that most impalpable of mediums, consciousness itself. Meaning is transmitted obliquely, in the sharing of a mystery between father and daughter, where to speak may be to betray what can only be communicated indirectly, with circumspection. The child too will one day love the herb, as he does. That future will be as mysterious for her as the present is now for him, founded in an indefinable past. Now, the child too experiences 'nothing' as she tries to penetrate to the essence of her experience:

> Often she waits there, sniffing the tips and shrivelling
> The shreds at last on to the path, perhaps
> Thinking, perhaps of nothing, till she sniffs
> Her fingers and runs off . . .

Memory for Thomas is frequently associated with elusive and tantalising scents which can never be defined in words, and, in 'The Word', he speaks of 'the wild rose scent that is like memory'. But the 'meaning' of the herb here lies as much in the future as in the past. The child's experience does not yet include language, for she, in this silent communion, partakes of a mystery older than speech:

> Not a word she says;
> And I can only wonder how much hereafter
> She will remember, with that bitter scent,
> Of garden rows, and ancient damson trees
> Topping a hedge, a bent path to a door,
> A low thick bush beside the door, and me
> Forbidding her to pick.

Her present will one day contribute to a mystery as profound as his past, yet it is not now mysterious to him, but mundane. All the wonder derives from those 'nothings' which invest the moment. The mystery he experiences is renewed for the child, and accumulates new significance for him in his wonderings about her half-known present and her unknown future. The sonorous echo of an earlier injunction in a garden is delicately subdued by the immediate sense of paternal complicity. He is no heavenly father, but a fellow-creature equally ensnared in the enigma and the temptation:

> As for myself,
> Where first I met the bitter scent is lost.
> I, too, often shrivel the grey shreds,
> Sniff them and think and sniff again and try
> Once more to think what it is I am remembering,
> Always in vain. I cannot like the scent,
> Yet I would rather give up others more sweet,
> With no meaning, than this bitter one.

In seeking its meaning, he is not remembering, but trying to think what he is remembering, to bring into consciousness something hovering perpetually on the edge of nothing. Yet the 'meaning', really, resides in this very impalpability; the pursued essence dissolves into the multitude of appearances. He has in one sense mislaid the key, but, in another, the scent

is itself a key which opens the door into a mystery beyond
language altogether, into a darkness that lies beyond the
garden and its illusory security:

> I have mislaid the key. I sniff the spray
> And think of nothing; I see and I hear nothing;
> Yet seem, too, to be listening, lying in wait
> For what I should, yet never can, remember:
> No garden appears, no path, no hoar-green bush
> Of Lad's-love, or Old Man, no child beside,
> Neither father nor mother, nor any playmate;
> Only an avenue, dark, nameless, without end.

There is nothing in the past that can subdue the
overwhelming sense of loss the scent provokes. Only the
repeated 'I' insists on the continuity of selfhood, in short, crisp
clauses, but this confidence too slowly dissolves through the
longer clause which moves from the emphatic immediacy of
fact (albeit negative) of 'sniff', 'think', 'see and hear', to a
perpetually transitive, participial world ('seem to be listening,
lying in wait . . .') in which a subjunctive reality is forever
pitched just beyond apprehension, in a nameless dark where
past and future merge. In the last four lines, those
accumulating negatives can totally overwhelm the painfully
preserved sense of identity, transforming the whole solid world
of fact into mere hypothetical, unembodied absences,
perpetually denied real existence.

In its hesitant, uncertain rhythms, the subtlety of its
discriminations, and its deference before the mystery of a
world at once strangely alien and frighteningly familiar, the
poem offers a personal myth which is at the same time
symptomatic of a general crisis. It is the diffidence, the sense
of frailty in face of a world never wholly contained within
consciousness, always finally other, which predominates in
the poem. It embodies as myth the crisis of liberal humanism
before the vastness and impenetrability of a world it can
hardly begin to understand. The very seclusion and privacy
are themselves part of this structure of feeling. The ontological
wondersickness is something released, not in a garden
mysteriously insulated from an arbitrarily displaced 'external

world', but at the dispossessed heart of this culture. The suppressed social dimension survives in that passage in *The South Country* which is one of the earliest sources of the poem:

> Perhaps the happiest childhoods are those which pass completely away and leave whole tracts of years without a memory . . . I watch the past as I have seen workless, homeless men leaning over a bridge to watch the labours of a titanic crane and strange workers below in the ship running to and fro and feeding the crane. . . . I recall many scenes: . . . lads-love and tall, crimson, bitter dahlias in a garden. . . .

The opening section of *The Heart of England* (1906), 'Leaving Town', generalises a similar sense of estrangement to reveal the historic matrix from which it arises. Here it is the 'multitudes entirely unknown to me' which overwhelm, in a city where men take on the same abstract, quantifiable homogeneity that afflicts language. Like an unknown language, they withhold their meanings, cannot be read, in a city which has become Babel. They are 'human faces that were at that moment expressing innumerable strange meanings with which I had nothing to do'. That transmission of meanings so precariously maintained as a private transaction by discretion and obliquity is here no longer possible:

> These streets are the strangest thing in the world. They have never been discovered. They cannot be classified. There is no tradition about them. Poets have not shown us how we are to regard them. They are to us as mountains were in the Middle Ages, sublime, difficult, immense; and yet so new that we have inherited no certain attitude towards them, of liking or dislike. . . . They suggest so much that they mean nothing at all. The eye strains at them as at Russian characters which are known to stand for something beautiful or terrible; but there is no translator: it sees a thousand things which at the moment of seeing are significant, but they obliterate one another.

This is the fissure in being through which filter the disabling negations of 'Old Man': 'They suggest so much that they mean nothing at all'. This reality is centreless because it is the chance aggregation of innumerable sub-cultures and locales now absorbed into one vast conurbation, which the marginalised 'superfluous man' roams in fascination and incomprehension. This social universe is a text without a cipher, intriguing and frustrating in its inviolacy. It insulates the self from the sign-systems of a pre-urban reality, landscapes which still speak a recognisable language, which it appears the vulnerable self can now discover only in an imaginary pastoral. This certainly seems to be the conclusion of the essay, in which the speaker 'reached a signpost that stood boldly up with undoubted inscriptions, one of them to London, and away from that I set my face'. Direction is discovered only be reaction and flight, and the world into which he moves seems to exist primarily as language, as wish and desire: 'Not for him hesitation and qualification; but to all men perplexed by definitions, testimonies, other prophets and their own thoughts, he cries "This is the way."' Meaning is recovered in a flight which is also a return home. But 'home' is precisely that Edenic garden 'Old Man' reveals to be already subverted by the perplexing serpent of a darkness beyond language.

Language and history are integrally related categories, 'The Word' seems to suggest; language opens right into that 'undefiled / Abyss of what will never be again' where history confronts silence. The poet's function, therefore, is a double one, as 'Words' makes clear, exploring the simultaneous plenitude and lack at the heart of language. Words, we are told, 'choose' the poet, but he also 'make[s] rhymes'. For all the humility of the poet's request to 'You English words' to choose him, 'As the winds use / A crack in a wall / Or a drain', he is not just the passive bearer of a tradition. He knows the words, has endowed them with values and associations out of his own life. Nevertheless, the words are at once 'familiar' and 'strange', living in an external element of which his own life is merely one brief moment. Even unused, they wait to be given a home and a formulation in an individual eye and ear, like 'the races / Of dead and unborn'; but, like them, they also dispossess as they offer a home. At the very moment that the individual finds his place in the order of language, there is the pang of nostalgia. These 'English words' are also the 'lost homes' of the permanent exile: at the very moment that they take a purchase on the earth, they also stand as a sign of our estrangement from it, never able to close the gap between 'the names, and the things, / No less':

> I know you. . . .
> Sweet as our birds
> To the ear. . . .
> Strange as the races
> Of dead and unborn:
> Strange and sweet
> Equally,
> And familiar,
> To the eye,
> As the dearest faces
> That a man knows,
> And as lost homes are:
> But though older far
> Than oldest yew, –
> As our hills are, old –
> Worn new
> Again and again:
> Young as our streams
> After rain:
> And as dear
> As the earth which you prove
> That we love.

The 'lost home' in which the self may stand 'Fixed and free / In a rhyme' can, it seems, only be found in that momentary 'ecstasy' of language which stands outside normal reality altogether.

What this poem expresses as a crisis in the poet's relation to language is also seen repeatedly, in Thomas's poems, as a crisis in social relations. 'Lob' explores the contradiction set out above. 'Lob' is the name given to the memory of an old countryman, encountered years before, whom the poet tries to track down in half-remembered regions. At first an apparently

real memory, he recedes, when pursued, into the realm of
myth. Different men recognise his description, but each with
equal conviction puts a different name to it. The confusion of
names is as great as that which prevented him turning back
years before, when his 'memory could not decide' between the
many similarly named villages where he may have
encountered Lob. It persists until one man volunteers advice.
Lob is likely to be one he too met in childhood:

> '. . . . The man was wild
> And wandered. His home was where he was free.
> Everybody has met one such man as he.
> Does he keep clear old paths that no one uses
> But once a lifetime when he loves or muses?'

'Lob' is a kind of English Prometheus, a fire-giver and a
light-giver, whose freedom lies in his adaptation to the land he
wanders. He is the epitome of the creative power of a people,
not one but many. 'Adam Walker', one suggested name, sums
up his genius: he is the wandering Adam who named the
places 'Marked on the maps', and thus claimed them to a
human use and meaning. 'He is English as this gate, these
flowers, this mire', an autochthonous figure of the fecundity
and inventiveness of a culture which makes the world dense
with language, the author of folk-wisdom, proverbs, tales and
weather-rhymes. His linguistic grasp is quick and intuitive:
the pragmatic value of 'thirteen hundred names for a fool'
excelling the abstract knowledge of the sage 'who knows all
languages'. Language is his only possession; but it is the only
faculty he needs to be fully human. 'Sometimes he is a pedlar,
not too poor / To keep his wit', or 'tall Tom that bore the logs
in', from whom Shakespeare learnt his art, and in these roles
he is opposed to the miserliness of the 'skinflint' housewife and
the miller 'who ground men's bones for flour'. This explains
his cavalier attitude towards property, which makes him stick
in the poet's mind in the first place ('All he said was: "Nobody
can't stop 'ee. It's / A footpath, right enough" ').

Yet the poem's conclusion is strangely equivocal. Its roll-
call of names denies that it is a coronach of a dying order.
Instead it celebrates a resilience and energy capable of

withstanding the corrosive changes hinted at by the overflying aeroplane and the dust of the busy road. Lob stands for an irrepressible cultural essence which, revealed through successive generations of Englishmen, is not ultimately historical at all but biological, rooted in the flesh and blood of men and women and the land from which they spring, and transcends all merely transient social categories ('clown', 'squire', 'lord'). Despite its deep conservatism, this populist mystique of England has a radical inflection, with its implied hostility to a utilitarian, capitalist ethos that would 'grind men's bones for bread':

> 'Do you believe Jack dead before his hour?
> Or that his name is Walker, or Bottlesford,
> Or Button, a mere clown, or squire, or lord?
> The man you saw, – Lob-lie-by-the-fire, Jack Cade,
> Jack Smith, Jack Moon, poor Jack of every trade,
> Young Jack, or old Jack, or Jack What-d'ye-call,
> Jack-in-the-hedge, or Robin-run-by-the-wall,
> Robin Hood, Ragged Robin, lazy Bob,
> One of the lords of No Man's Land, good Lob, –
> Although he was seen dying at Waterloo,
> Hastings, Agincourt, and Sedgemoor too, –
> Lives yet. He never will admit he is dead
> Till millers cease to grind men's bones for bread,
> Not till our weathercock crows once again
> And I remove my house out of the lane
> On the road.' With this he disappeared
> In hazel and thorn tangled with old-man's-beard.
> But one glimpse of his back, as there he stood,
> Choosing his way, proved him of old Jack's blood,
> Young Jack perhaps, and now a Wiltshireman
> As he has oft been since his days began.

For all the confident assertion, what is most striking is the *elusiveness* of Lob. Affirmation in this final speech has to be set against his immediate flight (so reminiscent of Arnold's 'Scholar Gipsy'). The dual movement of this poem enshrines a real cultural dichotomy. Lob is evasive, can never be pinned down for more than an instant, any more than those English

words courted in 'Words'. The ideal of spontaneous intuitive
life he embodies is a rarity, the power of language not to be
presumed upon. The need to search for him is indicative:
though 'His home was where he was free', Lob's whereabouts
and identity are increasingly problematic. His stature and
territory seem diminished since the days of those primordial
folk-tales, for he has to be hunted right into the 'heart of
England', until his pursuer is lost in a swirl of place-names
and faces, deep in the recesses of a receding world. He is
propertyless, but also dispossessed, 'one of the lords of No
Man's Land'. The battle of Sedgemoor, in 1685, ended in a
massacre of West Country peasants forced into insurrection
by economic and social forces they could not begin to
understand, rallying round the pretender Monmouth as the
equivocal focus of their confusedly radical and conservative
desires. In 1904, the Whig historian G. M. Trevelyan, in
England Under the Stuarts, had suggested a link between the
French peasants who fought for Napoleon at Waterloo and
those who had flocked to Monmouth's cause, speaking of the
vigour and 'love of liberty' of 'the old peasant life, since passed
away into the streets and factories, suffering city-change', and
concluding 'The land of England was not then owned by the
few'. At a time when the rural crisis had produced massive
popular agitation and the widespread demand for land
nationalisation, Thomas's reference to Sedgemoor is a highly
topical one, underwritten by those passing references to Jack
Cade and Robin Hood, with their hint of medieval jacqueries.
In this light, Lob's advice, ' "Nobody can't stop 'ee" ', takes
on a new significance.

   The crisis in the poet's relation to his language and culture,
his sense of frailty before an external landscape from which he
is readily estranged, yet which means much to him, has a
deeper, material base, hinted at in this poem. 'Nostalgia' is
right at the heart of the poem ' "Home" ', as is the whole
problem of finding an authentic language in which men may
speak to each other. In a review of Yeats in May 1908,
Thomas had discussed the idea that all symbolic art arises
from a shared community of belief, and felt compelled to add
that, in Yeats's work, 'The individual is everything in it:
society has not been considered. But then society is not alive,

it is a lump that exists. Reform society, not the artist.' The divorce of 'individual' from 'society', as subject set against object, is the source of that mutual estrangement which is the theme of ' "Home" '. None of the three individuals in this narrative feels that he belongs to a genuine community with the others. Each sees the other two as part of that external world, composing with the snowbound landscape an alien unity set over against his own isolate subjectivity. Such a perception arises from the unexplained yet tyrannous external 'necessity' which turns each life into a Babylonish captivity. Approaching 'the cold roofs where we must spend the night' –

> . . . 'How quick', to someone's lip
> The words came, 'will the beaten horse run home!'
> The word 'home' raised a smile in us all three,
> And one repeated it, smiling just so
> That all knew what he meant and none would say.
> Between three counties far apart that lay
> We were divided and looked strangely each
> At the other, and we knew we were not friends
> But fellows in a union that ends
> With the necessity for it, as it ought.

Despite the repeated 'we', there is no real fellowship. The others lack real singularity: the generalised, detached statement, with its impersonal pronouns and its passive voice, imputes a world where identity is reduced to anonymous uniformity as the snow levels the landscape to a homogeneous white. 'Someone' speaks; 'one' responds: in either case, the speaker might have been the narrator himself. Emotion remains furtive: distrusting the good faith of the others, each shrinks from the dangers of self-disclosure. The poem is full of interrupted flows: between motive and act, impulse and destination, internal 'need' and external 'necessity'. But it is in the gulf between experience and utterance that the chance of a deeper fellowship founders. The one line of speech at the heart of the poem comes with an unsolicited directness that startles with the shock of recognition. But it cannot close the gap between common knowledge and private acknowledgment ('all knew what he meant', but 'none would

say'), and the interrupted flow is repeated in the lines which
close the poem:

> Never a word was spoken, not a thought
> Was thought, of what the look meant with the word
> 'Home' as we walked and watched the sunset blurred.
> And then to me the word, only the word,
> 'Homesick', as it were playfully occurred:
> No more.
>   If I should ever more admit
> Than the mere word I could not endure it
> For a day longer: this captivity
> Must somehow come to an end, else I should be
> Another man, as often now I seem,
> Or this life be only an evil dream.

This is a deadlock where revolt and impotence cancel each
other out, in the failure to recognise the common ground of
their actual vagrancy: the shared language and landscape
where their private needs and memories converge. The
snowfall is not accidental. It is because the land is rendered
'strange' that the men can come to look 'strangely each /   At
the other'. The snow intervenes between mind and landscape
as the mutual distrust of the travellers stifles authentic speech.
The result is a paralysis in which they become helpless
dependents of a massively exterior world.

A similar subordination to a nature shorn of human
meanings occurs in 'Wind and Mist', a conversation between
a passer-by and a second man, the poet, who is wrapped up in
a private anguish which makes him loquacious but
unsociable. The object of their discussion is the hilltop house
which, it turns out, was the poet's home. His self-absorption
issues in a kind of speculative, proprietorial idealism in which,
speaking of the surrounding Downs, he feels 'as if /   He had
just created them with one mighty thought'. But the pride of
this naive idealism had led to its opposite, in which mind was
reduced to a desperate, embattled centre, threatened by the
primordial formlessness of nature – 'mist /   Like chaos surging
back' – so that it felt 'Alone in all the world, marooned alone'.
At other times, it seemed that 'the wind and I /   Between us

shared the world, and the wind ruled / And I obeyed it and forgot the mist'. Yet the dialogue, perfunctory though it is, keeps open a vital social dimension. The poem had opened with a subtle negotiation of points of view, in which the depressing view from the house itself is contrasted with the more benign prospect it offers from a distance. The poem ends by hinting at a further, social relativity which is the unacknowledged bedrock of the poet's fluctuating subjectivity. In despairing of contact he unwittingly demonstrates its possibility. The unexpected, begrudging admission of the close, as if on an afterthought, finally concedes this:

> 'Now you may say that though you understand
> And feel for me, and so on, you yourself
> Would find it different. You are all like that
> If once you stand here free from wind and mist:
> I might as well be talking to wind and mist.
> You would believe the house-agent's young man
> Who gives no heed to anything I say.
> Good morning. But one word. I want to admit
> That I would try the house once more, if I could;
> As I should like to try being young again.'

The poet vacillates between a stubborn isolationism and a desperate need for contact, retracting his abrupt 'Good morning' with an equally abrupt postscript which subverts the whole tenor of his previous monologue. Yet the tone of incipiently paranoid querulousness prevents any real exchange, half dissolving the world of human sympathies, with its many overlapping conversations, back into the alien and oppressive conspiracy of wind and mist. Like the snow in '"Home"', the elements here intrude not only between man and nature but between men and men, and the two movements are integrally related.

Although written in 1915, 'Wind and Mist' recalls that house in Wick Green, Hampshire where, in September 1911, Thomas suffered the nervous breakdown which was the inevitable product of years of overwork and chronic financial anxiety, sustained by tireless reviewing and the writing of innumerable pot-boilers. The birth and subsequent illness of his third child, in August 1910, extended his obligations at a time when the inflation which characterised the whole pre-war period had doubled the annual rate of increase of the cost of living (from four per cent in 1908 to nine per cent per annum between 1909 and 1913). Thomas's earnings not only failed to keep pace with this rise, but may actually have declined.

The period was one of desperation for Thomas, as the essays published at the time reveal. One scarcely fictionalised piece in *Light and Twilight* (1911) records a suicide attempt. In *Lafcadio Hearn* (1912) he wrote bitterly of 'European civilisation, with "unlimited individuality" to starve or purchase a peerage', and added, pointedly:

> Hearn saw the horrors of this free society, but dreaded Socialism, which he called a 'reversion towards the primitive conditions of human society'. . . . He foresaw 'a democracy more brutal than any Spartan oligarchy'. . . and this he confused with Socialism.

In February 1911 Thomas had written in *The Bookman* of the 'inevitable exile' and the 'feeling something like paralysis' of the poet in modern society, and had spoken warmly of William Morris's 'faithful Socialist' attempt to read the ambiguous message of the March wind, blowing from 'the "shabby hell" of the city', but presaging 'a union between love of one woman and of the world'. In January, he had selected as one of the 'essential things' in Stephen Graham's book *A Vagabond in the Caucasus* a remark which obviously cut deeply into his own sense of social vagrancy:

> You English have forgotten that you are brothers. Money has come between you, and money has made you work. You are all gathered together not out of love, but out of hate. In England, gregariousness; in Russia, conviviality.

Aggregation without community characterises the social relations of both poems discussed above. In 'Wind and Mist', the anguish of that period has been sublimed into a sense of metaphysical persecution. It is not necessary to foist a crude allegorical meaning on the symbolism of wind and mist. They stand for vast impersonal forces beyond the power of individual wills to control, in a world where 'The flint was the one crop that never failed'. But it would be foolish to ignore the extent to which the symbolism is imbued with personal, obsessive intensity by the experience of financial insecurity, 'living in clouds, on a cliff's edge almost', in a world rocked by inflation. It is no accident that the poem gravitates from the realm of misty metaphysics to the bathetically actual world of 'the house-agent's young man'. The wishful proprietorial pride with which the poem opens and the humiliating insinuation of financial duress with which it closes are intimately related. He had sought to monopolise the landscape, from his cliff-top vantage. The undefined, all-pervasive 'necessity' of ' "Home" ", which enforces his homesickness, is the same force that here intrudes between poet, questioner and house-agent's young man, and between the father and the child who is born in the house ('Never looked grey mind on a greyer one / Than when the child's cry broke above the groans'). It is the power of money, which taints all conviviality with the sordid and estranging smell of death, of petty and personal interest, turning genuine mutuality into the improper and obfuscating exchanges of drudgery, debt and bargaining, converting a world of shared meanings into the collective alienation of a 'league of snow', owned by none and interrupted only by the 'cold roofs where we must spend the night'. The house, as so often in Thomas's poetry, is then the whole dilapidated culture in which he finds himself, as in 'Gone, Gone Again', 'the old house, / Outmoded, dignified, / Dark and untenanted' with which he feels inevitable identification, even though he is 'Still breathing and interested / In the house that is not dark', in a new social order that might lie on the other side of a war which has begun 'to turn young men to dung'.

In a variety of poems, Thomas explores these estranging exchanges between individuals, which express the crisis of a whole culture. In 'The Gypsy', the flirtatious begging of a gypsy woman adds the *frisson* of sexuality to what is also a class encounter. In three poems for his children, he examines the absurdities of property relations in a world where one cannot be content, in the words of his *George Borrow* (1912), to see a larch wood in October 'described as so many poles growing in three.acres of land, the property of a manufacturer of gin'. 'If I should ever by chance grow rich', says the first poem in the sequence, he would buy the land around only to let it to his daughter for a rent of 'Each year's first violets'. By the end of the poem, he has promised to give the land away without any rent at all. The poem mocks the clauses of a legal contract, for instead of imposing qualifications on the original agreement each new clause enlarges the largesse, making the conditions less and less stringent. The repetition of the names of places and flowers is the real inheritance, the gift of a common language in which the world can be named. 'What shall I give?' carries this logic into outright renunciation, refusing to give anything to his younger daughter of a world already 'shared', at its deepest levels, with all the other creatures who inhabit it: 'Her small hands I would not cumber / With so many acres and their lumber', for it is already 'her own world'. 'If I were to own this countryside' evokes a sardonic hint of earlier enclosures (riding the bounds) before giving all the lands around to his son, providing 'he would let me any one / For a song, a blackbird's song, at dawn'. The mysterious transfiguration of personal possession in a mutual giving with which the poem ends is sustained by a syntactical ambiguity which allows the song to be both the son's payment for the whole and the father's rent for part. This seems to be an extension of that whimsical idealist communism Thomas had adumbrated in an early essay, speaking in *Rose Acre Papers* (1904) of a country estate whose 'gardens are really mine':

> Go when you will – except at the garden party – and you will see that I alone am lord of the roses and all the grass. I have sometimes wondered when the 'owner' will acknowledge my right. Yet I am in no haste to enter into possession: that in itself would be barbarous. . . . I prefer to be outside, innocently investing the place, never demanding capitulation or storming the wall. I am well provisioned with pride, and am content to see the great man go in and out, ignorant of rivalry. Never was such cheerful communism, such wholesome confusion of *meum* and *tuum*.

The idea of property intrudes deep into the heart of

Thomas's sense of Englishness. Enclosure is an 'un-English' act, to be replaced, here, by a kind of perceptual usufruct cognate with the poaching of the old tramp 'Jack Noman' in the poem 'May the Twenty-third'. Nature is restored to its intrinsic wholeness only when it is secluded from all property relations as, in *The Heart of England*, a disused road can be described as 'the innermost kernel of the land, because nobody owns and nobody uses it'. Perhaps this explains the ambiguity of Lob, his remoteness and unsociability. Epitome of the creative spirit of the English people, Lob is a homeless vagrant, 'one of the lords of No Man's Land'. 'His home was where he was free', but such territory has dwindled to those 'old paths that no one uses / But once a lifetime when he loves or muses'. As Thomas's radical solution to the land problem – nationalisation – in the study *Richard Jefferies* (1909) reveals, there is a sterner aspect to this 'cheerful communism', which persists as the lurking but suppressed dimension of one of his most powerful poems.

'Up in the Wind' is a poem which, opening with the ahistorical melancholy of ' "Home" ', slowly unfolds the social aetiology of the poet's 'homesickness', relating it to a wider history of deracination and dispossession. Implacable and absorbing, for the lonely country girl who has returned from a good job in London to keep the forest inn which is her birthplace, the wind bodies forth the mysterious power of an uncomprehended but accepted destiny. Her resentment cuts across the poet's picturesque melancholy, which peoples the abandoned landscape with ghostly but to him congenial company. Her Cockney accent, like the roads around, leads away to unfamiliar distances. It embeds her social history as absolutely as the landscape breathes its past.

Destinies of poet and girl have converged momentarily in a shared dispossession. He seeks the lost, traditional home of which an urban career has robbed him, here in this public house hidden from the road, yet 'homely, too, upon a far horizon / To one that knows there is an inn within'. She regrets the loss of that newer world, in Kennington, which offered her a fulfilment denied her here, in her ancestral home. Yet her tale unfolds a destiny which encompasses both of them as totally as the wind which surrounds the house.

Déraciné urban intellectual and *déclassée* 'peasant' girl share a
common legacy just as the vagrant tramp and the touring
motorist, despite their different motives, are the only other
users of these roads besides the poet and 'A market waggon
every other Wednesday'. Though the poet has constructed a
landscape of imaginary neighbours, the wildness of the place
is real, to be possessed, not as property, but only in its own
terms, by 'life that loves the wild'. The girl herself, like Lob,
is 'wild', almost as if she belongs to that world beyond the inn
which is untouched by human demarcations:

> But the land is wild, and there's a spirit of wildness
> Much older, crying when the stone curlew yodels
> His sea and mountain cry, high up in Spring.
> He nests in fields where still the gorse is free as
> When all was open and common. Common 'tis named
> And calls itself, because the bracken and gorse
> Still hold the hedge where scythe and plough have chased
> > them.

The only land that remains 'free' is that too 'wild' to be
economically viable and therefore worth enclosing. The house
itself was once 'public' in this sense, defined by the network of
paths which converged on it. A vast social transformation can
be deduced from the girl's private chronicle. The inn was once
a smithy; the smith's widow married again:

> 'Years ago, when this was all a wood
> And the smith had charcoal-burners for company,
> A man from a beech-country in the shires
> Came with an engine and a little boy
> (To feed the engine) to cut up timber here.
> It all happened years ago. The smith
> Had died, his widow had set up an alehouse –
> I could wring the old thing's neck for thinking of it.
> Well, I suppose they fell in love, the widow
> And my great uncle that sawed up the timber:
> Leastways they married. The little boy stayed on.
> He was my father.'

Most of the land has been enclosed; the forest is depleted to the few trees around the inn; the charcoal burners are long gone; now and again the traces of their fires are ploughed up. The roads have fallen into disuse because a community has exhausted its resources and disappeared, and the deforestation testifies to some self-destructive urge closely bound up with the economics of commodity exchange:

> 'My father, he
> Took to the land. A mile of it is worth
> A guinea; for by that time all the trees
> Except these few about the house were gone.'

The final note offers a tenuous personal resolution in which, as in 'The Gypsy', sexual undercurrents eddy briefly across the social gulf between them. A common experience has been delineated in the girl's monologue, and it draws the poet out of his romantic musings on the landscape into a momentary exchange with the real person before him. Two roads have crossed; for a moment, doors have opened for each onto illimitable vistas. Beyond these two isolated and marginal figures lies a world extensive in space and time, a history of wandering men and temporary settlements and of an inheritance transmitted uninterruptedly despite all obstacles. The wind, in the end, is the image of a humanly created and humanly chosen destiny, not a cosmic absolute, and the recognition gives a richer, humanising irony to the line in 'Wind and Mist': 'My past and the past of the world were in the wind'. The poem closes with a double directive which transcends, briefly, the social segregation of man and woman. The inn is deserted, but the roads are open: it is, after all, 'a public house and not a hermitage' (line 79):

> 'Look at those calves.'
>   Between the open door
> And the trees two calves were wading in the pond,
> Grazing the water here and there and thinking,
> Sipping and thinking, both happily, neither long.
> The water wrinkled, but they sipped and thought,
> As careless of the wind as it of us.
> 'Look at those calves. Hark at the trees again.'

It is a consummate ending. Here, in this pastoral seclusion, a small space is cleared out of the wind of history, where a man and woman divided by class and culture may, for a moment, share what Thomas in a 1901 review called 'a sense of common things' – of ordinary things, of things held, and experienced, in common. Yet this is a 'public house'. The very structure of Thomas's liberal humanism acknowledges this social dimension which is the source of its being: men and women are made what they are by the whole weight of an incumbent history. The landscape is shared and yet ultimately belongs to neither: 'Common 'tis named / And calls itself'. The land withdraws into itself, in the very moment that the vagrant self seeks to touch it, to make contact with its inhabitants. The only way forward from here, which would make this brief encounter permanent, would involve the making actual of that spectatorial 'cheerful communism'. Thomas's poetry everywhere acknowledges this, in its celebration of an England that cannot be parcelled up into private plots and private persons. For Thomas himself, the war and enlistment seemed a way out of that 'captivity' in which he found himself, a superfluous man in a dilapidated culture. His death at Arras in 1917 in a way consummated without resolving the contradictions of his life, putting an end to that conflict of populism and isolation, tradition and radicalism, nostalgia and hope which, in the poetry, exists as lived tensions and anxieties, doubts, hesitations and bewilderment, speaking with the obliquity of 'a language not to be betrayed'. For the culture of which he was the expression, the way forward was to lead from the trenches to a larger waste land.

4

T. S. Eliot: Lengthening Shadows

(The lengthened shadow of a man
Is history, said Emerson
Who had not seen the silhouette
Of Sweeney straddled in the sun.)

Eliot's parenthetical insertion in 'Sweeney Erect'
(*Poems – 1920*) indicates the ambivalence of his attitude
towards history. History is a recurring theme of the volume,
whether in the assertion in 'Gerontion' that 'History has many
cunning passages', or in the despairing vision of 'Time's ruins'
which concludes 'Burbank with a Baedeker'. Two years later,
in the opening section of *The Waste Land*, Eliot was to repeat
the shadow motif, in a passage in which the purblind visionary
Tiresias promises to show us:

> . . . . something different from either
> Your shadow at morning striding behind you
> Or your shadow at evening striding to meet you;
> I will show you fear in a handful of dust.

In 'Sweeney Erect' the mood is not fear, but closer to the
hysteria of the epileptic woman in the shady hotel, which
'does the house no sort of good', and is reinforced by the
language of the poem itself – at once highly mannered and
riven by a frozen and immobilised violence. The tone is set by
the opening stanza:

> Paint me a cavernous waste shore
> Cast in the unstilled Cyclades,
> Paint me the bold anfractuous rocks
> Faced by the snarled and yelping seas.

The oddity of 'anfractuous', like the past participle turned
into an adjective in 'unstilled' and 'snarled', suggests, even as
the meaning of the words denies it, a world turned to stone by
the glare of Medusa. The transfixed pastness of 'lengthened'
has the same effect, as do the changes of tense of a dislocated
sentence structure. In the fourth stanza, for example, the
subject of the sentence, 'This withered root of knots of hair',
does not find a main verb. Instead the sentence shifts to
another subject – 'The sickle motion from the thighs'. The
dislocation is compounded by this repeated use of
metonymy – the part for the whole – so that we are left with a
sense of Sweeney as no more than a disorderly assemblage of
parts and actions, an 'oval O cropped out with teeth', a
'Gesture of orang-outang' rising from the bed, a sickle motion
that 'straightens out from heel to hip'.

The apelike Sweeney and the Transcendentalist Emerson,
the bestial parody of the human and the high-flown
spirituality of the American puritan tradition, represent the
two extremes of Eliot's vision, the Scylla and Charybdis
between which, throughout his poetry, this reluctant
Odysseus is forced to sail. The way in which the parenthesis
intrudes into the squalor of the poem – like '(Nausicaa and
Polypheme)' later – suggests a central disjunction in Eliot's
view of the world. There is the immense panorama of futility
and anarchy of which he spoke in discussing Joyce's use of the
Odysseus legend – an everyday, squalid, precarious life,
always close, it seems, to madness. And there is the painted,
artificial world, where even apeneck Sweeney and the
hysterical 'woman on the bed' can be verbally transformed
into creatures of myth. Everyday life, in all its grossness,
contains within it these little bracketted moments of beauty
and transcendence. But this world is a constructed scene, as
the opening injunctions remind us: 'Paint ... Cast ...
Paint ... Display'. Both realms in the end are equally unreal.
Whether we inhabit the world of Sweeney or of Emerson, of
everyday life or of the spirit, we live in the 'Unreal City'. All
these things, in the words of 'Preludes', are no more than
'masquerades / That time resumes'.

In a talk called 'What Dante Means to Me' in 1950, Eliot
explained that his borrowings from Dante were intended to

'establish a relationship between the medieval inferno and modern life' in the reader's mind. In particular, he referred to 'the vision of my city clerks trooping over London Bridge from the railway station to their offices' in *The Waste Land,* and to 'the hallucinated scene after an air-raid' in *Little Gidding.* (The lecture is reprinted in *To Criticize the Critic,* 1965). Characteristically, Eliot begins his talk by speaking of two other poets, apparently remote from Dante, whose work nevertheless offers a similar critique of the diabolic modern world, Laforgue and Baudelaire. The remarks are of some interest for this discussion:

> I think that from Baudelaire I learned first, a precedent for the poetical possibilities, never developed by any poet writing in my own language, of the more sordid aspects of the modern metropolis, of the possibility of fusion between the sordidly realistic and the phantasmagoric, the possibility of the juxtaposition of the matter-of-fact and the fantastic. . . . I learned that the sort of material that I had, the sort of experience that an adolescent had had, in an industrial city in America, could be the material for poetry; and that the source of new poetry might be found in what had been regarded hitherto as the impossible, the sterile, the intractably unpoetic. That, in fact, the business of the poet was to make poetry out of the unexplored resources of the unpoetical; that the poet, in fact, was committed by his profession to turn the unpoetical into poetry.

It may be, he continues, that Baudelaire's lines about the swarming city, the city full of dreams, where the spectre accosts the passer-by in broad daylight, gave him everything that he needed. 'I knew what that meant, because I had lived it before I knew that I wanted to turn it into verse on my own account.'

What Eliot evinces here is that doubleness at the heart of his perception of contemporary history. On the one hand, it is 'sordid' and to be reviled. On the other hand, it is fascinating in its swarming, corrupt phantasmagoria, and the poet's only business. But at the same time that it enters intimately into the poet's mind it must be kept at a fastidious aesthetic distance by his handling of it. Attention must not be confused with endorsement.

The discussion of Eliot's cultural patrimony has frequently assumed a simple opposition between the rival claims of English domicile and New England descent – between the Anglo-Catholic, Royalist classicism he espoused in 1927, and the Calvinist and Transcendentalist inheritance represented by Emerson. Eliot's own writings have encouraged this tendency. Overtly, they invite us to observe the landscape of London and rural England, or the family snapshots of haut-bourgeois Massachusetts, as in 'The Boston Evening Transcript', 'Aunt Helen' or 'Cousin Nancy', a world where Emerson and Matthew Arnold kept watch on the bookshelves, 'guardians of the faith, / The army of unalterable law'. The St Louis of his childhood rarely occurs in his poems. Even when it does, as in the image of the river as 'a strong brown god' which opens 'Dry Salvages', our attention is directed away from the Missouri *mise-en-scène,* with its unsavoury properties ('the river with its cargo of dead negroes, cows and chicken coops'), to the spiritual symbolism offered by the dangerous rocks off Massachusetts, which provide the title to the poem.

Yet Eliot's mid-western origins are not merely a matter of 'background': they are a central part of the meaning of his poetry. If, for Eliot, 'history' usually means the fallen world of the modern industrial city, it was in St Louis that he came to consciousness of this history, and it is the image of the city given him by that provincial metropolis around the turn of the century which colours all his subsequent perceptions. In one of his few references to these origins, a lecture on 'American Literature and the American Language' delivered at Washington University, St Louis, in 1953, Eliot admitted as much, in speaking of his own upbringing and the involvement of his 'family and personal history' with that of the city and the university (*To Criticize the Critic*).

In that address, Eliot speaks of his paternal grandfather, W. G. Eliot, who died a year before his birth, but who remained for young Eliot 'still the head of the family – a ruler for whom *in absentia* my grandmother stood as viceregent'. The 'standard of conduct' in the household, he says, was dictated by the upright Unitarian tradition inherited from New England, whose foremost precept was the 'Law of Public Service'. In a few suggestive paragraphs, Gabriel Pearson has sketched in some of the less recondite implications of this 'background' (see Graham Martin, ed., *Eliot in Perspective*, 1970). W. G. Eliot, as one of the founding fathers of St Louis in the boom years that followed the American Civil War, invested his family's reputation in the city's success. The Eliots became a kind of 'practical aristocracy', with considerable prestige and patronage and the permanent visibility that, in a provincial setting, usually accompanies them. Unitarianism here survived its Eastern demise, to provide moral spine for that sense of specialness, of election, which underwrote a paternalism realised through 'public service'. Yet in the poet's adolescence there was a painful clash between image and reality, as the disclosures of the muck-raking journalist Lincoln Steffens between 1902 and 1904 'revealed St Louis flagrantly boss-ridden and corrupted'; 'the Eliots were apparently involved' in the subsequent clean-up. When Eliot left St Louis in 1905, at the age of seventeen, to attend school in Massachusetts, he took with him an image of the City tarnished by a corruption which inevitably rubbed off on the good name of its founding fathers and founding principles.

Brought up, in his own words, 'to reverence such institutions' as Church and City, and 'taught that personal and selfish aims should be subordinated to the general good which they represent', the adolescent Eliot can only have experienced the betrayal of these institutions as a personal betrayal. At this moment of maximum self-consciousness, the young Eliot experienced the self's involvement with history as one in which visibility meant exposure, and service meant vulnerability to an immediate, smearing otherness. For Eliot, henceforth, there was always to be a clash between ideal and actuality, between impeccable principle and motive and its realisation in the sordid, polluting world of history. Even to see such a world, in Eliot's poetry, is in some way to be tainted. Its very contingency demonstrates one's fallenness, the inescapable dependence on 'The thousand sordid images / Of which your soul was constituted' ('Preludes'). The given world is oppressive simply because it *is* given, in Eliot's early poems, that St Louis which for the young poet, in his own words, was 'the beginning of the Wild West'. It is a dead-end world, where the wind blows 'grimy scraps / Of withered leaves about your feet / And newspapers from vacant lots', and newspapers are automatically linked with danger and disintegration, with those threats to dignity and self-possession that the speaker of 'Portrait of a Lady' reads of in the park:

> Particularly I remark
> An English countess goes upon the stage.
> A Greek was murdered at a Polish dance,
> Another bank defaulter has confessed.
> I keep my countenance,
> I remain self-possessed. . . .

The very need to make this last affirmation suggests an anxiety that he too may become a victim of some inexplicable moral collapse or exposure. For this is a world where, as in 'Aunt Helen', one is no longer securely in control. The servants will lose all discretion as soon as one is out of the way and unable to exercise proper authority, a world where democracy, with its demeaning impertinences, threatens to overthrow all decorum:

> And the footman sat upon the dining-table
> Holding the second housemaid on his knees –
> Who had always been so careful while her mistress lived.

Such improprieties are the privileges of a fallen world. Should one be tempted, like Prufrock, to indulge in them, to dare 'disturb the universe', one will be exposed at once to the ridicule of inferiors, will see 'the moment of my greatness flicker / . . . the eternal Footman hold my coat and snicker'. One then has a right to be 'afraid', confronted by the whole exterior world of time and history as one gross, uppity servant.

The consciousness that animates 'Preludes' experiences this doubleness – at once superior and elect, and derided and put-upon – right at the heart of its identity. On the one hand, it is merely an object in a landscape, among many others – broken blinds and chimney-pots, lonely cab-horses and the other 'burnt-out ends of smoky days', in a run-down

world. On the other hand, it is the subjective arena for all
these phenomena, the place where 'smell of steak in
passageways' is experienced, where 'The morning comes to
consciousness / Of faint stale smells of beer'. The phrasing,
which makes 'morning' and 'consciousness' coterminous,
indicates the inseparability of subject and object-world. This
is a world drowning in plurality, 'With all its muddy feet that
press / To early coffee-stands', where 'One thinks of all the
hands / That are raising dingy shades / In a thousand
furnished rooms'. And yet at the same time the self is a
solitary and melancholy subject, the only real radius within
which these other lives and things 'come to consciousness'.

'Prelude' IV opens with an image of a spatially inclusive
consciousness which registers the strain and vulnerability of
the elect self. This self is simultaneously superior, embracing
the whole world as if it were his spiritual parish, and fallen,
trodden underfoot. 'His soul stretched tight across the
skies / That fade behind a city block', in a way which suggests
the anguish of a dutiful public responsibility. But this soul is
then 'trampled by insistent feet', imposed upon in some way
the syntax doesn't make clear by the 'short square fingers
stuffing pipes, / And evening newspapers, and eyes / Assured
of certain certainties'. There is a significant link between the
eyes and the newspapers, as there is a reassuring contrast
between the vulgar certainty of those eyes and the 'infinitely
gentle / Infinitely suffering thing' of its fantasies. Only by
becoming 'The conscience of a blackened street / Impatient to
assume the world' can the stricken but elite consciousness
recover some hint of its elective grace, through a superior,
patrician knowledge which acknowledges its own complicity
in, and adulteration by, this world:

> And when all the world came back . . .
> You had such a vision of the street
> As the street hardly understands;
> Sitting along the bed's edge where
> You curled the papers from your hair,
> Or clasped the yellow souls of feet
> In the palms of both soiled hands.

These hands may not bear stigmata, but their owner's elect consciousness certainly has something in common with that first trampled and crucified suffering servant. Unlike Christ, however, it is not in submission but in rejection that he finds release from this world, in an act of brutal dismissal which is simultaneously arrogant and self-deprecating, parodying the cynicism of those around, and refusing to be caught out in either pity or self-indulgence:

> Wipe your hand across your mouth, and laugh;
> The worlds revolve like ancient women
> Gathering fuel in vacant lots.

The mood of this perhaps explains why exile was not for Eliot an alienating but a liberating experience, offering a reassuring anonymity in which to construct a new, self-made identity. There is an unmistakable relish in Eliot's account of his own deracination, in a 1928 letter to Sir Herbert Read (cited in Allen Tate, ed., *T. S. Eliot: The Man and His Work*, 1966):

> Some day I want to write an essay about the point of view of an American who wasn't an American, because he was born in the South and went to school in New England as a small boy with a nigger drawl, but who wasn't a southerner in the South because his people were northerners in a border state and looked down on all southerners and Virginians, and who so was never anything anywhere and who therefore felt himself to be more a Frenchman than an American and more an Englishman than a Frenchman and yet felt that the USA up to a hundred years ago was a family extension.

To be rootless is to be free from the constraints of unreal cities, able to reduce their actual inhabitants to the wraithlike crowds that flow over London Bridge, whose downturned gazes pay one no attention. Yet Eliot's flight from a contingent landscape which imposes identities and obligations on the self is tinged also by the pride of a 'young pretender'. The self remains the 'prince over the water' for whom 'the USA up to a hundred years ago was a family extension'. Such a double attitude, at once renouncing and laying absolute claim to reality, lies at the heart of all the tergiversations through which a fastidious Prufrock passes, wondering whether he dare 'Disturb the universe'; it lies, too, behind Eliot's idea of 'Tradition' and the interior landscapes of a symbolist poetic for which he opted from 'The Hollow Men' onwards; and it accounts for the peculiar condition of Tiresias in *The Waste Land*, at once 'the most important personage in the poem. uniting all the rest' and yet no more than 'a mere spectator and not indeed a "character"' at all.

Throughout Eliot's poetry the self is both the absolute, judicious circumference of events and, at the same time, forever at risk, in danger of being overwhelmed by the thousand sordid images which constitute its experience. The world is simultaneously *out there* and threateningly alien to the self, and *in here,* entering into all the intimacy of personal consciousness. In 'Gerontion', this leads to a radical renunciation. If the self is 'adulterated' by its sense impressions, escape requires a flight from contingent being altogether, into a spiritual vacuity withdrawn from material things and their polluting messages, which accost one, like the spectres and prostitutes of these early poems, in broad daylight, through all the tainted portals of the body:

> I that was near your heart was removed therefrom
> To lose beauty in terror, terror in inquisition.
> I have lost my passion: why should I need to keep it
> Since what is left must be adulterated?
> I have lost my sight, smell, hearing, taste and touch:
> How should I use them for your closer contact?

In 'Portrait of a Lady' the young man is reproached for being 'invulnerable', having 'no Achilles' heel'. This is only partially correct. His vulnerability, in fact, lies in his urgent need to 'remain self-possessed', to preserve himself from pollution by a demeaning world, that makes demands upon his attention and allegiance. Thus, he is caught off-guard by the lady's shrewd remarks, just as he feels himself threatened by the 'mechanical and tired' street piano, which 'Reiterates some worn-out common song', or by the smell of hyacinths across the gardens, 'Recalling things that other people have desired'. Sharing in these 'common' experiences does not, as for Thomas, transcend the terrifying isolation of the self in an alien world, restoring a sense of momentary community which releases the self from bondage. On the contrary, it reinforces the terror of this self, by robbing it of its sense of specialness and election, tainting it with the squalor of the ordinary, reducing it to the status of those self-betraying fools assembled, trapped and diminished in the columns of the popular press. The association of desire with a tawdry mechanical music, easily repeated and dismissed, recurs at that crucial moment in *The Waste Land* when the 'lovely woman', harried into indifferent submission by the 'small house agent's clerk' – 'One of the low on whom assurance sits / As a silk hat on a Bradford millionaire' – recovers from her seduction and 'smoothes her hair with automatic hand, / And puts a record on the gramophone'. Her fall, significantly, is couched in class terms.

In 'Portrait', the young man seeks to escape from these humiliations by flight – literally, by going abroad, metaphorically, by envisaging the lady's death, in what seems almost a wishful symbolic homicide. Compelled to 'borrow every changing shape / To find expression', to 'dance / Like a dancing bear, / Cry like a parrot, chatter like an ape', his revolt against such demeaning contiguity cannot be final. Imagining the lady's death, he finds himself wondering whether this may not, after all, leave her with the final advantage, and him not even knowing what he should feel, or whether he is 'wise or foolish, tardy or too soon'. Even death, it seems, may simply be a tactic for trapping the self into commitment, forcing it to feel, involuntarily and therefore vulnerably.

In a poem such as 'Prufrock', ironic self-deprecation is one way out of this compromising dilemma. Prufrock adopts deliberately a protean changeableness, refusing to be caught out in romantic attitudinising. It would be easy for this exceptional and self-conscious young man to identify with Prince Hamlet. But such an act would be folly, exposing him to the ridicule of his spiritual and social inferiors. The strategy of extrication is a simple one, which begins with outright denial of any grandiose ideas:

No! I am not Prince Hamlet, nor was meant to be;
Am an attendant lord, one that will do
To swell a progress, start a scene or two,
Advise the Prince; no doubt an easy tool,
Deferential, glad to be of use,
Politic, cautious, and meticulous;
Full of high sentence, but a bit obtuse;
At times, indeed, almost ridiculous –
Almost, at times, the Fool.

I grow old. . . . I grow old. . . .
I shall wear the bottoms of my trousers rolled.

Far from being what Hugh Kenner in *The Invisible Poet* (1959) calls the '*non sequitur* of an aging Bostonian', this shift of tone emerges directly from what precedes it. Prufrock sees himself as a marginal, superfluous man, and this precludes him from any easy identification with the central figure of Shakespeare's play. Yet Hamlet's dilemma too is that he is marginalised in a world which should be his 'family extension'. Prufrock's descent of the Great Chain of Being seems to take him further and further away from the wronged Prince, to a suspect absurdity whose natural conclusion is the Fool. But Shakespeare's Fools are cleverer than their patrons. The Fool in *Hamlet* is not just the dead father-figure Yorick but also the living Gravedigger, who lives to bury most of his superiors. Hamlet comes closer to the Fool than to any one else, when he assumes an 'antic disposition' to elude the prying eyes of a cynical and manipulative court. The vulnerably balding Prufrock is not going to be caught out in romantic posturing, with his 'white flannel trousers' around his Achilles' heels. But in a sense, like Hamlet, he is a prince in hiding, the true heir to history, just as, earlier, he had denied being a prophet while self-deprecatingly conceding that 'I have seen my head [grown slightly bald] brought in upon a platter', like John the Baptist, and has also toyed with the idea of being Lazarus, back from the dead, 'Come back to tell you all'. All these denied analogies combine the sense of having an exclusive and elite knowledge with a fallen vulnerability. Prufrock shifts into apparent *non sequitur* at the moment that he seems in danger of giving his ruse away. Absurdity, the comic pose, is adopted skilfully in order to extricate the self from its ludicrous involvement in a world of snares and delusions, where 'perfume from a dress' can make one so digress. The strategy is that pre-emptive counter-encirclement spelt out earlier:

> I have known the eyes already, known them all
> The eyes that fix you in a formulated phrase.

Seeing in advance the way in which those others will look on him, he disengages himself from their humiliating gaze. As Eliot observed in his doctoral thesis on the idealist philosopher F. H. Bradley, carrying a social strategy into the realm of metaphysics: 'To realise that a point of view is a point of view is already to have transcended it.' Putting all those eyes into their place, as spatially relative subjects, objects of his own gaze, Prufrock here manages to maintain his final transcendence of all their limiting and demeaning contiguity. He remains the ultimate subject; and the perpetual circlings of his consciousness, constantly shrinking back from the point of action – where he would have to justify himself, succeed or more likely fail in his attempt 'to force the moment to its crisis' – preserve this spectatorial aloofness and election. As long as he does not commit himself to action, he is safe. Abstention becomes the guarantee of the self's privileged, aristocratic status, in a world of contaminating mediocrity.

Such a dilemma issues in that fear of visibility as tainting and corrosive which haunts Eliot's work, and explains that recurrence of the imagery of eyes which many critics have noted. Eliot's work on the philosophical idealism of Bradley and Leibniz is an attempt to explore the metaphysics of such a recognition, and frequently returns to the more immediate, and more immediately disturbing, implications of this for the self trapped in a 'common world' whose genesis 'can only be described by admitted fictions', where the objects we see are 'only "intellectual constructions" out of various and quite independent experiences'. So, he goes on, in this 1916 essay in *The Monist* (reproduced in *Knowledge and Experience*, 1964):

on the one hand, my experience is in principle essentially

public. My emotions may be better understood by others than by myself; as my oculist knows my eyes. And on the other hand everything, the whole world, is private to myself.

The rigid antitheses, so typical of Eliot's thought, demarcate that gap in being between 'internal' and 'external' 'points of view' where the lonely subjects of his poetry squirm in perpetual fear of being caught out, seen through. There is no way of resolving these discrepant perspectives. The self walks in lonely solipsistic anguish, knowing 'on the one hand', with Edward in *The Cocktail Party* (1950) that

> Hell is oneself,
> Hell is alone, the other figures in it
> Merely projections,

and, 'on the other hand', permanent exposure in a world of reproachful, judging, retributive others, symbolically embodied in the persecuting but ultimately just Furies of *The Family Reunion* (1939):

> How can you sit in this blaze of light for all the world to look
> at?
> If you knew how you looked, when I saw you through the
> window.
> Do you like to be stared at by eyes through a window?

In *The Waste Land* these two curses are combined in the figure of Tiresias. If all the men are one man, and all the women one woman, 'and the two sexes meet in Tiresias', it is because he combines the impotence of one with the sterility of the other, in a way which is intimately bound up with his blindly prophetic knowledge of the world. Eliot refers us in his notes to the account of Tiresias in Ovid, but he teasingly leaves off his quotation at the point at which the tale of Tiresias' blinding is linked to another myth, that of Echo and Narcissus. The tale is crucial to understanding how 'the two sexes meet' in Tiresias. Tiresias had warned Narcissus against coming to 'know himself'. Falling in love with his own image in a pool ('Death by Water'), Narcissus drowns in self-love.

The fate of Echo is equally extreme. Falling in love with Narcissus, who ignores her, she wastes away until she is no more than a pile of petrified bones and the plaintive, attendant echo of other people's voices. Total absorption in the self, and total absorption in others, the poem suggests, are both equally destructive, and Tiresias' condition, of rootless sympathy and voyeurism, passively 'foresuffering' all, combines these two negative knowledges. The speaker of 'Portrait' is suddenly frozen by the glimpse of his own smile in a mirror; the speaker of 'Prufrock' is deterred from ever acting by having 'known them all already', known them all'. 'Between the idea / And the reality', as 'The Hollow Men' tells us, between motion and act, desire and spasm, between, that is, the internal and the external points of view, self and other, Narcissus and Echo, 'Falls the Shadow'. It falls, too, across Eliot's idea of history.

The fundamental structure of a difficult and allusive poem such as 'Gerontion' lies in its vacillation between public and private points of view. In one sense, all the multifarious bric-à-brac of the poem is no more than 'Thoughts of a dry brain in a dry season', images in Gerontion's head. On the other hand, Gerontion himself is no more than a minute centre of consciousness in a massive, exploding universe, merely 'an old man, / A dull head among windy spaces', and all the other mysterious and sinister characters in the poem are equally shut up in their separate rooms, unable to communicate with each other except in the agitated whispers of some arcane Black Mass. It is at this point in the poem that Eliot introduces his most concerted statement about history, and it is set in the context of a discourse on a knowledge which, in its very structure, carries with it both election – a privileged awareness – and degradation, a damnable exclusion from grace:

> After such knowledge, what forgiveness? Think now
> History has many cunning passages, contrived corridors
> And issues, deceives with whispering ambitions,
> Guides us by vanities. Think now
> She gives when our attention is distracted
> And what she gives, gives with such supple confusions
> That the giving famishes the craving. Gives too late

What's not believed in, or if still believed,
In memory only, reconsidered passion. Gives too soon
Into weak hands, what's thought can be dispensed with
Till the refusal propagates a fear. Unnatural vices
Are fathered by our heroism. Virtues
Are forced upon us by our impudent crimes.
These tears are shaken from the wrath-bearing tree.

It is a passage whose whole organising principle is
antithesis, both within sentences ('knowledge . . . forgiveness',
'gives . . . famishes', 'giving . . . craving', 'not believed . . . still
believed', 'fear . . . courage') and between sentences ('Gives
too late. . . . Gives too soon', 'Vices. . . . Virtues',
'fathered. . . . forced upon us', 'heroism. . . . crimes'). To live
in history is to live in a world structured by paradox, where
tears are the fallen fruit of the tree of wrath, where all that
imagery of sexual propagation (taking up the earlier images of
the Jew 'spawned' in Antwerp, the word 'swaddled' like a
child, and the deceitful 'flowering judas'), issues only in
sterility, defeat and denial. Thus from the image of Christ
being 'eaten, . . . divided, . . . drunk' by his celebrants we
move automatically to its reverse, 'The tiger springs in the
new year. Us he devours'. To participate in history is to be
devoured by it. For history is a maze of insatiable feminine
snares, its 'cunning passages' and 'contrived corridors' (with
their subliminal puns) a series of *vagina dentata* which threaten
the itinerant self with castration. The 'supple confusions', the
lustful 'craving' she evokes, like that 'cauldron of unholy loves'
which tempts St Augustine at Carthage, in *The Waste Land*,
become the images of a larger danger, in which the individual
may lose his autonomy and coherence: 'The awful daring of a
moment's surrender / Which an age of prudence can never
retract', where the self founders in apostasy. So, in 'Rhapsody
on a Windy Night', the whore 'Who hesitates toward you in
the light of the door / Which opens on her like a grin' becomes
a siren tempting to dereliction and self-betrayal, whose eye
'Twists like a crooked pin', leading the poet to think of
'twisted things' thrown up high and dry on the beach of
memory, of a branch 'polished / As if the world gave up / The
secret of its skeleton', of a rusted broken spring the strength

has left, and of other images of inadequacy, failure and threat. Foremost of these is the 'automatic' hand of a child, of whom he observes: 'I could see nothing behind that child's eye'; and this terrifying vacuity at once calls up an even more macabre image of an alien and hostile otherness, that of the crab in a pool which 'Gripped the end of a stick which I held him'.

Eliot's universe is one beset by mysterious powers that threaten to engulf or castrate the reprobate self, as if in punishment for some failure of responsibility, some denial of obligation. In 'Gerontion', this failure may be related to those rejections of an importunate historical world spoken of negatively in the opening lines:

> I was neither at the hot gates
> Nor fought in the warm rain
> Nor knee deep in the salt marsh, heaving a cutlass,
> Bitten by flies, fought.

It has been suggested that the 'wilderness of mirrors' in which Gerontion is trapped is the Hall of Mirrors at Versailles, where the Peace Treaty was signed in 1919, and certainly Eliot, while he was writing this poem, was involved in working out for Lloyds Bank the financial implications of the Treaty for the settlement of pre-war debts (as he wrote to his mother in letters of 15 and 25 February, 1920). But this wilderness is a much larger one, in which the 'shuddering atoms' of individual selves repeatedly rebound upon, mirror and echo back all those others who comprise their world, that 'common world' of which he speaks in his essay on Bradley, where 'The self is a construction in space and time . . . an object among others', and at the same time 'a universe in itself'.

If Christ in 'Gerontion' is a devouring tiger, the Virgin in *Ash Wednesday* (1930) is more Belle Dame Sans Merci than Madonna, accompanied by voracious leopards which dismember, devour and disgorge the penitent self. The third section of the poem reverts to the image of a voracious female sexuality to describe the sensual snares of the temporal world, speaking of a stair, dark 'Damp, jagged, like an old man's mouth drivelling, beyond repair, / Or the toothed gullet of an aged shark', and linking this repulsive aspect of sex immediately with its traditional romantic ones:

At the first turning of the third stair
Was a slotted window bellied like the fig's fruit
And beyond the hawthorn blossom and a pasture scene
The broadbacked figure dressed in blue and green
Enchanted the maytime with an antique flute.
Blown hair is sweet, brown hair over the mouth blown,
Lilac and brown hair;
Distraction, music of the flute, stops and steps of the mind
                                        over the third stair,
Fading, fading; strength beyond hope and despair
Climbing the third stair.

Even Eliot's anti-semitism seems to have had its source in the infantile sexual anxiety, of engulfment and castration, indicated here: Rachel née Rabinovitch, in 'Sweeney Among the Nightingales' (with its memories of the murdered husband Agamemnon) 'Tears at the grapes with murderous paws'; while the Russian Grishkin, in 'Whispers of Immortality'. is compared to a 'couched Brazilian jaguar' with a 'rank . . . feline smell'. But from *Ash Wednesday* onwards the poet seems to have come to terms with this world. The poem celebrates an exorcism. At the beginning of Lent, it looks forward to the death and rebirth of Easter, and records the dying of that self which once 'strove to strive towards such things' but has now renounced 'The vanished power of the usual reign'.

From *Ash Wednesday* onwards there is a transformation in Eliot's vision of history. It is no longer a dimension in which the boundaries between subject and object might suddenly be overthrown, and the self drowned by vanities and deceptions not of its making. Rather the historic world of men is now massed, objectified, set over against the self at a calm and composed distance. Unlike Hardy, Eliot does not yearn across this gap, to the world he has lost. Instead, the self frees itself from its contingent being, seeking to evacuate all the 'empty forms' from its solitude. Only briefly 'the lost heart stiffens and rejoices / . . . And the weak spirit quickens to rebel' to recover the sensations of this renounced world. The yearning now is for reunion with a power beyond history altogether, for that 'silence after the viaticum' of which 'Animula' (1929) speaks.

In a way, this spiritual disengagement reflects the changes in Eliot's own predicament, no longer a struggling, aspirant writer, part of an avant-garde set against the old men of a moribund culture, and yet also seeking entrée to the world he despises. Instead Eliot himself has become part of that cultural establishment, a conversion ratified by that joint surrender to Church and State in 1927 which was also a Declaration of Independence – the refusal of a given, contingent identity as an American. The assumption of a new, self-made identity was at the same time the endorsement of that 'Tradition' he had been engaged on inventing from his earliest critical writings, a rejoicing in 'having to construct something / Upon which to rejoice'.

Eliot's poetry in the interwar years becomes the figure of a larger condition, where a ruling class smelt its own supersession, in the words of 'Journey of the Magi' (1927), 'no longer at ease here, in the old dispensation, / With an alien people clutching their gods', and admitting, in 'A Song for Simeon' (1928), that 'I am tired with my own life and the lives of those after me'. 'Animula' abolishes both the historic self and the history which constructs it as no more than mutually sustaining illusions, 'Shadow of its own shadows, spectre in its own gloom'. Eliot's intensely ascetic form of Christianity in this period becomes an inflexion of that larger nihilism which afflicted the European ruling classes of the day, abdicating their responsibilities to the marching men of an insurgent fascism in a poem such as *Coriolan* (1931), with its final cry of the exasperated spirit: 'RESIGN, RESIGN, RESIGN'.

'Burnt Norton', appearing in 1935, however, heralds a shift from total renunciation, in the final redemptive change that transforms 'the waste sad time / Stretching before and after' into another pattern, in which 'through time time is conquered'. The remaining three of the *Four Quartets*, appearing in 1940, 1941 and 1942, required the visitation of the war to bring them to birth; but what they enshrine, at a cool, as if retrospective distance, is a prolonged meditation on the concept of history, quickened by that dark midnight of the century in which they were conceived.

The eternal present tense of these poems has an anterior time, beyond the poem itself, in that sordid world which is negated, transcended, by the very process which transforms world into word, history into story. This is the struggle consummated in 'Burnt Norton' by that 'concentration / Without elimination' which gives

> .... both a new world
> And the old made explicit, understood
> In the completion of its partial ecstasy,
> The resolution of its partial horror.

But it is a struggle which also continues, as the last section records, with its admission that 'Words strain, / Crack and sometimes break, under the burden, / Under the tension'.

The 'Shrieking voices / Scolding, mocking, or merely chattering' which assail 'The Word in the desert', 'voices of temptation, / The crying shadow in the funeral dance' initiate a motif that runs through the *Quartets*. The immaculate Word, represented throughout the poem by the concept of the 'barely prayable / Prayer', is beset on the one hand by distracting voices – in 'Dry Salvages', for example, by the 'sea voices', 'The sea howl / And the sea yelp' – and on the other hand by silence, 'the oppression of the silent fog'. Between these two distractions, the authentic word has to chart its course, succumbing neither to 'the voiceless wailing' nor to 'The loud lament of the disconsolate chimera'. The poet wins through in 'Little Gidding' to a vision of English history and of Christian revelation 'where every word is at home, / .... Every poem an epitaph', in 'a pattern / Of timeless moments' where, in a secluded chapel, 'History is now and England'. At the moment that this destination is reached, 'the voice of this Calling' finds its perfect utterance, in 'A condition of complete simplicity' where silence and speech are reconciled. That is the formulaic pattern of the poem; but its resolution is achieved only at the expense of evacuating that actual history of all real substance.

History in 'Little Gidding', for example, is 'only a shell, a husk of meaning' until it is resurrected to symbolic resonance by the presence of the individual talent of the poet-pilgrim. Just as prayer is more than an order of words, 'the sound of the voice praying', so 'what the dead had no speech for, when living, / They can tell you, being dead'. Seeking a tradition, the peripatetic self can stand in unambiguous relation to dead men, whose communication may be 'tongued with fire beyond the language of the living' but who tell no tales and certainly don't answer back, unless they are the 'familiar compound ghost' the poet invents in the dawn light after an air-raid, or the 'voice descanting (though not to the ear, / The murmuring shell of time, and not in any language)', in the rigging of the ship in 'Dry Salvages'. In all these moments of 'intersection time / Of meeting nowhere, no before and after', the self extricates itself from the ravelling, intricate filaments that reach back into the waste sad time of a collective history. In devaluing the merely contingent, the poem hovers between meaninglessness and the infolding of all meanings, place dissolved in grace. The inclusiveness of Eliot's vision is self-negating: 'I am here / Or there, or elsewhere', 'England and nowhere. Never and always', 'Whether on the shores of Asia or in the Edgware Road'. Contempt for the specific leaves the poem always on the point of action, never actually soiled by commitment.

Nowhere is this truer than in Eliot's reflections on that watershed in the formation of modern English society, the English Civil War. The poem sifts out a coterie of exceptional individuals from the collective turmoil of that epoch, only to set them in the timeless apotheosis of their common election. That they belonged to opposing sides, or to none, is unimportant. They have become emblematic figures, whose actual deeds are transformed, uprooted from their actual divisive history, and 'folded in a single party' in that 'constitution of silence' imposed upon them by death, but also by the poet's resurrecting voice. The Blitz likewise, the importunate violence of a given world, can be transmuted into the muted urgency of a spiritual messenger: 'the dark dove with the flickering tongue'. This struggle has no victors and vanquished: rather it produces the settlement of a unitary, undivided Englishness: tradition.

Four Quartets offers a world curiously empty of people. A deliberate abstractive movement evacuates the human from a reality which is on the one hand focused in moments of privileged ecstasy and, on the other, a series of massed, generalised, impersonal processes. In 'East Coker', history is condensed to a sequence of images which assume a fetishised autonomy, enforced by the passive voice, that seems to have dispensed with flesh and blood agency:

> In my beginning is my end. In succession
> Houses rise and fall, crumble, are extended,
> Are removed, destroyed, restored, or in their place
> Is an open field, or a factory, or a bypass. . . .

That inert 'Is', so effectively positioned, denies the active, substantial remaking involved here, plucking as if by magic sesame, field, factory and bypass out of thin air, and then successively cancelling them. Men appear concretely in this world of almost totally automated process only as the nutrient humus of tradition, 'Bone of man and beast, cornstalk and leaf', or as shadowy fictions reconstructed from past literature. 'Houses live and die' in 'a time for building / And a time for living and for generation' which is actually disaffiliated from the ragged, disparate, untidy rhythms of work and sexuality and mundane living. The anthropomorphising tendency substitutes throughout the poem for the absence of any real human activity of a concrete kind. 'The deep lane insists on the direction', for example, with a quirky peasant idiosyncrasy; but 'you lean against a bank while a van passes' which seems to be driving itself.

Only momentarily do we glimpse other faces, and at once they are dispersed into the mere appurtenances of a lapsed alien world, evaporating into abstraction and the shabby landscape, as the elect consciousness plays over them:

> Only a flicker
> Over the strained time-ridden faces
> Distracted from distraction by distraction
> Filled with fancies and empty of meaning
> Tumid apathy with no concentration

Men and bits of paper, whirled by the cold wind
That blows before and after time,
Wind in and out of unwholesome lungs
Time before and time after.
Eructation of unhealthy souls
Into the faded air. . . .

The tossaway correlation of 'men and bits of paper', the linking of diseased lungs to diseased air, as if its victims were really its causes, and the final collapse into an incantatory listing of suburban tube-stations, each with its cliché associations, cunningly detaches the observing mind from the masquerades he observes.

What is missing throughout Eliot's work is a substantial middle ground, of language, of meaningful social forms, of what Raymond Williams has called a 'knowable community', that would mediate between detachment and attachment, self and others, the rigid antitheses of a split being. For all his lifelong attempt to fabricate a social identity, the painful subordination of the self to the minutiae of religious and social observance, this middle ground eluded Eliot. Even when, like Thomas or Hardy, he seems in pursuit of a place, such as Little Gidding, in which the past will come alive, his quest in the end is not a *recherche* of lost time, but a self-sufficient act, in a moment which absorbs all time into itself: 'You are here to kneel / Where prayer has been valid'. In this silent communion with another order than that of time, the individual talent celebrates his own communion with the tradition he has invented.

The gap between the individual and society is dramatically embodied in *Murder in the Cathedral* (1935) in the estrangement of Becket from the Chorus. Becket's way only becomes clear after the Women of Canterbury have petitioned him to reach a compromise that would exempt them from the need to abandon their happily mediocre routines, 'living and partly living'. Becket insists on equating the real with the intense ('Human kind cannot bear very much reality') and it is contempt, finally, for their soiled importunate averageness which drives him on. They, too, must suffer 'to the sword's point', or acknowledge their unworthiness. Compromise would be false charity, allowing them to sink back into the slough of history. That this last, unnumbered temptation, to which Becket succumbs, emerges unintentionally from the inner logic of his monodrama, makes it all the more revealing. When Becket, in one of the few actually *dramatic* moments in the play, rounds on the audience and, in a series of punctuated jabs, rams home their complicity, he speaks with the sublimated venom of the wronged aristocrat, forced to participate in the ludicrous caper of history, finally extricating himself with a vengeful supercilious disowning:

> You, and you,
> And you, must all be punished. So must you.

The spleen of the Missouri Eliots, men of quality in a shabby world, able in the end to blame their dereliction on the circumstantial rot, is what surfaces here, as it does in those vignettes of metropolitan squalor in *Four Quartets,* where the brittle exasperation of the voice rises to a familiar arrogance, denouncing with an irascible quaver 'fools' approval' and raging impotently at 'human folly', including one's own. For, in recognising 'the shame / Of motives late revealed', in acts 'Which once you took for exercise of virtue', what really rankles is that, all along, others may have had you sprawling on a pin, fixed in a formulated and dismissive phrase, without your ever knowing.

Eliot never finally came to terms with the tangible material world he so substantially inhabited, as merchant banker, eminent man of letters, generous patron of arts, chairman of many committees. All these were little more than masquerades that time resumed. In *The Use of Poetry and the Use of Criticism* (1933) he spoke of Coleridge as one 'haunted' by the Muse, 'a ruined man', whereas Wordsworth 'had no ghostly shadows at his back, no Eumenides to pursue him'. For Eliot too, the shadow repeatedly fell across the page. In *On Poetry and Poets* (1957) he wrote of poetry as both exorcism and conjuration of those shadows, 'unknown, dark *psychic material* . . . the octopus or angel with which the poet struggles'. The poet

is oppressed by a burden which he must bring to birth in

order to obtain relief. Or he is haunted by a demon, a demon against which he feels powerless, because in its first manifestation it has no face, no name, nothing; and the words, the poem he makes, are a kind of form of exorcism of this demon.

The punishment of the possible uxoricide in that Eumenides-haunted play, *The Family Reunion* (1939), is described in terms very similar to this account of the poetic vocation:

> It is possible that you have not known what sin
> You shall expiate, or whose, or why. It is certain
> That the knowledge of it must precede the expiation.
> It is possible that sin may strain and struggle
> In its dark instinctive birth, to come to consciousness
> And so find expurgation. It is possible
> You are the consciousness of your unhappy family.

'Come to consciousness' recalls that image of morning in 'Preludes', evoking a mid-western world which 'up to a hundred years ago was a family extension', but from which the elite soul has now been expelled, for some unspecified sin of omission, some failure of responsibility. In many ways, Eliot's poetry is an attempt to settle scores with that world, to be the conscience of a blackened street, and to justify his unhappy family and its high reputation. But in that struggle, he became, too, the spokesman of a larger attempt at justification, in which the tradition, the culture, of bourgeois Europe had to vindicate its continued claims to a once undisputed inheritance, in that haunted era of the thirties when it was threatened on all sides by fascism and communism, by its own failures and apparently imminent collapse, and by the new social forces massing within it.

In the end, it was not a calling which Eliot could fulfil. The past could not be justified, it could only be negated, as in that moment in 'East Coker' at which the poet sees his own identity, and the historical stage on which it appears, as no more than a theatrical sham, a play of lengthening shadows:

> I said to my soul be still, and let the dark come
>   upon you

Which shall be the darkness of God. As, in a theatre,
The lights are extinguished, for the scene to be
                                        changed
With a hollow rumble of wings, with a movement of
                                darkness on darkness,
And we know that the hills and the trees, the
                                distant panorama
And the bold imposing façade are all being rolled
                                        away. . . .

It could be that the desire for supersession is the deepest impulse in Eliot's poetry, as 'Words, after speech, reach / Into the silence'. In this, Eliot's poetry expresses, with great beauty and precision, a profound crisis in the bourgeois soul in this century, a crisis as yet still unresolved. Poetry, Eliot says in *The Use of Poetry,*

> may make us from time to time a little more aware of the deeper unnamed feelings which form the substratum of our being, to which we rarely penetrate; for our lives are mostly a constant evasion of ourselves, and an evasion of the visible and sensible world.

Eliot's poetry in fact explores the processes of evasion themselves, as it explores the violations imposed upon the self, in its very inception, by that visible and sensible world. Yet it is characteristic of Eliot that, having ventured so much, he should himself close the book with a similar side-stepping, an evasion which nevertheless is also a kind of confession: 'The sad ghost of Coleridge beckons to me from the shadows.' It is in the abdication of the *agent,* the contemplative abstraction of the subject, that Eliot's poetry finds its representative power, as the expression of an age when bourgeois culture entered into what looked like a terminal paralysis. It is in the lengthening shadows of history – of Emerson, Coleridge, and Sweeney – that in the end we must leave him, in a merely human darkness.

5

A Lesson Half Learned: Ezra Pound

'Yeats said to me that if they knew what we thought, they'd do away with us. They want their poets dead.' Ezra Pound took no pains to conceal what he thought and, sure enough, found himself at the age of sixty in the death-cells at Pisa – open-air cages, exposed to the elements, with only a pup-tent for shelter – facing the possibility of execution for treason as a result of his war-time broadcasts on Italian radio in support of Mussolini and fascism. Instead, he was consigned to thirteen years in St Elizabeth's mental asylum, Washington, medically diagnosed at his trial as a man 'afflicted with a paranoid state of psychotic proportions', and judged 'of unsound mind' by a jury which took three minutes to reach its verdict.

Perhaps that is the significant phrase. Yeats's remark was romantic braggadocio: for 'do away' we should read 'put away'. Pound's treatment, after the initial atrocities of the Pisan cage, which induced an arguably long-imminent nervous breakdown, was lenient enough, in conventional terms, and in comparison with the treatments handed out to millions by those regimes whose cause he had so vigorously espoused. But to see Pound's beliefs as a logical development from his starting-point, to see that 'paranoid state' as having its origins in a real cultural history, was too risky an option in the war-ravaged Europe of 1945, where already former fascists were being rehabilitated to prop up the administrations of the occupied zones, and fend off the prospects of communist takeovers. Many of those litterati who spoke up for Pound, after all, had had their own flirtation with fascism. Eliot himself, whose loyalty to his old friend shines through these times, had spoken with equivocal sympathy of Mussolini in the columns of his journal *The Criterion,* and in *After Strange*

Gods (1934) had only just managed to mute the querulously reactionary tone of his invective with that pontifical irony which everywhere allows him egress from too stern and compromising a commitment.

What distinguishes Pound is not the nature of his political sympathies – in one form or another they were echoed fairly widely throughout the British and American establishments in the thirties – but the quixotic stubbornness of his fidelity, and the shrill insistence of his genius. But in a sense this difference in tone did make for a difference in politics. Pound actually did believe in the rhetoric of renewal, the language of revolt which made fascism a *popular* ideology. Unlike Eliot, who saw in such systems merely one more convenient prop for the status quo, Pound remained firm in his faith in the *radical* possibilities of fascism: the world was to be remade, and to be remade nearer the heart's desire, nearer the ruthless clarity of art. Pound's broadcasts were made precisely because he believed, with almost naive conviction, in the inseparability of his social and aesthetic responsibilities. When in 1943, he followed the retreating fascist regime north, to Salo, it was because he felt a duty 'to educate the still educable masses' in the superiority of fascism over bourgeois democracy and, as he wrote in an article, one of many, in 1945, over 'that form of economy praised by the usurocracy and eulogized by the dirty *Times* of London, by Lippman and other filthy jews, covered with excrement'. He was, in his own mind, simply doing his duty as an artist, cashing that claim for 'the damned and despised *litterati*' made years before, in *How to Read* (1928):

> When their work goes rotten . . . , when their very medium, the very essence of their work, the application of word to thing goes rotten, i.e., becomes slushy and inexact, or excessive and bloated, the whole machinery of social and individual thought and order goes to pot. This is a lesson of history, and a lesson not yet half learned.

His admiration for Mussolini expresses the same moral-aesthetic pre-occupation: 'Mussolini speaking very clearly four or five words at a time, with a pause, quite a long pause, between phrases, to let it sink in. . . . The more one examines the Milan Speech the more one is reminded of Brancusi, the stone blocks from which no error emerges, from whatever angle one looks at them'. He might almost be describing the typographic layout of the *Cantos*. Mussolini's continuing artistic and political revolution, he wrote in *Jefferson and/or Mussolini* (1935), had the 'material and immediate effect' of 'grain, swamp-drainage, restorations, new buildings, and, I am ready to add off my own bat, AN AWAKENED INTELLIGENCE in the nation and a new LANGUAGE in the debates in the Chamber'. Similar preoccupations are proclaimed in some of his finest verse, as notably, in the Usura *Cantos,* with their insistence that 'with usura the line grows thick / with usura is no clear demarcation'. And these lucid expositions not only co-exist, but are structurally integrated with, the 'slushy and inexact, or excessive and bloated' anti-semitic mouthings which recur throughout the later *Cantos,* integrated by image and allusion, echo and cadence. This inseparability of excellence and scatological obscenity, of 'Crystal waves weaving together toward the gt / healing' in *Canto XCI,* with the vision of 'Democracies electing their sewage / . . . a dung flow from 1913' in the same *Canto,* cannot be ignored, for it is central to the crisis both Pound and Eliot explored, and for which each, in different ways, could find no satisfactory solution, other than in art.

Pound's immediate perceptions of the iniquity of usury seem to have been crystallised by the Great War, which took away from him the irreplaceable genius of friends such as the sculptor Gaudier-Brzeska and the littérateur T. E. Hulme. *Hugh Selwyn Mauberley* (1920), with its attack on democracies founded in demagogy, where 'lies' and 'mendacities' corrupt both present and past, is the first overt political statement of what was to become an obsessive fixation, but it is coloured, still, by the tone of plangent elegy. If the debasement of language is presented, in section three, as a political process, in a world where 'We have the press for wafer; / Franchise for circumcision', and thus 'choose a knave or an eunuch / To rule over us', it is nevertheless the elegiac anger – a recurring note in Pound – of stanza four which, rightly, predominates in our memory of the poem:

> Died some, pro patria,
> non 'dulce' non 'et decor' . . .

walked eye-deep in hell
believing in old men's lies, then unbelieving
came home, home to a lie,
home to many deceits,
home to old lies and new infamy;
usury age-old and age-thick
and liars in public places.

And against such nightmares can be set the vision of Beauty, 'Braving time', of the 'Envoi', surviving amidst the dust of history, 'Siftings on siftings in oblivion'. As in the *Cantos* later, the righteous fury and the phrase-making clarity of the language disguise the lack of discrimination, the crudity even, of the thought, in a strangely tranquil confusion of radical and reactionary impulses.

In *Gaudier-Brzeska, A Memoir* (1916), Pound identified the decay of language as the cause rather than the consequence of historic decline, in a 'ply over ply' of cultural moments which links the decline of the Renaissance with the 'siftings on siftings' of earlier civilisations:

> And in the midst of these awakenings Italy went to rot, destroyed by rhetoric, destroyed by the periodic sentence and by the flowing paragraph, as the Roman Empire has been destroyed before her. For when words cease to cling close to things, kingdoms fall, empires wane and diminish. Rome went because it was no longer the fashion to hit·the nail on the head.

An essay in *The Egoist* in February 1917 even went so far as to argue that 'The hell of contemporary Europe is caused by the lack of representative government *and* by the non-existence of decent prose in the German language', attributing to 'the mush of the German sentence' the 'befoozlement of Kultur and the consequent hell', as the rhetoric of later Rome was 'the seed and the symptom of the Roman Empire's decadence and extinction'. Pound's conclusion, that 'A nation that cannot write clearly cannot be trusted to govern, nor yet to think', might seem to be little more than opportunistic, taking advantage of current sentiments to propagate a case for the

clear-thinking of poetry. Yet this linguistic idealism –
attributing the real processes of a material, practical history to
some prior cause in the ideal forms of language – is reiterated
with absolute seriousness throughout the critical writings and
the *Cantos*. *Canto VII*, written about this time, sees the 'Dry
professional talk' of modern scholarship, of a usurpatory
academic elite, as the cause of a modern hell, where men and
language alike are emptied of substance:

> Thin husks I had known as men,
> Dry casques of departed locusts
>   speaking a shell of speech . . .
> Propped between chairs and table . . .
> Words like the locust-shells, moved by no inner being;
>   A dryness calling for death.

The discontinuance of Pound's graduate fellowship by
Pennsylvania University in 1907, and his sacking from his job
at Wabash College, Indiana, by just such prudent, dry-as-
dust professors, may have added an edge of personal venom to
such an account-settling, but there is a larger cultural
significance to such invective. The tone of Pound's early
writings is insistently that of an arrogant counter-elite,
excluded from the centres of power and culture, but not, like
Prufrock, seeking ironic solace in its marginality. In Pound,
the 'superfluous man' finds his articulate and contentious
spokesman, finds that purchase on historical reality which, in
the pre-war and war-time conditions of Hardy, Thomas and
early Modernism, was yet to come into its own. In Pound, the
new sensibility, deracinated, fractious, torn by contradictions,
yearning both for reconciliation and apocalypse, demanding
its inheritance, was an idea whose moment had come. It is not
an edifying spectacle.

Pound's essays in *The Egoist* in the last few months before
the outbreak of war are full of the straining at the bit of an
avant-garde which is yet excluded from cultural power. In
'The New Sculpture' on 16 February 1914, discussing Hulme
and Wyndham Lewis, for example, Pound suddenly breaks
into a fury of exasperation that 'The artist has been for so long
a humanist!' Awoken at last to the reality of his situation, the

artist has begun to realise that 'his only remedy is slaughter'. An artist is not elected but born, and his links are with the Tahitian savage and the Bushman: 'He must live by craft and violence. His gods are violent gods.' Without 'strife in the arts' artists are 'uninteresting'. Epstein and Gaudier-Brzeska alone have talent, and derive their energy from their anti-humanism. This sculpture, with what Pound calls 'its general combat', may sound revolutionary enough. It may represent a generation in revolt against an establishment mediocrity in art and society alike, in terms which recall a nihilistic Dadaism, so that Pound can proclaim: 'my generation is not the generation of the romanticists. . . . We do not believe in Eutopias. . . . To the present condition of things we have nothing to say but "merde"; and this new wild sculpture says it.' But the radical intensity of this is matched by another moment, which takes the rebellion out of time altogether: 'These men work in an unchanging world'. To have 'dabbled in democracy' would be as invidious for such an artist as being 'at peace with his oppressors'. Like Thomas's superfluous men, they stand at the interface of the two major classes, with loyalties to neither. Instead:

> We turn back, we artists, to the powers of the air, to the djinns who were our allies aforetime, to the spirits of our ancestors. It is by them that we have ruled and shall rule, and by their connivance that we shall mount again into our hierarchy. The aristocracy of entail and of title has decayed, the aristocracy of commerce is decaying, the aristocracy of the arts is ready again for its service.

Prufrock, we might say, has begun to part his hair behind, like some latterday Leonidas at Thermopylae; has begun to consider that he might, after all, dare to disturb the universe.

Coming to Europe in 1908 from an Indiana he described as 'the sixth circle of desolation', Pound, like Eliot, turned his back on a philistine continent symbolised by the figure of Walt Whitman, whose 'crudity is an exceeding great stench'. Fascinated from the beginning by the old stately aristocratic forms – Provençal poetry, Japanese Noh plays, 'Attic grace' – Pound remained enough of an American to combine this love with what in *Homage to Sextus Propertius* (1917) he calls

'savage indignation at pomp and official stupidity'. The two
moods, of rebellious outrage and aesthetic refinement, find
their unity in the cult of a past, a tradition, at once savage and
aristocratic, irrational and disciplined. As a failed college
lecturer turned bohemian and freelance writer, endowed with
the entrepreneurial skills of a pioneering business family,
Pound's class ambiguities found their expression in that
ability, in the early verse, to assume *personae* as distinct as the
medieval French poet-criminal Villon and the Chinese poet-
emperor-bureaucrat Liu Ch'e. The combination of
aristocratic and bohemian is fused perfectly in those Provençal
troubadours, high-born vagabonds, hard men with rarefied
sensibilities, who stroll through his early volumes, like
Bertrans de Born in 'Near Perigord', whose love poem may
also be a song of war, a coded message of intrigue and strategy
as well as poetic craftmanship.

Pound's cultural bolshevism, right from the start, is bound
up with a reactionary cult of tradition, the seeking out of
legitimate ancestors in a culture from which the true heirs
have been expelled by the usurper and the fraud, the
demagogue and the career scholar. The revolution then
envisaged is no more than a *restoration*, in which the
dispossessed will reclaim that which is rightly theirs, as 'The
New Sculpture' promises:

> Modern civilisation has bred a race with brains like those of
> rabbits and we who are the heirs of the witch doctor and the
> voodoo, we artists who have been so long the despised are
> about to take over control.
>
> And the public will do well to resent these 'new' kinds of
> art.

The fine equipoise of that delicate poem 'The Garden'
(*Lustra*, 1916) conceals deep social ambivalences. The upper-
class woman who walks by the railing of a path in Kensington
Gardens is initially dismissed with the full contempt of the
energetic parvenu. Like her civilisation, she is 'dying
piecemeal / of a sort of emotional anaemia', and the speaker's
sympathy seems to lie, democratically, with the 'rabble / Of
the filthy, sturdy, unkillable infants of the very poor' round
about her – though that third adjective raises a doubt which

tends to be confirmed by the ironic close of the second movement: 'They shall inherit the earth'. In reality, it is the excluded middle, the poet himself, who is the rightful inheritor, as emerges in the third and final movement:

> In her is the end of breeding.
> Her boredom is exquisite and excessive.
> She would like someone to speak to her,
> And is almost afraid that I
> will commit that indiscretion.

The speaker despises both worlds equally. Yet he is prepared to invoke the sturdiness of the rabble as an ally against the woman's anaemia. At the same time, 'the end of breeding', with its *double entendre* ('end' as goal or as finish, 'breeding' as refinement or procreation) suggests that, subliminally, he endorses and would encourage her extinguished yearning. The balancing act of 'exquisite and excessive' suggests more than one kind of excess. He also is 'almost' ready for a liaison; but not to make the first move. 'I', pausing in the exposure of the line-ending, almost tips into action, only to be reined in by the complexities of 'commit' and the diminuendo of 'indiscretion'. To remain superior, and therefore worthy of her wish, he must refrain from the very act which, in breaking with gentility, would ensure fulfilment. Pound offers here in miniature a figure, not only of the excluded artist as true synthesis of refinement and vigour, avoiding the excesses of both, but also of the hair's-breadth distance that separates possibility from actualisation, in a culture too anaemic to take risks any more.

The mood is very close to that of 'Prufrock' and the end of *The Waste Land,* and it expresses the same delicately poised cultural conjuncture. Unlike Eliot, however, Pound's somewhat less genteel background makes him less likely to hang around forever. 'Further Instructions', in the same volume, envisages his own poems as a gang of unemployed street-corner bohemians, poised between the 'baser passions' of its opening line and the gentility he lays claim to in its last, dismissing the gossip that 'we are lacking in taste / Or that

there is no caste in this family'. With droll topicality, the poem
pinpoints its own social nexus:

> Come, my songs, let us express our baser passions,
> Let us express our envy of the man with a steady job
>   and no worry about the future.
> You are very idle, my songs.
> I fear you will come to a bad end.
> You stand about in the streets,
> You loiter at the corners and bus-stops,
> You do next to nothing at all.
>
> You do not even express our inner nobilities.

Writing of Wyndham Lewis on 15 June 1914, in *The Egoist,*
Pound returned to vituperation against 'the man in the
street, . . . who is only in the street because he hasn't
intelligence enough to be let in anywhere else, and who does
not in the least respect himself for being in the street'. Such
democratic fetishes carry with them a further threat to art:

> The rabble and the bureaucracy have built a god in their
> own image and that god is Mediocrity. The great mass of
> mankind are mediocre, that is axiomatic, it is the definition
> of the word mediocre. The race is however divided into
> disproportionate segments: those who worship their own
> belly buttons and those who do not.

Kicking against the marginalisation imposed by an indifferent
society, Pound speaks in terms of a generational revolt against
mediocrity, represented by Wyndham Lewis:

> If a man have gathered the force of his generation or of his
> clan, . . . expressed the sullen fury of intelligence bafflled;
> shut in by entrenched forces of stupidity, if he have made [of
> it] a type emotion and delivered it in lines and masses and
> planes, it is proper that we should respect him in a way that
> we do not respect men blaring out truisms or doing an
> endless embroidery of sentiment.

Wyndham Lewis is 'not a commentator but a protagonist. He
is a man at war'. He declares 'that the intelligent God is

incarnate in the universe, in struggle with the endless inertia' – a struggle which has obtained since the beginning of the world, 'of driving the shaft of intelligence into the dull mass of mankind'.

This is Pound's particular version of that struggle we have encountered repeatedly in the poetry of the period: a struggle to overcome the separation of mind and matter which, here in Pound's writing, is clearly and immediately related to a class struggle. For the direct opponent of art is that 'malebolge of obtuseness' represented by *The Times,* the smugness of a class society where mediocrity reigns supreme, and bureaucratic torpor is sustained by the inanities of a mass culture. Against such a profanity, Pound raises the prophetic voice of a new dispensation:

> Mr. Lewis has got into his work something which I recognise as the voice of my own age, an age which has not come into its own, which is different from any other age which has yet expressed itself intensely. . . . And we will sweep out of the past century as surely as Attila swept across Europe. We can therefore be content to live in our own corner, and to await to be pleased by the deaths of survivors of an age we detest.

The modulation from apocalyptic hysteria to a shrewd quietism is characteristic of the moment in which Pound is writing. The same pattern can be discerned, for example, in the quiet different work of Edward Thomas. But the contradictions here verbally resolved were to achieve their practical solution sooner than Pound could have realised. The same mixture of euphoria and fatalism was to send many of his contemporaries, within a few months, flocking to enlist in the ranks of the war to end all wars, and, as he was to write in *Mauberley:*

> There died a myriad,
> And of the best, among them,
> For an old bitch gone in the teeth,
> For a botched civilization.

In June 1914, it was little more than 'an annoyance to see

waterlogged minds in administrative positions', and simply a matter of being 'ineffably bored by these anomalies'. When Pound reprinted his essay on 'Vorticism' in the memoir for Gaudier-Brzeska, in 1916, these comments on Lewis's work had a new urgency of repetition. For now it was not simply a matter of 'the fury of intelligence baffled and shut in by circumjacent stupidity'; that stupidity had killed Pound's friends, and robbed civilisation forever of their uncreated art, 'For two gross of broken statues, / For a few thousand battered books'.

Mauberley begins, and almost finishes, with an obituary. The first is that intended for 'E.P.', the poet himself, a stubborn and virtually anachronistic fellow, 'out of key with his time', striving to resuscitate a dead art, 'fish[ing] by obstinate isles'. The last is that of a rather more insubstantial creature who nevertheless – since his author reputedly 'passed from men's memory' before the poem began – has to carry the full weight of the poem. This figure, Mauberley himself perhaps, is no more than 'A consciousness disjunct, / Being but this overblotted / Series of intermittences', and his epitaph is fitful enough:

> 'I was
> And I no more exist;
> Here drifted
> An hedonist.'

All that remains is for the poet to add his tailpiece, the clinching 'Medallion' which rounds off all these intermittent, half-hearted vignettes into the closure and the ruthless precision of art's 'suave bounding-line'. In the interval, the poem has been traversed by various denizens of this world's 'tawdry cheapness', exposed to the cynicism of the professional man of letters, 'Mr. Nixon', and heard the obituaries of a whole lost generation. It has also, in the figure of Lady Valentine, registered an upper class's uncertain response to the prospect of revolution. For Lady Valentine, the 'well-gowned' patron of art, poetry is a kind of vehicle for coming to terms with the fact of social change, a place to encounter such marginal, superfluous men as Pound and Mauberley:

> Poetry, her border of ideas,
> The edge, uncertain, but a means of blending
> With other strata
> Where the lower and higher have ending;
>   . . . Also, in the case of revolution,
> A possible friend and comforter.

'E.P.' and 'Mauberley' in a sense represent the two poles of Pound's artistic and political personality. The same antithesis can be found in the criticism, between the call to a generation to revolt and, in the same issue of *The Egoist* (16 March 1914), an affirmation of the aloofness of art from 'the pettiness and the daily irritation of a world full . . . of the constant bickering of uncomprehending minds'. Of Gaudier and Epstein Pound here affirms: 'Representing . . . the immutable, the calm thoroughness of unchanging relations, they are as the gods of the Epicureans, apart, unconcerned, unrelenting'. At the same time, that last adjective, with its insistence on artistic ruthlessness, explains how the attitude of withdrawal can easily flip over into that of violent confrontation. In Gaudier, he says, one sees 'an austerity, a metaphysic, like that of Egypt'; in Epstein, 'the planes of [his] work seem to sink away from their outline with a curious determination and swiftness'. Writing of Arnold Dolmetsch's music, in *The Egoist* in August 1917 he makes the same point. A work of art 'is a compound of freedom and order', and 'hangs between chaos on one side and mechanics on the other'. To attempt to 'restore' the sense of major form 'is branded as "revolution". It is revolution in the philological sense of the term'; and the artistic revolutionary, 'the heretic, the disturber, the genius, is the real person, the person stubborn in his intelligent instinct or protected by some trick of nature, some providential blindness or deafness even, which prevents him from being duped by a fashion'. His 'unsocial surliness' is the ground of his social utility.

Writing of Dolmetsch again, in *Pavannes and Divisions* (1918), he relates this to a major distinction between 'myth' and its debasement, for purposes of social or moral propaganda, into allegory or fable, which was 'the beginning of the end. And the gods no longer walked in men's gardens'. The true myth is that 'impersonal or objective story woven out of [the artist's] own emotion', that 'equation', 'a pattern of notes or . . . arrangement of planes or colours' which 'throws us back into the age of truth'. In Dolmetsch's music, one finds oneself 'in a reconstructed century – in a century of music, back before Mozart or Purcell, listening to clear music, to tones clear as brown amber'.

It would be wrong to see what Pound envisages here as an essentially historical regression; it is, rather, a recovery of that primal world represented everywhere throughout the *Cantos* by light and sounds with a crystalline perfection, 'a sound which is undoubtedly derived from the Gods'. But it can nevertheless be translated into the myth of an historical Fall, 'from the pleasure of . . . the pre-Cromwellian many' into a debased 'democracy'. And Pound can end this essay with a series of rhetorical questions which indicate the political as well as the aesthetic drift of this logic, in a vision simultaneously radical and reactionary, which inveighs against an existing aristocracy 'too weakened, and too unreal to perform the due functions of an "aristocracy"'; in the name of an alternative spiritual elite able to fulfil this task. Could it be, he asks, that 'the quattrocento shines out because the vortices of social power coincided with the vortices of creative intelligence?' And 'Is it that real democracy can only exist under feudal conditions, when no man fears to recognise creative skill in his neighbour?' In 1917-18 the moment of revolution had arrived. That for Pound it led, not to bolshevism, but to fascism, illuminates both the past and the coming two decades of English and American culture.

Fascism was not a 'pure' doctrine, but a deeply contradictory amalgam of ideas, the momentary reconciliation of profound social antagonisms. It is essentially a 'politics of conjuncture', the momentary resolution of fissures and tensions in that 'muddy, confused, hesitating mass, of small courage though much endurance' of which Thomas spoke in *The South Country,* those suburban middle-strata who 'neither produce like the poor nor consume like the rich' and from whom, by and large, the technical, cultural and administrative intelligentsia is recruited. Such strata, often first-generation recruits from the classes above or below them, may feel, like Thomas's superfluous man, that they 'belong to no class, or race, and have no traditions', and so may cling all the more vehemently to the values of the class from which they have emerged, or to some synthetic 'tradition' invented out of the circumstances, social and cultural, of the strata to which they now belong. In the immediate post-war period, as Robert Wohl has shown in *The Generation of 1914* (1980), movements such as that of an insurrectionary fascism offered, to deracinated ex-combatants and to the rootless lumpen-intelligentsia of a culture in ruins, lost in a waste land, a rhetoric of renewal and of social transformation capable of uniting their disparate needs against a common enemy – the 'old men' responsible for the war and for the shabby peace that followed. The rhetoric of a 'lost' or 'betrayed' generation, let down by the generals, the politicians, the Jews, then became a heady brew for befuddling the real divisions of interest between men of widely differing social backgrounds, in a political programme which fused elitism and populism, the cult of a revolutionary avant-garde with that of an insurgent people.

C. David Heymann argues in *Ezra Pound: The Last Rower* (1976) that Pound was essentially 'an old-fashioned agrarian populist who had outlived himself and the bulk of his generation', seduced into temporary alignment with fascism by his own eccentric and relentless intellectual consistency. Pound in some respects was certainly an American small-town boy who believed he'd found, in the 'Social Credit' theories of Major Douglas, the final solution. They were first peddled by Pound as an alternative to 'Soviets or red shirts or polygamy or free beer or free divorce or guillotines, or any of the more decorative paraphernalia of ancient and modern revolution' in the columns of *The Athenaeum* in April 1920. His lobbying of Mussolini with ideas of monetary reform – what he called 'Volitionist Economics' – reveals a familiar autodidactic megalomania.

But Pound's cranky, myopic innocence – the *idées fixes* of a parochial fanaticism – was merely a context for his later development. His grandfather, whose lumber company issued its own paper scrip (a 'certificate of work done', Pound wrote to Mussolini) had been a campaigner for the Greenback Party, whose mixture of agrarian and labour groups, Heymann observes, 'corresponded to the poet's ideal of an agrarian-guild craftsman economy. In this sense Ezra Pound had never abandoned the frontier'. Such populist movements, deeply imbued with syndicalist ideas, already at the turn of the century contained in embryo the ambiguities of a mature fascism, which it would take the war fully to bring to fruition. As can be deduced from Norman Pollack's *The Populist Response to Industrial America* (1962), such movements combined a hatred of federal bureaucracy, the finance houses and the big trusts with a frequent anti-semitism and an equivocal attitude towards organised labour, sometimes using it, in a cautious alliance, at other times shrinking from its revolutionary potential. The rhetoric of such movements expresses the anti-capitalism of the small capitalist, the resentment of entrepreneur, farmer and professional middle-class against the centralised and nationwide agencies that shape their destinies – agencies made more powerful and all-embracing by the growth of the state apparatus in the period before and during the war, and by that concentration of monopolistic financial and industrial power brought about by the recessions which had swept the western world from the 1880s onwards.

With the Great War, bringing in its wake first bolshevism and proletarian revolution and then their near-universal defeat, the provisional alliance of such groups with labour could not survive, and populism underwent that mutation from radical to reactionary forms that carried such men as Mussolini from socialist to fascist politics – defections to be repeated on a mass scale throughout the following two decades. Pound's collocation of federalist democracy with Blackshirt dictatorship in *Jefferson and/or Mussolini* (its pivotal hesitation catching the mood perfectly) thus contains a nugget of historical truth. Fascism was the escape-hatch for a frightened, insecure petty-bourgeoisie whose opening to the Left had been closed by the concerted defeat of outright socialist revolutions in Italy, Germany and Hungary. An ascendant working-class might have led such strata towards socialism, as Thomas seemed to envisage. In defeat, it offered only decades of ineffectual struggle and deepening immiseration. It was a change in the historical configuration within which Pound's aesthetics were articulated that accounts for the rapid acceleration of his ideas towards fascism.

This shift, not of particular ideas, but of the constellation in which they operate, can be traced fairly accurately in his work. In 1922, the year of Mussolini's March on Rome, Pound could still write in *The Dial* with brilliant acuity of Joyce's *Ulysses,* with its 'ubiquitous' Jewish hero:

> He has presented Ireland under British domination, a picture so veridic that a ninth rate coward like Shaw (Geo. B.) dare not even look it in the face. By extension he has presented the whole occident under the domination of capital.

The same essay shows Pound already looking towards a wilful aristocracy of supermen capable of ruling through 'the public utility of accurate language' – 'the succinct J. Caesar, or the lucid Macchiavelli, or the author of the Code Napoléon, or Thos. Jefferson, to cite a local example'. And Jefferson 'was perhaps the last American official to have any general sense of civilisation'.

Pound insisted at his trial on his long-sighted patriotism, and the transcripts of his broadcasts reveal the same urge – 'to save what's left of America and to help keep up some sort of civilisation somewhere or other'. What haunted him most was a sense of betrayal: the old, federalised America was small and beautiful – 'Boston was once an American city; that was when it was about the size of Rapallo'. But it is no longer 'the domination of capital' – a systemic evil – which he attacks, but 'usurocracy', an alien, personalised conspiracy that *distorts* that system – the lies put out by 'Mr Squirmy and Mr Slime' from 'every one of the Jew radios of Schenectady, New York and Boston', which have created and sustain megalopolis. Pound's patriotism is for a mythical homeland enshrined 'ply over ply' in the paradisal moments of the *Cantos*, where the landscapes of America, Italy and the Orient constitute a kind of visionary palimpsest, charged with the accumulated wisdom of the ages.

The populist elements certainly recur throughout his work: in *Canto LXXIV* he speaks of Mussolini's fall as 'The enormous tragedy of the dream in the peasant's bent shoulders', and in one of his last letters to the Italian Minister of Popular Culture, in 1944, he insisted that it was 'The monopolists betrayed Fascism; they were ready to sell the country down the river.' But in that same *Canto,* another aspect of Pound's intellectual personality is revealed, as he rounds on Eliot – 'Old Possum' – to declare, combatively:

> . . . but the twice crucified
> where in history will you find it?
> yet say this to the Possum: a bang, not a whimper,
> with a bang not a whimper,
> To build the city of Dioce whose terraces are the colour of
> stars . . .
> What you depart from is not the way. . . .

It is the quietism of Eliot's response to a fallen world which is rejected here, in the name of an active remaking of that world. The same point is made even more forcefully in that famous sequence in *Canto LXXXI* of the *Pisan Cantos,* where Pound salvages, from the wreckage of his hopes and the vanity of human projects, a renewed vision of the order and the tradition, with that repeated insistence: 'What thou lovest well remains . . . What thou lovest well is thy true heritage'. Pride is here recovered out of the very acknowledgment of vanity:

> But to have done instead of not doing
> this is not vanity. . . .
> To have gathered from the air a live tradition
> or from a fine old eye the unconquered flame
> This is not vanity.
> Here error is all in the not done,
> all in the diffidence that faltered. . . .

Even in the humility of 'a beaten dog beneath the hail',

Pound's posture remains the antinomian self-righteousness of an unacknowledged and excluded elite, an unshakable faith in his own inner light. Italy for him, like Paris and London and Provence before it, has become the spiritual home of his 'live tradition', its past everywhere apparent in the present. And here, with fascism, had come a *Risorgimento* which confirmed his deepest convictions. His articles in 1944 for the newspaper *Il Popolo* reiterate all his earliest beliefs:

> The Fascist dictum was defined years ago; we believe in the freedom to express an opinion on the part of those qualified to hold an opinion. . . .
> Do you believe in law? Very well, but remember the eternal law of nature; the strong shall dominate the weak. . . .

It is the traditional arrogance of the déraciné bohemian, scornful of the class which produced him, its demeaning contiguity and compromising claims on his loyalty—a disdain apparent even in his remorse, in a 1962 conversation with Allen Ginsberg, for 'that stupid, suburban prejudice of anti-Semitism'. In reaction, he aligns himself with a timeless excellence which constitutes true aristocracy, just as, in the *Cantos,* sequence and distance are compacted and overthrown in a mind out of key with its time, which moves effortlessly and at its own pace through other histories and cultures. The young Pound found in Vorticism the aestheticisation of reality, the cult of hard edges and dynamic energies, the aristocratic anti-humanism, which were to shape both his poetic and political beliefs. But again, this was no mere personal discovery, but the trajectory of a class. In his rejection of the philistinism and timidity of the petty-bourgeoisie, Pound remained ironically typical of that class, large sections of which found, in the glamorous melodrama of fascism, a similar intoxication and excitement, the thrill of living out its own most dangerous impulses and denying its own deepest anxieties, rebelling and conforming at once in a sinister euphoria of communion.

This political contradiction is inscribed right in the heart of Pound's aesthetics, in, for example, his definition of 'the Image'. In 'A Few Don'ts', published in *Poetry* in March 1913, he had emphasised the instantaneity of the Image, its power to make time stand still and to compound space: 'An Image is that which presents an intellectual and emotional complex in an instant of time'. His essay on 'Vorticism' in the *Fortnightly Review* in 1914, however, stressed its dynamism:

> The image is not an idea. It is a radiant node or cluster; . . .
> a VORTEX, from which, and through which, and into which, ideas are constantly rushing. In decency one can only call it a VORTEX. . . .

Ostensibly, the 'Imagist' poem is a short, timeless *aperçu*, an epiphanic instant detached from the continuities of historical and social time. Yet if we look closely at the poem Pound cites to illustrate his theory, 'In a Station of the Metro', we can see that it is in reality a pattern of historical perception:

> The apparition of these faces in the crowd:
> Petals on a wet black bough.

This is certainly that 'direct treatment of the "thing", whether subjective or objective' of Pound's Imagist manifesto. But there is also a larger abstracting movement which takes the 'thing' up into a luminous transcendence of particulars like that which recurs throughout the *Cantos*. There is an unremitting withdrawal, from the specificity of the title, through the first line, which already renders the historical ghostly in that word 'apparition', stressing the abstractive power of perception, to the conclusion, which has transformed the metonymy of 'faces' into the generalising metaphor of 'petals', and the collective 'crowd' into the singular and remote 'wet black bough'. The human has been translated into the impersonal, the ebb and flow of metropolitan crowds into an aesthetic 'equation'. An underground station – a vortex into which man and woman are constantly rushing – becomes, first, the halls of Hades and then, in the completion of its movement, the static balance of light and dark in a Japanese print, an almost abstract counterpoint. What remains as the link between the concrete actual scene and the abstracted image is no more than an equals sign, underwritten by the resonantly ambiguous 'apparition'.

Pound compares such procedures to the equations of algebra, in which the image, like an algebraic sign, has a 'variable significance', in contrast to the symbol, which has 'a fixed value, like numbers in arithmetic'. This 'variable significance' is determined by the place the image occupies in the 'toneless phrase' or 'rhythm-phrase' of the poem. It is out of such equations that the *Cantos* are constructed, translating the particular moments of an open-ended, anterior history into the variable signs of a closed equation.

In 'Vorticism' Pound had seen such algebraic equations as 'the thrones and dominations that rule over form and recurrence, And in like manner great works of art are lords over fact, over race-long recurrent moods, and over tomorrow'. In *Thrones de los Cantares* (1959) the powers which prevent such an order are of course those counterfeiters, false coiners, 'money sellers', hoarders, people who buy cheap and sell dear, who deny 'the idea of just price' through monopoly, adulteration, and abuse of power. In their subordination to 'the stench of the profit motive' they corrupt not only social relations and the money supply but language itself, introducing mendacity and deceitful eloquence into human communications.

For Pound, there is a profound correspondence between the exchanges of money, of language, and of human intercourse, particularly at the level of sexuality. As he says in *Guide to Kulchur* (1938):

> Until the power of hell which is usura, which is the power of hogging the harvest, is broken, that is to say until clean economic conditions exist and the abundance is divided in just and adequate parts among all men, legal enforcements and interjections of the legal finger in relations between man and woman will be deformation and disease.

The tenor of this is very close to Thomas's correlation of the gulf between men and women with a social and ultimately economic gulf in 'Up in the Wind'. Indeed the *Guide*, in an unexpected and moving tribute to the 'clean wording' of Hardy's poetry, links this 'clarity' to a far-sighted 'rebellion against the sordid matrimonial customs of England' and concludes that 'The code of Hardy's time and Hardy's plots all imply monetary pressure.' Yet the radicalism of Pound's position, which responds, rightly, to that implicit in the Hardy tradition, has undergone a significant mutation, in the twenty years of English and European history that have elapsed since the main work of Hardy and Thomas. This mutation has exposed, worked through, some of the ambiguities held in sustained equipoise in their work. Pound, in the *Guide,* can talk of discovering 'the true bases of credit, to wit the abundance of nature and the responsibility of the whole people', but this is no longer a radical humanist project. It is, rather, the context of a quite different task: 'And can we', he asks, 'at this distance, abstain, to any good end, from taking totalitarian hold on our history?' The only way forward now, it seems, lies in one form of terror or another, if the human world is to be reappropriated, made new.

The contradiction between Pound's authentic radical impulse here, and the cause in whose service it is placed, a contradiction which lies at the heart of his poetics and his idea of history, has a complex genesis. Compelled to deny the Marxist theory of value which, as he says towards the end of *Guide to Kulchur,* attributes the creation of wealth to the labour of the proletariat, he has nothing to replace it with except a 'Physiocratic' notion of wealth which is simultaneously – in its rhetoric at least – anti-capitalist and anti-socialist. 'Work does not create wealth,' he says, 'it *contributes to the formation of* it. Nature's productivity is the root'. This idea, adduced for example in *Cantos XXXVIII, XLVI,* and *LXXVII,* affirms unequivocally that ' "the earth belongs to the living" ', rather than to 'the buggering bank', which levies 'interest on all it creates out of nothing'. This claim to create *ex nihil* is the sin of usury. The crime of socialism, however, is that it sees all wealth as generated by the productive manual labourer, thereby excluding such intermediate strata as the organisers and distributors of wealth (precisely those middle strata to which Pound, like his populist forebears, still belonged): 'Economic injustice consists in allowing claims to come into the hands of those who have contributed nothing either to production, or to getting things to those who need them'.

Pound can reconcile Jeffersonian federalism with Mussolini's corporate state, with its social base in the small peasantry and the administrative strata of the provinces, because both – in theory – lump together the interests of producers and distributors in a system set against the inequities of the rigged, monopolistic market: 'Nature overproduces', he says, and 'Overproduction does no harm until you overmarket (dump)' (*A B C of Economics*, 1933). The primal sin arises, not in the exploitation of labour at the point of production, but in a maldistribution of the surplus, through the invention of false credit, middle men 'clogging the circulation of goods and money' (*Guide*). In this, as *Thrones* makes clear, the struggle of the working class to raise its wages – 'inane loquacity hoisting the wages' – is as vicious as the irresponsibility of the bureaucrat who 'Without perfect style / might not notice punctuation and phrases / that alter the sense, / and if he writes down a variant / his sponsors will be responsible'. And, once again, the coiners of false language, the meretricious artists, 'those who deform thought with iambics', are as guilty of a political crime as the coiners of false money, for they 'destroy the five human relations'.

In *Thrones,* the sum of wisdom is 'get a dictionary / and learn the meaning of words', 'cut some of the cackle', and 'State the laws in clear language', for ' "That you should hear it unblurred" ' is the prerequisite of a healthy body politic. In *Canto XCIX* Pound reiterates this, in an imagistic instant of time that harks back to a lifetime's preoccupations:

> To see the light pour,
>   that is, towards sinceritas
> of the word, comprehensive
>   KOINE ENNOIA
> all astute men can see it encircling.
> Chou saw it, my SIRE also,
> With splendour,
>   Catholicity,
> Woven in order. . . .

In *Mauberley,* Pound had spoken of 'tò kalón, the Greek principle of beauty, being 'Decreed in the market place'. In the *Guide to Kulchur* he comes to a new and more comprehensive view of the term, influenced by Rackham's 'perhaps brilliant translation of KALON as nobility' as well as 'beauty or order'. It is in this complex sense that, at the end of *Jefferson and/or Mussolini,* speaking of 'the permanent elements of sane and responsible government', he can invoke the same concept:

> Towards which I assert again my own firm belief that the Duce will stand not with despots and the lovers of power but with the lovers of

> ORDER
> tò kalón

> .... These things being so, is it to be supposed that Mussolini has regenerated Italy, merely for the sake of reinforcing her with the black death of the capitalist monetary system?

All the discrete historical moments evoked in the *Cantos* are no more than collective *personae,* masks, in which the present is re-presented. But that 'present', with its perpetual conflict between 'beauty' and infernal reality, had shifted drastically in the half-century during which the poem was written and rewritten, and in the final *Cantos* Pound returns to the question of Mussolini. *CXVI,* the last complete *Canto,* is an admission of defeat which retracts as it confesses. For if the poet can say: 'But the beauty is not with the madness / Tho' my errors and wrecks lie about me. / And I am not a demigod, / I cannot make it cohere' – he can go on to insist:

> i.e. it coheres all right
>   even if my notes do not cohere.
> Many errors,
>   a little rightness,
> to excuse his hell
>   and my paradiso. . . .

The analogy has already been made at the beginning of the *Canto:*

> These concepts the human mind has attained.
> To make Cosmos –
> To achieve the possible –

Muss., wrecked for an error,
But the record
  the palimpsest –
a little light
  in great darkness –

Mussolini too is only 'wrecked for an error', a mere aberration from a norm which can be blamed on 'circumjacent stupidity'. Adhered to, it would have brought perfection; it is, really. history which is to blame. There is no real contrition, no sense that the vision was flawed from the start.

Here, too, persists Pound's continuous parallel between reality and text: history, like Pound's poem, is a 'palimpsest', a series of overlaid texts. 'A thousand candles together blaze with intense brightness. No one candle's light damages another's. So is the liberty of the individual in the ideal and fascist state'. Thus, under the heading 'Fascio', opens Pound's 1942 manifesto, *A Visiting Card,* setting out the utopian vision at the heart of the *Cantos* in terms of an historical dialectic of infernal and paradisal energies, 'one that divides, shatters, and kills, and one that contemplates the unity of the mystery'. In the *Cantos* several discrete, occasionally overlapping histories are heaped together to make a 'fascio', or bundle of luminous instances, 'a thousand candles together'. The dilemma of form in the *Cantos* is that they are intended to embody at one and the same time the incoherence of history and the coherence of a contemplative unity, 'the tradition of the undivided light'.

The realm of history is 'beclouded', 'overgrown', he had told us in *Guide to Kulchur,* in words immediately relevant to his epic:

whole beams and ropes of real history have been shelved, overclouded and buried. . . . We know that history as it was written the day before yesterday is unwittingly partial; full of fatal lacunae; and that it tells us next to nothing of causes.

If the 'muddling and muddying terminologies' which dissemble this history are to be purged, one must not simply breathe in the superficial air of the *'Zeitgeist',* but dig for its

'*Paideuma*' – 'the tangle or complex of the inrooted ideas of any period'. Such digging links the poet with the peasant; but the active, dynamic nature of the 'paideuma' links him also to the cadres of the fascist movement. The 'paideuma' is 'the gristly root of ideas that are in action'; the artistic avant-garde is 'interested in ideas that are going into action'.

What Pound is struggling with here, as throughout his work, is the obligation of the artist to participate actively in the history of his period, and to reconcile this participation with his commitment to an unchanging, timeless order of things. 'It is difficult to write a paradiso, when all the superficial indications are that you ought to write an apocalypse', he said in his *Paris Review* interview, and the *Cantos* everywhere show the strain. They reproduce a decentred, fractured, schismatic world, but they also endeavour to point beyond it. The three phases of the modern era identified in *Guide* repeat themselves endlessly as an equation within *Cantos* and between them: 'The sorting out, the *rappel à l'ordre,* and thirdly the new synthesis, the totalitarian'. The difficulty of the poem arises from the fact that this is not a dialectic of sequence, but of instantaneity: the sorting out is simultaneously a call to order and both moments together *constitute* the active making of that 'new synthesis', as the mind abstracts a muddied 'history' into an incandescent 'tradition'. History contracts to the eternal co-presence of all events within the constituting mind of the poet, or of the man of destiny, and within the 'corporate state' of language itself. In a sense, Pound puns on the concept of 'totalitarian', fusing political hegemony with the idea of an aesthetic 'totality'. The mind orders its experience as the state orders civil society, as syntax, image and ideogram order language into poetry; for, as we are told in the *Guide,* 'poetry is totalitarian in any confrontation with prose'.

The final words of *Canto CXVI* are a pertinent epitaph on the failure of this particular tradition:

> But to affirm the gold thread in the pattern. . . .
> To confess wrong without losing rightness:
> Charity I have had sometimes,
>   I cannot make it flow thru.

A little light, like a rushlight
    to lead back to splendour.

The pattern here is still that of the Imagist equation: an
abstractive movement, a recession from the infernal, avernal
darkness of real time, into a visionary, a paradisal splendour.
The gold thread is both a pure design woven into the contrary
pattern of events, and the thread of Ariadne (line 36) which
leads Theseus out of the labyrinth, from error into light. Yet
the distressed admission, 'I cannot make it flow thru',
suggesting an almost physical blockage and impotence,
endows with negative intensity the only sentence in these
closing lines which actually reaches its conclusion, which has
a main verb. All the other sentences are disjunct, unfinished,
like their theme: questions left hanging in air, suspended
affirmations, or like the last lines of the poem, a wishful
infinitive that gestures towards a consummation not yet
reached.

Reducing the faces in the crowd to 'apparitions' and then to
petals on a wet black bough, detached from all their historical
dynamism, Pound cannot make it cohere, for he excises from
history precisely that *momentum* in which it both realises and
loses its particular moments. Intensity in the noun or image
compensates for fragmentation and dispersal in the sentence
as a whole, as a rhetorical activism justifies the practical
quietism of the artist's vocation. The spots of time in which
time is transcended are paid for at a high price. The poem
closes with the errant soul still in the dark tunnels of a history
that knows no end, as if frozen to stone.

Pound's politics and his art record a symptomatic destiny,
in an era when the western intelligentsia was collectively
drawn to totalitarian and irrationalist allegiances of one kind
or another, as part of a wider crisis of disintegration and
polarisation in the class of its origin. The attraction of both
fascism and Stalinism for the intellectuals *'entre deux guerres'*
registers a deepening and a clarification of the contradictions
in the western cultural tradition. On the one hand there is a
yearning for community and wholeness and, on the other,
heightening of elitism and self-regard – an insistent self-
assertion experienced as self-abnegation and sacrifice. This

pattern transcends the formulaic differences of Left and Right, and explains an Auden as much as a Pound. Similar men, from the same class, were to be attracted to one cause or the other for what in the end were essentially similar, socially determined reasons. An account of Pound's career is not finally a parable of personal aberration and redeeming genius, but the analysis of the contradictions of an epoch, containing a lesson as yet still only half learned.

6

History to the Defeated:
the Poets of the Thirties

In a review of Marianne Moore's poetry, in *The Dial* in December 1923, T. S. Eliot distinguishes two kinds of supposedly 'proletarian' art – that which is really rooted in middle-class values, and that which aspires beyond them:

> So far as a proletariat [sic] art is art at all, it is the same thing in essence as aristocratic art; but in general, and at the present time, the middle-class art . . . (the proletariat *is* middle class in America) is much more artificial than anything else; it plays with sham ideas, sham emotions, and even sham sensations. On the other hand a real aristocracy is essentially of the same blood as the people over whom it rules: a real aristocracy is not a Baltenland aristocracy of a foreign race. This apparently purely political definition applies to art as well: fine art is the *refinement,* not the antithesis, of popular art. . . .

It is a useful distinction to remember when we consider the politically committed poets of the thirties, for here, more than anywhere, the complex problems of reconciling an 'aristocratic' aesthetic with a radical populist politics reveal some of the contradictions built into the English tradition, to which, in one sense, 'Modernism' was a shock reaction. The early poetry of W. H. Auden, in particular, is aggressively, even provocatively difficult, resistant to interpretation, tightlippedly refusing to give up its secrets. And this is a refusal of that compact with the general reader which allows a middle-class audience to find reassurance in the familiarity of second-hand sham ideas, sham emotions, sham sensations. If, like Marianne Moore in Eliot's description, Auden combines 'a quite new rhythm' with 'an almost primitive simplicity of phrase', and 'a peculiar and brilliant and rather satirical use of what is not, as material, an "aristocratic" language at all, but simply the curious jargon produced ... by universal university education', this does not make him a poet of the demotic muse. Indeed, Auden's primitive simplicity of phrase in his early poems only deepens their obscurity, by setting up a disturbing strain between the casual, conversational tone of his idiom, the originality of his rhythm, and the intractability of his meaning. The jargon of psychoanalysis which lards the poetry is of only secondary significance, compared with this deeper elusiveness.

The attempt to reconcile an elitist aesthetics with a socialist politics can lead to some improbable theses. Michael Roberts, for example, that indefatigable literary entrepreneur of the thirties, can argue in his famous Preface to the *New Signatures* anthology in 1932 that 'the poems in this book represent a clear reaction against esoteric poetry in which it is necessary for the reader to catch each recondite allusion'. The revolt against the elitist poetics of Pound and Eliot is manifest. Yet, faced by the packed opacity of William Empson's verse, Roberts can only revert to sleight of pen. Empson's poetry 'may still be difficult', but it 'is definitely trying to say something to an audience'. Its 'obscurity is due solely to a necessary compression':

> In Mr Empson's poetry, there is no scope for vagueness of interpretation, and its 'difficulty' arises from this merit. Apart from their elegance, their purely poetic merit, they are important because they do something to remove the difficulties which have stood between the poet and the writing of popular poetry.

Robert employs a characteristic strategy of the Auden generation here. The inverted commas around 'difficulty' detach the speaker from the attitude discussed, and devalue that attitude, as a specimen of middle-brow prejudice to be disposed of as quickly as possible. The real problem is the 'difficulties' placed by the previous generation in the way of authentic communication between poet and people. Eliot and Pound offer real and obstructive 'difficulties', intended to preserve the inscrutability of an elite. The 'difficulty' of

Empson, as of Auden, Day Lewis and Spender, is both imaginary and necessary. In order to be truly poets of the people, they must separate themselves not only from the elitism of Pound and Eliot but from the superficial attitudes which object to intellectual strenuousness. They constitute, that is, a true elite, which is struggling to overcome its isolation.

Robert's argument, in fact, is a continuation of Eliot's. The true poetic aristocracy arises from and refines the language of the commonalty. It is not set in exotic and usurpatory authority over it; nor does it vulgarly court favour from the mob. The delicate balance between 'aristocracy' and popular base is defined with a characteristically arch analogy in Auden's essay on 'Writing', in *The Dyer's Hand* (1962):

> *My language is the universal whore whom I have to make into a virgin* (KARL KRAUS). It is both the glory and the shame of poetry that its medium is not its private property, that a poet cannot invent his words and that words are products, not of nature, but of a human society which uses them for a thousand different purposes. In modern societies where language is continually being debased and reduced to nonspeech, the poet is in constant danger of having his ear corrupted, a danger to which the painter and the composer, whose media are their private property, are not exposed. On the other hand he is more protected than they from another peril, that of solipsist subjectivity; however esoteric a poem may be, the fact that all its words have meanings which can be looked up in a dictionary makes it testify to the existence of other people. Even the language of *Finnegans Wake* was not created by Joyce *ex nihilo;* a purely private verbal world is not possible.

The transformation of universal whore into virgin, of popular speech into inviolable voice, is clearly more difficult than a change in the other direction: the 'decay' and 'corruption' of language, for Auden as for Pound, is something endemic to its nature. Yet Auden's terms are subtly different from Pound's. For Auden, this debasement is both the 'glory' and the 'shame' of language: it actually gains from its promiscuous slumming.

Throughout his long career, this ambiguous double endowment has disclosed his own mixed attitudes to reality, which is both a reluctant virgin to be mastered and a luxurious whore to succumb to. The two attitudes are reconciled in a larger aloofness of the poetic self from its materials, both as language and events. Auden's poetry moves repeatedly between renunciation and indulgence, at once delighting in the variegated richness of an abundant world, and keeping it at arm's length with a deliberate, defamiliarising self-consciousness and artificiality. Ransacking the dictionary for arcane or archaic usages, or decked out with magpie gauds and macaronics, nonce-words and neologisms, his poems call attention to their artifice, their status as linguistic objects, in a way that sets a cautionary distance between their words and the things to which they refer. In the same way, the speaker of the poems, his portentous polysyllables switching to sudden racy slang, by turns demotic and hieratic, shocking and coy, shifting peremptorily in rhythm, tone and register, demonstrates his mastery of a world in which all hierarchies of class and authority are in the melting-pot, and therefore at the mercy of any individual single-minded enough to lay claim to the linguistic (and political) inheritance. Skittish, hoydenish or haughty, polyglot and jargonish, ruminative and aphoristic, the poet and his language alike affirm that easy mélange of aristocratic disdain and populist humility which characterises the political stance of the thirties leftist. Such a stance easily outlived that decade of strenuous commitment to become a habit of the soul, even when the poet had relapsed into quietism, Christianity and post-war retrenchment. Beneath the changing ideological personae lies a personality which, though it mellows, does not really change in its most fundamental patterns. It is to this that we should look to understand that brief closing of the rift between poet and history in the 1930s, and its equally abrupt surcease.

The poets of the thirties imagined that they had a special relationship with 'History' – conceived of as some absolute dynamic of events – and the very potency of this infatuation accounts for the vehemence of their subsequent recantations. In a world dominated by economic depression, the rise of fascism, wars and rumours of war and what Auden, in 'September 1 1939' called 'Imperialism's face / And the international wrong', the identification of the 'aristocratic' poetic sensibility with working-class politics was never, however, unproblematic. Stephen Spender wrote of some of these problems in an article called 'Poetry and Revolution', in *New Country* in March 1933:

> . . . . the artist today feels himself totally submerged by bourgeois tradition, he feels that nothing he can write could possibly appeal to a proletarian audience, and therefore he finds himself becoming simply the bourgeois artist in revolt, in short, the individualist. He feels that nothing of revolutionary interest can be produced within his tradition, and yet there is no way of getting outside of it. All his judgments are ruled by it, and to be an exception is only a way of emphasizing his individuality.

His dilemma is compounded by the fact that 'the proletariat has no alternative tradition which he could adopt'. But 'Art can make clear to the practical revolutionaries the historic issues which are in the deepest sense political', by saving the language from 'degenerating' and offering 'the language of moments in which we see ourselves . . . in our . . . true relation to humanity or nature'. In this sense, poetry is necessarily 'counter-revolutionary', for it expresses a classless compassion. The writer who sympathises with communism cannot escape 'his individuality, his isolation'; for, in remaining economically dependent on the old order, 'he must be a rentier or a hireling'. He can however make clear 'the causes of our present frustration' and 'prepare the way for a new and better world'. This necessary class-ambiguity places him always, as the title of one of Auden's plays suggests, *On the Frontier* (1938), perpetually preparing to embark but, in the words of that other play, *The Dog Beneath the Skin* (1935), 'caught in the teap of his terror, destroying himself', 'divided always and restless always', 'An isolated bundle of nerve and desire, suffering alone'. The poetry thus inscribes in its contradictions two competing social moments. If, as Spender says, 'Revolution is to be accomplished by an act of will on the part of some, a paralysis of it overtaking others', the poetry of

Auden and his contemporaries records both together, in the
nerve endings and sinews of a divided intelligentsia.

Such divided loyalties are admitted in C. Day Lewis's
poetry with a directness of allegory which illuminates the
obscurer corners of Auden's more cryptic verse. The poems in
A Time to Dance (1935) for example, speak of a civil war in the
self, both prefiguring that Spanish conflict soon to erupt and
harking back to the imagery of the conflict which still
overshadowed so many of the thirties writers, that Great War
brought alive for a new generation by the memoirs of its
survivors, many of which were first published in the formative
years of their admirers' adolescence. 'In Me Two Worlds'
speaks of a class war between a bourgeois past and a
proletarian future which takes place in the poet's own
consciousness, in his very body. The self here fluctuates
between being a neutral terrain invaded by alien forces, and
something *constructed* out of the very terms of the conflict:

> In me two worlds at war
> Trample the patient flesh,
> This lighted ring of sense where clinch
> Heir and ancestor. . . .
>
> The armies of the dead
> Are trenched within my bone . . .
>
> But see, from vision's height
> March down the men to come,
> And in my body rebel cells
> Look forward to the fight. . . .
>
> So heir and ancestor
> Pursue the inveterate feud,
> Making my senses' darkened fields
> A theatre of war.

Whereas for Pound this conflict could still be resolved – or
so it seemed – in a synthesis which reconciled both halves of
the struggle, for the thirties marxist, one half of the self has to
be expunged, overthrown, by rebel cells which, the pun
unwittingly seems to imply, are not healthy cells at all, but a

life-consuming cancer. What is significant here is the reduction of the self that takes place between the opening stanza's 'lighted ring of sense' and the 'senses' darkened fields' of the end, where the lights have gone out all over a microcosmic Europe. The trampling of the 'patient flesh', recalling Eliot's 'Preludes', suggests that the long-suffering poet, and the culture he represents, is the only real victim of this struggle.

In 'The Conflict' this self initially feels caught 'between two massing powers . . . / Whom neutrality cannot save', and the movement of the poem enacts the reluctant surrender of the lonely, poised pride of the liberal tradition to 'the red advance of life'. If he is not to become a posthumous relic, like those displaced survivors of an earlier war, he must choose a new allegiance:

> Move then with new desires,
> For where we used to build and love
> Is no man's land, and only ghosts can live
> Between two fires.

Stephen Spender could speak in similar terms in 'Variations On My Life' (*The Still Centre*, 1939). Here, entry into history is seen as an addition of self to an already constituted discourse:

> That is to walk in a sacred grove
> And pluck the ripened voices with their ears
> Bound into sheaves filled with the sun
> Of summers that spoke and then went on;
> And among them to place
> My own posthumous voice. . . .

The imagery of harvest plenitude pulls against the sense of constriction and constraint, in which the new voice is posthumous almost before it has spoken, already taken up into a completed past, merely waiting to be plucked. 'The Human Situation' frets even more uneasily against the limits of a given, an inscribed being, where freedom shrinks to the mere mispronunciation of a predetermined script – one's class and family identity, in an image which recalls Hardy:

My history is my ancestry
Written in veins upon my body:
It is the childhood I forget
Spoken in words I mispronounce:
In a caligraphy of bones
I live out some hidden thought
Which my parents did forget.

Identity is oddly bound up with a forgetfulness transmitted
across generations, with a congenital faltering of being, for 'It
is impossible for me to enter / The unattainable ease / Of him
who is always right and my opponent', one of those 'victors of
history' associated with the 'law-giving, white-bearded father'
and legendary heroes of an earlier stanza. Before these others,
the incompetent self is shamefaced and irreconcilable, 'forced
on to my knees, / On to my real and own and only being / As
into the fortress of my final weakness' before an inimical
world. Faced by 'This aristocrat, superb of all instinct, / With
death close linked' of his *Poems* (1933), he turns in revolt to
identify with an alternative, revolutionary elite, who turn
weakness into strength, in the words of a title in *The Still
Centre:* 'Exiles from their Land, History their Domicile'. Such
leaders 'Purify the achievement of their lives / With human
bodies as words in history / Penned by their wills'. Yet
identification with them is difficult and improbable, lived out
in the illusions of a metaphor which moves, as in Hardy's
verse, between the tangible hardness of carving, through the
ambivalence of the uttered word, to the bondage of script
('Penned' is a resonant ambiguity). The future here can be
evoked only as question and invocation, and it brings with it
the groves of a petrified tradition:

What miracle divides
Our purpose from our weakness? . . .
Who carves
Our will and day and acts as history
And our likeness into statues
That walk in groves with those that went before?

O utter with your tongues
Of angels, fire your guns – O save and praise –

Recall me from life's exile, let me join
Those who now kneel to kiss their sands,
And let my words restore
Their printed, laurelled, victoried message.

At the heart of this apocalyptic yearning, in fact, is a dream of return, a vision of restoration and reconciliation. The imagery itself represents this equivocal vocation, moving between violation and exultancy as in the convolutions of the opening lines, which shift abruptly from fixity to turmoil in an unstable oscillation, to come to a momentary point of rest, history's exiles long returned no longer rootless, to her printed page, in 'one / Balancing present sky'.

To enter history is to be recruited from volatile freedom to the defined and finished, quite literally *conscripted* from speech to print, an image that is poignantly realised in the play *Trial of a Judge* (1938):

He's dead. His living was one word
Influencing surrounding speech
Of a crowd's life, printless until
The words of all this time are frozen
By all our deaths into the winter library
where life continually flows into books.
For us the blood still melts
We breathe a ripe or sparse or torturing air
And are the cursive act of history
Moving with fever, like distraction
In waves. I with dead sight
          . . . . read
In your faces and your actions
Present history, and, in the reading, I shall write.
Myself a word amongst existing words
Reading your words, I see in them death's orders.

In the context of the play, this is a moment of affirmation and revolt, of renewed commitment. But the language in which it is couched pulls against this, suggesting a world already pre-empted, in which the rebellious self is already set down in the books, his acts appropriated to an effacing history, in the words of the play's last act, to 'Freeze time suddenly into a single crystal / Where history is transparent', but where it is also a realm of defeats, violence and hatred transmitted from generation to generation, until the children's faces 'become that single face / We gave our lives to kill'. The pessimism, the defeatism, the sense of failure before starting out, is present everywhere in this poetry which speaks, not of a new order coming to birth, but only of the endlessly deferred death of the old.

The persona of Auden's first volume, *Poems* (1930), is torn between two stances toward a world which, like Eliot, he sees as a natural inheritance from which he has been mysteriously excluded. This inexplicable gap between potential and actual is summed up in 'Missing' in the very movement of the gaze, as the 'leader looking over / Into the happy valley' turns away to observe instead 'The slow fastidious line / That disciplines the fell'. What is missing in the landscape and accounts for this bitter exile is a sense of purpose that would give direction to its heroes. It is a world full of 'angles unforeseen', whose streams 'are acrid yet / To an unaccustomed lip'. The sense of a destiny as yet undefined extends to the vision of leadership itself: to what end and with what destination in mind? The 'tall unwounded leader' has 'doomed companions'. The heroic 'voices in the rock / Are now perpetual', speaking for a past tradition that had value and depth. But such men were 'Fighters for no one's sake, / Who died beyond the border'. Lack of motive is implicit in all their eager motion. The tradition and its current bearers share a common perplexity:

> Heroes are buried who
> Did not believe in death,
> And bravery is now,
> Not in the dying breath
> But resisting the temptations
> To skyline operations.

Survival, for a purpose unspecified, means not aspiring to that upright posture which makes one a target for snipers. And 'leaders must migrate', in haste, under cover of dark, to some unspecified bourne which becomes the larger figure of a

class defection. The host, in the last line of the poem, returns
'Alive into the house'. The leader, by contrast, is almost a
posthumous man already.

There is a great deal of restless, troubled activity in these
poems yet the overall impression is of a kind of hysterical
stasis, what the poem '1929' calls the 'restlessness of
intercepted growth'. Confronting a dismantled, comatose,
abandoned landscape in 'The Watershed', the automatic
response is:

> Go home, now, stranger, proud of your young stock,
> Stranger, turn back again, frustrate and vexed:
> This land, cut off, will not communicate.

Yet even this abrupt injunction cannot move the poem out of
its sense of blocked purpose into that unobstructed renewal
envisaged near the end, 'Where sap unbaffled rises, being
spring'. The poem closes not with this hope, but with a more
urgent sense of deadlock, forever arrested at the point of
action, fraught with menace, as 'Ears poise before decision,
scenting danger'.

'No Change of Place' ends with another command to 'Turn
back!', but it is almost unnecessary. No one dares trespass too
far from the unfamiliar paths, or beyond the railhead or pier
end, 'Will neither go nor send his son'; and the sense here of a
younger generation arrested at the point of departure by a
withheld parental command is shrewd and precise as an
image of the thirties dilemma. In poem after poem, the eager
would-be voyager is held back by some external restraint, by a
past which cannot be abandoned, but whose derelictions, as in
'The Secret Agent', will finally betray him:

> At Greenhearth was a fine site for a dam
> And easy power, had they pushed the rail
> Some stations nearer. They ignored his wires:
> The bridges were unbuilt and trouble coming.

The power is there to be tapped, but not the facilities to realise
it; it is always already too late, and no amount of anxious
signalling will ever be heeded. He knows that control of the

passes is the key to this new district, but not who will get it.
The fine tradition has not prepared him adequately for these
new developments and dangers. Knowledge is not enough
without action, but the decisive break with inertia cannot be
made, as in 'Never Stronger': 'Each knowing what to do / But
of no use / . . . Saying good-bye but coming back, for fear / Is
over there'. As this poem stresses, 'the centre of anger / Is out
of danger'; but a comatose culture cannot be raised to the
anger that might liberate it.

The anxiety of transit and decline, of time running out and
an unheeded urgency, is strong in these poems. 'This Loved
One' speaks of 'mortaged lands' where the individual inherits
a family and a history only to find 'much to be done', and
'Frontiers to cross / As clothes grew worse / And coins to
pass / In a cheaper house'. 'Easy Knowledge', one of the most
cryptic of these early poems, holds the anxiety in a peculiar
arrested agitation which is enacted in the elisions and
dispersals of its syntax. Knowledge and action are at odds,
tugging against each other, in a 'mortal distraction' which
repeatedly deflects the impulse to make a break, to cut free.
The poem opens 'Between attention and attention, / The first
and last decision'. This intercalated region ('between' is a
favourite preposition in these poems) is the true human
condition. The poem comes alive in its refusal to define 'the
vague wants / Of days and nights, / And personal error' and,
as in *The Hollow Men,* metonymy breaks up the unitary self,
turning the personal into something remote and only
residually human. A semi-abstract vocabulary suggests a
world stripped of volition, moved by impersonal forces:

> And the fatigued face,
> Taking the strain
> Of the horizontal force
> And the vertical thrust,
> Makes random answer
> To the crucial test. . . .

The sentences lack the narrative thrust that would integrate
all these separate items into a causality that would respond to
the poem's stifled urgency. It is as if the poem itself makes

random answer to the crucial test. The disoriented speaker, a 'divided face', lacks the confidence of the 'snub-nosed winner', caught always on the threshold, neither rejecting nor returning to the fold:

> The opening window, closing door,
> Open, close, but not
> To finish or restore;
> These wishes get
> No further than
> The edges of the town,
> And leaning asking from the car
> Cannot tell us where we are. . . .

Human acts and features are barely distinguishable from things and processes in this depersonalised world. The self breaks up into a proliferation of parts, its wishes taking on a momentary autonomy only to succumb to baffled immobility. The dispersed self is perpetually poised 'Upon this line between adventure', where 'Forward or back are menaces', standing on narrowness, seeking relief in the shallow brightness of surfaces, 'No anger, no traitor, but peace'. But this peace is merely that 'neutralizing peace / And an average disgrace' spoken of in 'The Questioner Who Sits So Sly'—the peace that comes from acknowledging that there is 'No income, no bounty, / No promised country'. Even the 'nonchalant pauses' of 'A Free One' are really a 'balancing subterfuge'. The 'returning conqueror' may be the beggar's envy, but beneath the masterful manner lies a deep unsureness. He is not secure in his inheritance, but 'poised between shocking falls on razor-edge'. His 'accosting profile, . . . erect carriage' are confidence tricks, and 'the varied action of the blood' is merely a device to 'cancel the inertia of the buried'. In reality he is the hapless victim of impersonal forces, moved like a leaf on the stream of events, travelling from house to house in pursuit of 'an intrinsic peace', knowing love's fidelity and weakness. In a poem such as 'Family Ghosts', the personal and the political crisis come together amidst the privation and uncertainty of an assaulted city, surrounded by 'the watchfires of a stronger army' and threatened from within by 'subaltern mockery' and 'speeches at the corners'. Yet for all this sense of a personal and social order on the edge of catastrophe, the poem ends with the strange congealing of expectation into a vision of ' "... Massive and taciturn years, the Age of Ice" ', as if the impasse might last forever.

By the time of Auden's second volume, *Look, Stranger* (1936), such a predicament has been translated into the furtive heroisms and heroic subterfuges of Leninist romance in 'Our Hunting Fathers'. The fathers are the ancestral voices of the humanist tradition, in which man was secure in the 'personal glory', 'The liberal appetite and power', able to exercise the tolerance, pity and love which are 'reason's gift'. Such an assurance is denied their sons. The sense of election can now be preserved only by deliberately sinking it in collective anonymity, in communist conspiracy against the fine tradition which nurtured it, making its 'mature ambition / To think no thought but ours, / To hunger, work illegally, / And be anonymous'. Man, unlike the animal, does not have 'finished features'. He is able to transform himself, as, in the move from one collectivity ('Our hunting fathers') to another (thinking 'no thought but ours'), he redefines the whole meaning of the concept 'us'. That second, restricted franchise insists on a break with the past, and acceptance of guilt and of loss of individuality as the price paid for this. But the shift from the confident assertions of the first stanza to the uncertain questioning of the second indicates a larger ambivalence of mood. The poem is finely balanced between continuity and rupture, poised equivocally on the edge of rejection, defining its alternatives only in terms of what it rejects.

The class deadlock which afflicts Auden's early poems has here found issue in commitment to that 'final war / Of proletariat against police' spoken of in '1929'. But such a commitment involves a personal death too, for 'the destruction of error' cannot be accomplished without 'death, death of the grain, our death, / Death of the old gang'. If such a realisation puts an end to agitation, so that 'the loud madman / Sinks now into a more terrible calm', it does not solve the dilemma of the arrested agent. He is still transfixed, waiting for others to make the move: agency has passed elsewhere, to another class, to what 'Consider' had called 'the powerful forces latent' in diseased soils. This poem had spoken with unconcealed glee of this supersession, telling financier, Oxbridge don and all bourgeois seekers after happiness that 'The game is up for you and for the others' and that 'It is later than you think'. But the poem vibrates with the same anxiety of deadlock. The 'ruined boys' of Auden's generation may have gone over to the enemy, but their whole society is now arrested at the moment of flight, unable to escape even though they pack within the hour. 'Venus Will Now Say a Few Words' had made the point even more brutally:

> Do not imagine you can abdicate;
> Before you reach the frontier you are caught;
> Others have tried it and will try again
> To finish that which they did not begin:
> Their fate must always be the same as yours,
> To suffer the loss they were afraid of, yes,
> Holders of one position, wrong for years.

What distinguishes the dispossessed son of the ruling classes from his peers, however, is his knowledge. In 'A Communist to Others', a poem Auden later suppressed, his transit to freedom is enacted through a careful manipulation of personae. The poem is a dramatic monologue, attributed to one of those outsiders who look in with contempt and pity on the poet's privileged world. But the closing stanzas appeal to the 'unhappy poet' to defect, in an act of mutual benefit: 'You need us more than you suppose / And you could help us if you chose'. The very act of writing the poem confirms the appeal with which it closes. The speaker is simultaneously an outsider despising the bourgeois world and, in his intimate knowledge of its flaws and vanities, the insider-poet himself, a self-delighting traitor in the camp. (As Auden wrote in his also suppressed 'To a Writer on his Birthday', 'Our hopes were still set on the spies' career', where 'all the secrets we discovered were / Extraordinary and false'.)

Thus Auden settles some old scores with his own class in this poem at the same time that he dons a new identity whose prime attraction is that it carries over the conviction of specialness derived from his class inheritance. The 'splendid person' who is the epitome of the old order imagines he is the affianced of history, but he is deceived: 'She's not in love with you at all'. The legacy has passed elsewhere, and to remain one of the elect, one must follow it; for, in the last words of the poem:

> Remember that in each direction
> Love outside our own election
> Holds us in unseen connection:
>   O trust that ever.

Election is not of our choosing, but if it comes to us, we should accept it. And it is more likely to come if we predispose ourselves in its favour. What is figured here, at the core of Auden's most strenuous proclamation of commitment, is the passivity, the *attentisme,* waiting upon history, of the thirties poet.

In the subsequently suppressed 'Prologue' to *Look, Stranger,* the expected revolution is defined by a cluster of images which captures this contradictory mood. At the very moment that the poem wishes to speak of 'actual History' it takes us on a recessive detour further and further away from actuality, in a prolonged epic simile which moves from the remote geological past into the realms of Arthurian romance and Homeric epic, finally to leave us beached high and dry on a purely imaginary shore, far removed from the stubborn facts of 1936, and forgetful of our point of embarcation:

> Some possible dream, long coiled in the ammonite's slumber
> Is uncurling, prepared to lay on our talk and kindness
> Its military silence, its surgeon's idea of pain;
>
> And out of the Future into actual History,
> As when Merlin, tamer of horses, and his lords to whom
> Stonehenge was still a thought, the Pillars passed
>
> And into the undared ocean swung north their prow,
> Drives through the night and star-concealing dawn
> For the virgin roadsteads of our hearts an unwavering keel.

The same process can be found at work throughout the poetry of the period, where the use of geological and topographical imagery consistently displaces into a realm beyond human volition the very workings of that 'History' which is supposed to be a product of human choice. It is there, centrally, in the image of history presented in *Letters from Iceland,* which Auden produced in collaboration with Louis MacNeice in 1937. In the verse epistle dated 16 August 1936, at a moment of maximum volatility in European politics, a month after the outbreak of the Spanish Civil War, and with a newly elected Popular Front government installed in France, backed by extensive strikes and factory occupations, two moments are brought into conjunction.

The first, the ostensibly personal moment, is described in terms which combine biology and fairy tale, to suggest the miraculous waking of the self to its destiny:

> . . . . the crude
> Embryo rummages every latitude
> Looking for itself, its nature, its final pattern,
> Till the fairy godmother's wand touches the slattern
> And turns her to a princess for a moment. . . .

But this crystallisation of identity is linked to another process, which is precisely the reverse: the unfreezing of history from glacial deadlock into fluid but still destructive dynamism. The geological metaphor stresses the inevitability of this process, even as it places the self as both independent observer and yet vulnerable subject of these impersonal forces:

> Until indeed the Markafljot I see
> Wasting these fields, is no glacial flood
> But history, hostile, Time the destroyer
> Everywhere washing our will, winding through Europe,
> An attack, a division, shifting its fords.
> Flowing through Oxford too, past dons of goodwill.

In his retrospective of this period, in *World Within World* (1951), Stephen Spender used a similar image to describe his own pre-political perception of events:

> In general, I thought of public events as happening more or
> less incalculably. . . . As all political events, solid as they
> might seem today, appeared to liquefy in the uncertainty of
> tomorrow, it seemed to me enough that I should preserve a
> guileless attitude in relation to them.

The difficulty of maintaining such a position, he records,
finally led to that questioning of his own identity as possibly
'simply an expression of the class interest which I,
unknowingly and instinctively in everything I thought and
wrote and did, represented'; and this in turn led to that brief
communist commitment in which he struggled to make
himself 'its exact opposite – a function of the proletariat'.
External events, that is, are at once totally separate from the
self, and yet the most intimate source of its being. And the gulf
between these two aspects cannot be overcome without a total
remaking of that self, a willed transformation in which it
surrenders autonomy to the forces of 'History', represented by
its self-appointed agents, a Stalinist Communist Party.

Auden's 'A Summer Night', collected in *Look, Stranger,* had
already given a similar inflection to the image of the insurgent
flood. The protected upper-middle-class world of the English
country house, with its *hortus conclusus,* is there seen to be under
threat. The 'gardens where we feel secure' of one stanza are
seen to be founded on the wilful ignorance of the next, where
we 'gentle, do not care to know, / Where Poland draws her
eastern bow, / What violence is done'. The naming, in its very
rejection, of that supposedly exterior history prepares the way
for the next admission, of a direct causal link between the
innocence and the harm:

> Nor ask what doubtful act allows
> Our freedom in this English house,
> Our picnics in the sun.

The moon that looks down upon this tranquil English
pastoral also 'blankly as a butcher stares' on the art treasures
and atrocities of Europe. They are all, in actuality, part of the
same, interrelated world. But the poet, guiltily acknowledging
the walled-off gaze of other, less disinterested parties, cannot
rest at ease in such benevolent privacy:

> The creepered wall stands up to hide
> The gathered multitude outside
>   Whose glances hunger worsens;
> Concealing from their wretchedness
> Our metaphysical distress,
>   Our kindness to ten persons.

Such guilt, and such attempted self-justification, prepare the way for the apocalyptic prediction of that 'destructive element' in which, in the rhetoric of Spender's influential critical study of 1936, the bourgeois intellectual had to immerse himself, if he were to be saved:

> Soon, through the dykes of our content
> The crumpling flood will force a rent
>   And, taller than a tree,
> Hold sudden death before our eyes
> Whose river dreams long hid the size
>   And vigours of the sea.

Auden can still wish, at the end of the poem, that when the flood recedes the 'privacy' of the liberal individual and his 'river dreams' may be restored, so that the 'drowned voices of his parents', of the old tradition, may once more 'rise / In unlamenting song'. In Day Lewis's 1936 political morality play, *Noah and the Waters,* the same outcome is suggested: it is the intellectual elite, represented by Noah, which will inherit a world cleansed by catastrophe. But once again, the actual timing of that flood, of that breaking of the dykes, is not a matter for the intellectual's practical concern. He can only wait passively for it to happen, and in the meantime, enjoy the delights he dreads to lose.

Perhaps the most articulate deployment of that more precise metaphor for historical process, the thawing glacier, is offered by John Cornford's poem of the Spanish campaign, 'Full Moon at Tierz' (1936), where, as in Auden's poem, the same moon looks down upon the whole of a Europe where 'our freedom's swaying in the scales'. The experience of being a combatant (the poem is subtitled 'Before the Storming of Huesca') has closed the gap between personal agency and historical process for Cornford, and this new urgency makes his use of the analogy precise and alive. It is no mere Romantic symbol drawn from Shelley's 'Mont Blanc', but a powerful embodiment of the paradoxes of a history which is simultaneously responsibility and burden, nightmare and bequest. The very acknowledgment, at the end of the opening movement, that the analogy will not hold, the shift from metaphor to plain statement, reinforces the assumption of personal responsibility it describes. 'Time future has no image in space.' Some pre-emptive topographical figure would only create new confusions (between, for example, the visually unresolvable 'crooked' and 'straight'). To give it metaphoric and visual embodiment would be to deny its openness, its *Undefined* status as sheer potential, that which *may* be. It can be expressed only by two terse, unmetaphoric utterances, one a statement of fact, the other a simple injunction, in which the human is by turns subject and object of the historical process, for it is a matter of plain, collective choice:

> The past, a glacier, gripped the mountain wall,
> And time was inches, dark was all.
> But here it scales the end of the range,
> The dialectic's point of change,
> Crashes in light and minutes to its fall.
>
> Time present is a cataract whose force
> Breaks down the banks even at its source
> And history forming in our hand's
> Not plasticine but roaring sands,
> Yet we must swing it to its final course.
>
> The intersecting lines that cross both ways,
> Time future, has no image in space,
> Crooked as the road that we must tread,
> Straight as our bullets fly ahead.
> We are the future. The last fight let us face.

Here, the poem continues, the rhetoric and political decisions of his party find their real 'testing', along with the men who adhere to them: 'If true, if false, is live or dead, / Speaks in the Oviedo mausers' tone'. But, with great honesty, Cornford refuses the empty heroism of an undivided commitment, confessing not just to his membership of an elite, a political vanguard, but also to the isolation and fear it carries with it. Nothing is certain, if the future is really open, and the claim to represent 'History' has to be vindicated by action. 'Now, with my Party, I stand quite alone', and the 'private battle with my nerves', 'The loneliness that claws my guts', are overcome only by a real inner struggle to fuse them 'in the welded front our fight preserves'. The fight is conducted within the self as well as in the outside world. But there is not here a simple separation of struggling individual and massive externality. For the struggle in the self is conducted as part of a collective struggle, to forge a fighting unit out of disparate individuals, to overcome separateness in a group endeavour. Hence 'Freedom was never held without a fight'; it is not an abstract condition, a state to enter into, but a dynamic *holding* of contrary forces.

If the poem closes with an affirmation of abstract principles which in retrospect seem naive and sadly frustrated, they have nevertheless been fought for throughout the poem, which is itself the site of a struggle between the fragile individual being and the terrors of a real and unaccommodating history. The ending comes as the climax to a crescendo of wishes translated into imperatives directed not only at the self (which can try to do something about them) but also at a world beyond presided over by the indifferent moon, and, in that larger invocation, they turn back into mere wishes, mere hopeful appeals to a fairy-godmother history. The poem ends not in triumphant affirmation of a banal faith, but in a *negative* acknowledgment, that real victory is a long way off. The proud abstractions of the last line have to be set against the merely putative nature of the occasion they summon up, out of the unimagined, imageless future. The poet does not in fact speak them here and now. He imagines them being expressed, both as oath and act, in that future. But the very imagining establishes a covenant between then and now, fact and possibility:

Freedom is an easily spoken word

But facts are stubborn things. Here, too, in Spain
Our fight's not won till the workers of all the world
Stand by our guard on Huesca's plain
Swear that our dead fought not in vain,
Raise the red flag triumphantly
For Communism and for liberty.

In the 'Foreword' to his *Collected Shorter Poems, 1927–1957*
(1966), Auden wrote dismissively of his most famous
suppressed poem, *Spain*, published separately as a fund-
raising pamphlet in 1937. For the worldly-wise and world-
renouncing Christian Auden, the last lines of that
poem – 'History to the defeated / May say alas but cannot
help or pardon' – were 'shamefully dishonest', equating
'goodness with success'. Yet if we put this poem beside
Cornford's, we can see that its purport is quite different, and
also that it carries within its contradictory impulses that
larger uncertainty of purpose and confusion of motives which
find their neutralising peace in the relaxed aristocratic
postures of Auden's later poems, and the disingenuously
candid recantations of his 'Foreword'.

Auden's poem also begins with a résumé of 'all the past'
which dismisses as it defines all that transpired in a series of
accumulated 'Yesterdays'. When 'today' and its 'struggle'
finally emerge, it is the individual visions of the intellectual, of
poet and scientist, which step forward to distinction from an
array of generalities; but their specialised knowledges then
have to be completed, at once, by that of 'the poor in their
fireless lodgings'. All the particular desires and deprivations
converge in a collective yearning:

> . . . .'Our day is our loss, O show us
> History the operator, the
> Organizer, Time the refreshing river.'

The poem speaks of a repeated appeal to some external
agency to 'Intervene. O descend as a dove or / A furious papa
or a mild engineer, but descend', only to refute such faith in a
deus ex machina capable of resolving the dilemmas of men. This
fantasised 'History', created by men and women out of their

own needs and deeds, 'if it answers at all, replies from the heart / And the eyes and the lungs' of the actual city. Yet in putting words into the mouth of this fetish, Auden also breathes life into it. Like Hardy's Immanent Will, it comes alive in the very denial of its existence. Auden's literary device, that is, ratifies that separation of 'History' from human wills which the whole poem, at the level of its ideas, is struggling against, and in doing so, catches a larger contradiction of thirties marxism, its uneasy amalgam of voluntarism and fatalism. History's knowingness here is part of its fateful charm, but it evinces, too, the poet's superior scepticism about human motive:

> 'O no, I am not the mover;
> Not today; not to you. To you, I'm the
>
> 'Yes-man, the bar-companion, the easily-duped;
> I am whatever you do. . . .
>
> I am your choice, your decision. Yes, I am Spain.'

The poem at once concedes and refuses too much. Just as the earlier sections had filtered out a generalised list of 'progressive' moments in the spread of knowledge and the abolition of error, speeding them up within an evolutionary momentum that condensed whole millennia to a few sentences, and admitted no contrary movement, so here, men are at once the sole instigators of their projects and, in the blasé perspective of a know-all History, helpless victims of their own obsessions. They have 'migrated like gulls or the seeds of a flower' from remote peninsulas or corrupt cities, in answer to the call of Spain, have clung like birds to express trains, floated over oceans, walked passes, as if drawn by some inescapable biological impulse, and the poet's abstracted distance enables him to totalise this movement in a way which empties it of all particular volition.

Such an evacuation of individual will from events is the necessary prelude to the sacrifice of self which follows: 'All presented their lives'. It is clear from the succeeding lines that Auden sees the alignment of private and historic planes not, as for Cornford, as the ground of a possible liberation, but as the surrender and submergence of one in the other. There is little difference between the political philosophy expressed here and the Christian doctrine of a service which is perfect freedom that he was soon to adopt. Spain is a place where 'Our thoughts have bodies; the menacing shapes of our fever / Are precise and alive'; where, that is, the subjective is bodied forth as history. But it is also the tableland upon which the subjective is extinguished by that history, where 'fears' become 'invading battalions' and 'our faces' 'Are projecting their greed as the firing squad and the bomb', instruments of our own destruction.

Time, in the last section, is reduced from that unfolding history held together by a cohesive narrative syntax of the early sections, into a series of disjunctive moments, 'moments of tenderness' that 'blossom / As the ambulance and the sandbag', 'hours of friendship' that turn 'into a people's army'. Despite the affirmation of the metaphor of natural growth, this fragmentary quality persists. The future likewise is a series of listed moments, lacking the narrative momentum of 'Yesterday all the past'. The present activities which may ensure that future fluctuate between the abstract callousness of 'The conscious acceptance of guilt in the necessary murder' and the 'makeshift consolations' of a world where individual agents have dispersed into their discrete acts, frozen into a catalogue of nouns, 'the shared cigarette, / The cards in the candlelit barn, and the scraping concert / The masculine jokes; . . . the / Fumbled and unsatisfactory embrace before hurting'.

The encounter of the individual and history has itself become a fumbled and unsatisfactory embrace, and the poem rises to real plangency in its conclusion, not in a 'dishonest' celebration of the doctrine of success, but in a lament for the solitude of history, the vulnerability and anxious urgency of the embattled self, conscripted to a process that supersedes it. Here lies the real nature of the thirties poet's brief engagement with history, and the reasons for his posthaste return to bourgois decency. It is the very honesty of its revelation which is painful for an older and wiser Auden; for the defeat has already occurred, before even starting out:

The stars are dead. The animals will not look.
We are left alone with our day, and the time is short, and
   History to the defeated
May say alas but cannot help or pardon.

7

Night is Always Close: Gunn and Hughes

'It was a violent time', as Thom Gunn observed of an earlier Elizabethan age, in 'A Mirror for Poets'. Again and again the writers of the 'Movement' – the name loosely and inaccurately applied to the English poetry of the fifties – returned to the theme of violence, yet shrank back from engaging with it. Gunn's own poetry, full of latent aggression, strove to contain its smouldering energy in couplets, formal stanzas and histrionic poses ('Even in bed I pose') as impersonal and self-disciplining as those Nazi uniforms and leather-jackets with which his poems abound. The motor-cyclists of 'On the Move' seemed to offer an adequate parallel to his own poetic stance:

> In goggles, donned impersonality,
> In gleaming jackets trophied with the dust,
> They strap in doubt – by hiding it, robust –
> And almost hear a meaning in their noise.

Much of the writing of the period tried to explore the barbarous hinterland recent history had shown to lie behind the genteel façades of western culture, but most of it had an air of 'donned impersonality' which suggested that this violation of assumed values could not yet be faced. The doubt was too profound, the revelations of depravity too recent and too raw, to make total candour possible. In the death camps of Hitler and Stalin the two alternatives to the bourgeois humanist tradition had shown their true faces. But, as the experience of both Ezra Pound and the marxists of the thirties had disclosed, such 'alternatives' were not simply antithetical to that tradition. Under pressure, riven by crisis, the tradition itself had mutated into these grotesque secrets of its senile dementia.

Robert Lowell christened this period of convalescence 'the tranquillised fifties'. Its tutelary deity was no longer 'the God that failed', 'History the operator, the / Organiser, Time the refreshing river' of Auden's 'Spain'. Instead, history is now that 'Madonna of silences' Auden addressed in 'Homage to Clio' (1960) 'to whom we turn / When we have lost control', to whom 'We look for recognition after / We have been found out'. Ashamed of a politics which subdued the individual conscience to 'conscious acceptance of guilt in the necessary murder', Auden now sought in the patience and the fortitude of everyday life the true historical experience. Such life, absorbed in itself, not comprehending the larger movements which impose upon it, nevertheless survives with dignity and pathos amid all the atrocities of the history-makers:

> .... I have seen
> Your photo, I think, in the papers, nursing
>   A baby or mourning a corpse: each time
>
> You had nothing to say and did not, one could see,
>   Observe where you were, Muse of the unique
> Historical fact, defending with silence
>   Some world of your beholding, a silence
>
> No explosion can conquer. ....

Many poets of the fifties turned to this world of the quotidian, of everyday life, as a refuge from history, seeking, in a strangely superannuated image of English life that seemed to hark back to a pre-1914 ethos, a reassuring and a consoling escape from the pressure of the times. Donald Davie admits as much in his 'Rejoinder to a Critic', arguing that 'recent history', the atom bombing of Japan, had revealed the dangers of 'feeling', of the Romantic tradition of self-fulfilment, and ending with the plaintive enquiry: 'How dare we now be anything but numb?' But beneath this preference for keeping the head down, the avoidance of 'skyline operations' in cautious self-protection, and the provincial pastoral of poets such as Philip Larkin, is another story, equally interesting.

The literature of the fifties insists on continuity, on, for example, a return to that literary traditionalism represented by Hardy and Edward Thomas, and a rejection of the innovations of a Modernism inseparable from the extremist vision. Yet underneath all this rediscovery of origins a real and profound transformation is taking place. For the writing of this period is that of an essentially *new* spirit, of that meritocratic self thrown up by the 1944 Education Act, the emergence of the welfare state, and the growth of an institutionalised cultural apparatus in education, the arts, the media. In its ideology, it combines an ethic of opposition derived from the thirties' assault on the 'Old Gang' – underwritten by grammar-school-boy resentment of inherited privilege – with an opportunist eye and a streak of ruthlessness, ready to seize its chances in this new world, and, on the basis of sheer native entrepreneurial talent, to carve out its own niche in it.

Both Thom Gunn and Ted Hughes remain ambiguously drawn to the dark proletarian underside from which this new sensibility, this ascendant ego, has emerged – a world viewed from a distance by Gunn as a violent terrain, inhabited by a free-floating lumpen of Hell's Angels, Nazis, and 'Lofty in the Palais de Danse': a world metaphorically represented, in Hughes's poetry, as a primordial realm of animal instinct and feudal barbarity. Both poets grasp unconsciously that the stabilised order which has brought achievement to the combative self is deeply rooted in violence. But – 'The self-defined, astride the created will' of 'On the Move' – the self-made heroes of their poetry never see their own egos as in any way problematic. The ego is a simple given, confronting an equally given world it aims to master. Gunn can claim 'I am condemned to be / An individual', as if identity were an easy and inescapable donnée. In his later, acid-trip poems in *Moly* (1971), written in the United States, this assurance dissolves, the constructed ego collapses, and a volatile self undergoes that centrifugal expansion into directionless, illimitable fields which, for Gunn, was a salutary experience. In a sense, such an experience provided the answer to certain dilemmas which had forced their way through the strictly disciplined forms, the 'Plan of Self-Subjection', of his earlier work, with all its insistence upon defining limits.

In 'To Yvor Winters, 1955', for example, Gunn had used a language heavy with ideological intent, to describe the older poet's conservative 'defence of reason':

> Continual temptation waits on each
> To renounce his empire over thought and speech,
> Till he submit his passive faculties
> To evening, come where no resistence is;
> The unmotivated sadness of the air
> Filling the human with his own despair.
> Where now lies power to hold the evening back?
> Implicit in the grey is total black:
> Denial of the discriminating brain
> Brings the neurotic vision, and the vein
> Of necromancy. All as relative
> For mind as for the sense, we have to live
> In a haif-world, not ours nor history's,
> And learn the false from half-true premisses.

The terms here are highly charged: the new, progmatic sense of relativity in social and political values, after the fanatical commitments of the thirties; and yet the steeling of the self to accept a system *as if* it were absolute; the conservatism, and that insistent emphasis on *containment* – both keeping *out,* and keeping *in,* those forces which threaten the delicate balance of 'Rule and Energy'. Noticeably, as in 'Homage to Clio', the self rises to combativity only in resistance and *defence.*

In a year that saw the resignations from leadership of two architects of that Cold War partition of the globe which had ensured an unstable peace – Malenkov, Stalin's successor, and Churchill – and saw, too, three Geneva Conferences aimed at reducing tension in a divided Europe, the imagery of Gunn's poem is rich with contemporary reference. When Gunn speaks of 'Ferocity existing in the fence / Built by an exercised intelligence', it is not difficult to see this as a version, not just of the 'Iron Curtain', but of all those defensive perimeters, in reality as in thought, which divide a delicately balanced world. Likewise, when he goes on to say that, 'Though night is always close, complete negation / Ready to drop on wisdom and emotion', it is still 'right' to persist in the raising of excellence, one can feel the full force of that threat of negation, not just as a personal collapse, but as a global catastrophe – nuclear holocaust. Yet when Gunn divides this half-world up, in the lines above, he makes the partition, significantly, one between 'ours' and 'history's', as if somehow history and 'the deliberate human will' are radically estranged. The identification of the girded self, only half-sure of its premisses, with a confident assertion of 'empire over thought and speech', since the only alternative is total, passive surrender, is a highly political choice.

The ideological function of such poetry can be encapsulated in a phrase coined by Herbert Marcuse: it speaks out of the experience of a *one-dimensional* universe. The geo-political settlement between the United States and the Soviet Union, conceived in 1945 at Yalta and Potsdam, brought to birth by Churchill in his Fulton speech about an 'Iron Curtain' descending over Europe, confirmed by the Truman Doctrine, and never disturbed by any subsequent moment in the 'Cold War', created a social universe insulated from change, in which history itself seemed to have come to a stop. Nothing in the future, it appeared, could rescind the status quo established and consolidated by the Cold War. In the post-war era which is the subject of Marcuse's *One Dimensional Man* (1964) this political deadlock seemed to have been underwritten by the development of a technological apparatus of terror – the warfare state – intimately combined with that other instrument of social control, the welfare state:

> Technical progress, extending to a whole system, of domination and co-ordination, created forms of life (and of power) which appear to reconcile the forces opposing the system and to defeat or refute all protest in the name of the historical prospects of freedom from toil and domination. Contemporary society seems to be capable of containing social change – qualitative change which would establish essentially different institutions, as new direction of the productive process, new modes of human existence. This containment of social change is perhaps the most singular achievement of advanced industrial society.

This closed political universe necessarily entailed, too, a

closed emotional universe. Yet within the contained present, new modes of human existence were felt as pressing possibilities. Since these modes found no point of insertion into established reality, they lacked a language that would make sense of them. They manifested themselves, therefore, as a frustrated and aimless violence, like that 'posture for combat' revealed in the music of 'Elvis Presley' in Gunn's poem, which 'turns revolt into a style'. Such revolt, without apparent cause or object, 'generation of the very chance / It wars on', seems an ungrateful and irrational irruption into the commonsense world which gave it opportunity and occasion.

In the poetry of the period, this contradiction between the established rationality of the status quo and the nameless and undefined potentialities latent but deadlocked within it reveals itself in many ways. In Gunn's verse, it is there in the awareness of a 'ferocity' that has to be 'trained' and 'controlled', and in the unexpected image, in the last lines, of a 'carnivorous breath' that might descend on the stockade, on those 'accumulations that compose the self', the 'words' that 'maintain' and 'mark out our chosen lineaments'. The inner menace, which is usually allied with an outer one, and threatens to break down the barriers between the two – between 'self' and 'history' – is often projected in the image of the werewolf, that distorted representation of our dual nature. Gunn's 'Allegory of the Wolf Boy' is explicit about this, telling us that 'The causes are in Time; only their issue / Is bodied in the flesh, the finite powers'. This *alter ego* belongs not to us but to a history ('Time') conceived as *nature*, the inhuman and subhuman substratum of our being, which lies beyond the pale of a pacified contemporary reality: 'At tennis and at tea / Upon the gentle lawn, he is not ours, / But plays us in a sad duplicity'. In Hughes's poetry too we find the self assuming these 'wolf masks', overtly in 'A Modest Proposal' and 'Fallgrief's Girl-Friends', more generally, in strange, atavistic fantasies of animal violence and intensity, which burn their way through the fabric of everyday experience with memories of an older and more terrifying existence, in a world where 'night is always close'.

Ted Hughes's 'Pibroch' is a powerful evocation of a one-dimensional world – an unremittingly bleak landscape swept by the wind, 'Without purpose, without self-deception', where 'The sea cries with its meaningless voice' and the rock occasionally dreams it is 'the foetus of God'. This vision, of a cosmic order totally 'imprisoned' within itself, 'Created for black sleep', claims to make an inclusive statement about the human condition, as the last stanza indicates:

> Minute after minute, aeon after aeon,
> Nothing lets up or develops.
> And this is neither a bad variant or a tryout.
> This is where the staring angels go through.
> This is where all the stars bow down.

Yet it is most significant in its omissions. Organic life is almost totally absent from this landscape; that which intrudes is sterile, futile and alien, a tree struggling to make leaves like 'An old woman fallen from space / Unprepared for these conditions'. To admit organic life would be to recognise a different conception of nature, not as erosion and entropy, but as growth, exfoliation, fecundity, in a process in which the material world constantly remakes and renews itself. In such a world, time would be more than an inert perpetuation of the present.

What this poem catches, in fact, is the inner experience of an era of social impasse. A crucial part of that experience is the conviction that it has always been like this, and will always remain so. Translating the relative historical episode into the dimension of myth and metaphysics, the poem therefore underwrites that conviction. This is a world arrested beyond human agency to alter, and any aspiration beyond it, like the pebble's absurd dream, is a delusion whose only punishment will be to remain unfulfilled and ignored.

This is a repeated moment in Hughes's poetry, and its historical significance is perhaps confirmed by one of the few poems in his oeuvre which has an overt political reference. 'A Woman Unconscious' shows history stalemated, unable to move forward, before the prospect of a nuclear war which has eliminated the very possibility of change:

Russia and America circle each other;
Threats nudge an act that were without doubt
A melting of the mould in the mother,
Stones melting about the root . . .

From such a prospect of 'world-cancelling black', we're told,
'flitting thought' shies away. It has learnt that there's no
reliability in 'Dates when the world's due to be burned':

That the future's no calamitous change
But a malingering of now,
Histories, towns, faces that no
Malice or accident much derange.

The hypostasised 'History' of the thirties poets, converted
into a mere 'malingering of now', fragments into innumerable
private 'histories', which, for all their surface bustle, remain
fundamentally unchanged by the succession of accidents
which befalls them. There has been history, but there is no
more. Human agency is no more than a flitting thought which
casts a playing and playful shadow across the face of the
globe. But that 'shadow' is also the shadow of the nuclear
bomber which could cancel the whole world in one delicious
melting. Russia and America, in all their swarming human
plenitude, are reduced to the falsely concrete and diminished
emblem of two animals engaged in a fight. At the same time,
the focus and the emphasis shift to the prospect of personal
death, which alone seems real in such a world. What is out
there, in the meaningless devalued world, haunted by the
disabling prospect of its own annihilation, is less real than the
felt intensity of personal life:

And though bomb be matched against bomb,
Though all mankind wince out and nothing endure –
Earth gone in an instant flare –
Did a lesser death come

Onto the white hospital bed
Where one, numb beyond her last of sense,
Closed her eyes on the world's evidence
And into pillows sunk her head.

It is only in personal terms now, it seems, that time itself can unfold. The real individual death is more meaningful, more tragic, than the prospect of a collective death forever deferred into a hypothetical future.

The essentially totalitarian nature of the universe Hughes describes is revealed, in 'Hawk Roosting', through the figure of the arrogant and rapacious hawk which is a recurrent image in his early poetry. Such a figure combines medieval ruthlessness with a decidedly modern opportunism. Its all-seeing eye seems to identify it with the vigilant authoritarian state of Orwell's *1984;* at the same time, it is the self-centred individualism which is most distinctive about the bird. Unlike its prey, it is not distracted by any 'falsifying dream'; even its sleep, as it sits 'in the top of the wood', is dedicated to rehearsing its single-minded purpose: 'perfect kills'. Like the pushy meritocratic 'hero' of John Braine's *Room at the Top,* published in 1957, the same year as Hughes's first volume, *The Hawk in the Rain,* this bird defines the whole world in ruthlessly egocentric terms. Thus the trees offer 'convenience', the air's buoyancy and the sun's light 'Are of advantage to me', and the earth seems to turn its face 'upward for my inspection'. This, the self-styled ultimate heir of Creation, in whom, it seems, Creation has come to rest, is the epitome of simple, unreflective power, gloating over its own supremacy, and confirmed in its confidence by the whole weight of a universe which acknowledges the logic of success alone:

> My feet are locked upon the rough bark.
> It took the whole of Creation
> To produce my foot, my each feather:
> Now I hold creation in my foot
>
> Or fly up, and revolve it all slowly –
> I kill where I please because it is all mine. . . .

The bird does not need 'arguments' to assert its 'right', because the sun in a double sense, is 'behind' it. Descending on its prey out of the sun, it vindicates its mastery over the status quo by will and cunning: 'Nothing has changed since I began' because 'My eye has permitted no change'; and the bird's last words are a threat and a promise: 'I am going to keep things like this'. But there *are* limits to this power, as the sustained irony of the poem suggests, hinting that this hubris is the pride before a fall, that such solipsistic smugness – assuming that, for example, the objective rotation of the planet is produced by 'revolving' it in thought – may be the source of its undoing. The bird does not notice the ambiguity with which its feet are 'locked' on the branch. This may imply the despot's grasp, but suggests, too, the jesses of the falconer, which make the bird no more than a subjected sovereign, the slave of a higher power. The meritocratic free spirit may be the more securely enslaved by its ignorance of dependence on that 'Creation' it thinks it controls: it is free only to identify with the given, the achieved order of things.

This double perspective is confirmed by the unironic but contradictory image of the hawk in the title poem of *The Hawk in the Rain*. Whereas in 'Hawk Roosting' the bird's mastery resides in its identification with a rapacious reality, this hawk seems a symbol of a transcending freedom, escaping from the glutinous mud of a world where, at ground level, the poet's eyes are thumbed by the banging wind, his breath thrown and his heart tackled by it. The whole poem is structured round a polarity of images, of eye and mouth, which focus this opposition. While the 'earth's mouth' seeks to swallow the floundering individual, the bird 'Effortlessly at height hangs his still eye', in a contemplative freedom that distances it from this 'Bloodily grabbed dazed last-moment-counting / Morsel in the earth's mouth'. The hawk's wings 'hold all creation in a weightless quiet' and it is towards this 'master- / Fulcrum of violence where the hawk hangs still' that the struggling self strains, seeking to free itself from a one-dimensional world of violation and exposure, where such freedom can seem mere 'hallucination'.

Vision and detachment seem to be power, an achieved mastery of stillness in the heart of flux. But 'hallucination' is the appropriate word. The hawk is no more free from its environment than the poet, as a momentary lapse of vigilance or the failing of inner power would soon disclose. In time, it too will succumb to the pull of gravity, its 'round angelic eye' will be 'smashed' in the mire of the land. It will die, however, still locked in its illusion of autonomy, ostensibly meeting the weather 'Coming the wrong way' 'in his own time', suffering the air to 'Fall from his eye' feeling 'the ponderous shires crash on him'. Like the hawk roosting, this bird will persist to the last in its naive belief that the world is arranged for *its* convenience, and that all relations in space or time take *it* as their 'fulcrum'.

Hughes's poems repeatedly reach out to creatures which embody this tension between boundless inner potency and an external limitation. Recurrently, such a pattern involves a lack or surrender of discrimination which carries with it an allusion of omnipotence. 'The Jaguar' describes a zoo in which time itself seems incarcerated, where animal vitality has rotted in its own inertia, so that they have become merely creatures in a bestiary which 'might be painted on a nursery wall', or, like the boa-constrictor, 'coiled like a fossil', redundant in a tranquillised world. Amid this futility, one creature alone haunts the vacuous present with a mesmerising 'dream' of a lost and alien intensity: 'a jaguar hurrying enraged / Through prison darkness after the drills of his eyes / On a short fierce fuse'.

There is, for the jaguar, no gulf between intention and act: all meaning is incarnate here and now, with 'The eye satisfied to be blind in fire, / By the bang of the blood in the brain deaf the ear'. Its very stride is 'wildernesses of freedom', and the jaguar is no more confined in its cage than the visionary is imprisoned in his cell. But the paradox of the last line catches the illusory nature of a freedom that can only be bought by the blunting of discrimination. Instinct is deaf and blind, intoxicated by its own magnificence: 'Over the cage floor the horizons come'. This intensity of energy is in some way self-destructive: the eyes burn like fuses to a powder keg.

The same process occurs in 'Macaw and Little Miss'. The poem shudders with a suppressed, smouldering energy like that of the bird it describes. The language is dense, clustered and stubborn, unfolding slowly and painfully, as if reluctant or incapable of reaching any clear consummation, and with a stifling inertia that duplicates the suffocation of a creature that can only endure without realising its own diabolical intensity, 'in a staring / Combustion, suffers the stoking devils of his eyes'. This ferocity is grotesquely at odds with the shabby gentility of its setting 'In the old lady's parlour, where an aspidistra succumbs / To the musk of faded velvet'. Yet what is most striking here is the archaic nature of the imagery Hughes employs to describe this energy. The macaw hangs 'Like a torturer's iron instrument', 'Or like the smouldering head that hung / In Killdevil's brass kitchen, in irons', or 'a fugitive aristocrat / From some thunderous mythological hierarchy' caught by a little boy and put in a cage to sing. This ultimate reduction of the mighty and cosmic by a banal and spiteful act rounds off the whole sequence of images, and finds its parallel in the teasing cruelty of the old woman's grand-daughter. But at this point, the whole cycle of archaic violence is renewed.

The girl too is possessed by 'stoking devils'. Her incinerating passions, finding no outlet, turn back upon her in concupiscent fantasies of violation totally at odds with her genteel situation and innocent demeanour, a vision of a desired yet terrifying catharsis at once release and punishment:

> . . . . The girl calls him 'Poor Polly', pokes fun.
> 'Jolly Mop.' But lies under every full moon,
> The spun glass of her body bared and so gleam-still
> Her brimming eyes do not tremble or spill
> The dream where the warrior comes, lightning and iron,
> Smashing and burning and rending towards her loin: .
> Deep into her pillow her silence pleads.

Identity is a carefully sustained equilibrium – the unspilled brimming – of inner and outer pressures, achieved only at great cost in repression. Should that equilibrium be upset 'in a tantrum', the whole house may be shaken 'in conflagration and frenzy' by the macaw's shriek, wings, talons. Yet the dream of some return of the repressed, in which the frustrated instincts turn back upon themselves in an orgy of self-chastisement, has deep roots. In such a universe, self-affirmation seems to open the way, almost at once, for this vengeful return, and the poet is in some way its avatar, calling up memories, as in 'Famous Poet', of 'a time when half the world still burned', though he is now 'set / To blink behind bars at the zoo'.

In all Hughes's bestiaries this doubleness is recorded. His animals are never simply expressions of unalloyed instinctual *joie de vivre*. Most of them are deeply ambiguous creatures, poised between two worlds – voracious carnivores in suburban zoos or, like 'Esther's Tomcat', moving from the everyday domestic world into a night which is as old and dark as time. In the daytime, such a cat may seem 'a bundle of old rope and iron'; but at dusk, its eyes open 'green as ringstones', its mouth 'yawns wide red, / Fangs fine as a lady's needle and bright', and, automatically, the poem moves us into a feudal ethos of cruelty, superstition and barbarous grandeur in speech and gesture where hundreds of years ago 'A tomcat sprang at a mounted knight'. In 'An Otter', there is the same reversion, in which animal instinct calls up a lost, primeval world, 'Brings the legend of himself / From before wars or burials', crying without answer for 'Some world lost when first he dived, that he cannot come at since'. The amphibious nature of the animal then becomes a figure for a deep ambivalence in the self: it immerses itself in the dark stream, to avoid its hunters, as 'the self under the eye lies, / Attendant and withdrawn'.

In 'To Paint a Water Lily' the same ambivalence recurs. The plant floats at the intersection of two worlds, 'the two minds of this lady'. The air of consciousness is itself shot though with violence. But it is in those depths below, on the pond's bed, that the real horror resides:

> Prehistoric bedragonned times
> Crawl that darkness with Latin names,
>
> Have evolved no improvements there,
> Jaws for heads, the set stare,
>
> Ignorant of age as of hour. . . .

The present, tranquillised universe is haunted by glimpses of that dark ahistorical substratum of being in which it is rooted.

'Pike' is another such image of the attendant and

withdrawn self that lingers within the pool of the eye, biding its time, and Hughes here, briefly, links this personal moment to a larger cultural one. The pike lives in the 'Stilled legendary depths' of a pond 'as deep as England'. It is no ordinary fish but a symbol of some archaic modality of being 'so immense and old' the rational self shrinks from inviting it into consciousness. And yet its murderous fascination is irresistible; and when at the conclusion of the poem, as he sits past nightfall casting for it, it rises 'slowly towards me, watching', he in turn, as the ambiguous last participle suggests, has become the object, and not just the subject, of its alien and yet familiar gaze.

Hughes's poems are haunted by a nostalgia for a lost world of being in which the feudal, the archaic, and the prehistoric are associated with the instinctual and automatic, with a brutal realm of primary responses which, as here, is equated with the most ancient and abiding recesses of England itself. The mythos of all these poems, in fact, is a *recherche* for a lost unity of being back before the modern era, before two world wars which overthrew, as if for good, the real England. This is the burden of such poems as 'The Ancient Heroes and the Bomber Pilot'. For the latter, even though his bombs can turn the enemy capital to a fume and shake the huge earth, 'The grandeur of their wars humbles my thought', 'my heart / Is cold and small' compared with theirs. In those poems which return to the mass slaughters of the Great War, a similar note recurs. In 'Six Young Men' even the faded photograph of six casualties, their smiles 'Forty years rotting into soil', can unnerve the speaker with an emotion hardly to be borne:

> That man's not more alive whom you confront
> And shake by the hand, see hale, hear speak loud,
> Than any of these six celluloid smiles are,
> Nor prehistoric or fabulous beast more dead;
> No thought so vivid as their smoking blood:
> To regard this photograph might well dement,
> Such contradictory permanent horrors here
> Smile from the single exposure and shoulder out
> One's own body from its instant and heat.

Clearly, it is the present and vulnerable self which is here 'exposed', just as, in 'Griefs for Dead Soldiers', the intuition of 'some universal cataclysm' in the picture of bodies piled into graves is a 'Moment that could annihilate a watcher'. The imagery of this poem is apocalyptic, speaking of the opening of hell's gates, of an approaching planet, 'a half-day off', hanging huge in the sky; but it is apocalypse which opens in the heart of the everyday, 'Monstrousness of the moment making the air stone'. Thus, in 'Parlour Piece', two lovers sit 'chaperoned' by pale cool tea in teacups, while 'fire and flood' strain in their eyes. Love is anti-social, anarchic; it opens up the world of commonsense to dangerous, cataclysmic irruptions. Throughout Hughes's poetry, in fact, the intensity of emotion has to be kept on a tight rein, or its short fierce fuse will splutter to destruction. What is most noticeable about his creatures, perhaps, is their stifling self-containment, their solitude and self-absorption. Like the self, attendant beneath the eye, they do not venture into contact and communication, into a shared world.

Gunn, contemplating Nazi atrocities in such poems as 'Innocence', or the long sequence 'Misanthropos'(*Touch*, 1967), probes them for their meaning, their ironies, their insights into the human. Hughes, however, seems to feel too intimate an involvement with them to keep his cool, collected distance. It is a feature of his peculiar honesty that he accepts this intimacy, this complicity even. In *Crow* (1972), in raucous, acerbic tones, he submits all human pretensions to Crow's cold, nihilistic scrutiny, through the persona finally detaching himself from all evasiveness. For Crow, man is 'a walking / Abattoir of innocents', hypocritically justifying his lust for survival with a flood of words – lies, jests, vows, curses and prayers – all of which mask his deep viciousness. Crow, for whom even birth is a kill, who struggles into existence over the body of his mother, cannot afford such luxuries. Charity, compunction, love, remorse, forgiveness, are all denied him by life itself. To come into existence is to give pain, to survive is to survive at the expense of others: atrocity, madness, rapine are the very grounds of being, in a world racked by entropy, where all hierarchies of order and privilege break down into destruction, and survival, sheer brute continuance, is the nearest one comes to hope:

So the survivors stayed
And the earth and sky stayed.
Everything took the blame.

Not a leaf flinched, nobody smiled.

In earlier poems such as 'The Horses', Hughes had
envisaged the prospect of apocalypse, of the dawn sun
erupting, splitting open the 'Evil air, a frost-making stillness'
of a one-dimensional world, a 'world cast in frost', where the
breath itself congeals into 'tortuous statues' and light into
iron. Even there, such a vision could not be borne, so that the
self, desiring transcendence, nevertheless retreats from its
moor-ridge eminence, 'Stumbling in the fever of a dream', till
it comes upon the horses, standing 'Megalith-still' in the fields
below. Ostensibly the horses are offered as a climax to the
narrative crescendo, but their primary function is to provide a
reassuring diminuendo, an antidote to the futuristic terror of
'the big planets hanging' in the gulf torn open by dawn. This
cosmic convulsion has to be muted, subdued by the picture of
brute stoical endurance the horses stand for, 'Their heads
hung patient as the horizons'; and the poem ends with a wish
for a personal future in which 'In din of the crowded streets,
going among the years, the faces', he may 'meet [his] memory
in so lonely a place. . . . / Hearing the horizons endure'. Here,
the prehistoric immutability of the horses is their prime
reassurance. Drawn to the idea of an apocalyptic renewal, the
reality terrifies him, and it is no accident that the horses, in
their ability to outlive all cataclysms, should speak of a
reassuring solitude amongst multitude: the crowd and the
vision of the 'kindling tops' are intimately related. The poem
misplaces its centre, from the dawn to the horses, as if trying
to diffuse the full impact of that revelation.
   The revelation is even more insistent in 'Wind', with its
vision of the hills re-arranged by the storm, their 'tent'
drumming and straining on its guyrope, and 'The fields
quivering, the skyline a grimace, / At any second to bang and
vanish with a flap', so that the poem's conclusion envisages a
transformation of a fragile stasis by an enormous violence, in

which the house of civilisation is no more than some 'fine green goblet' about to shatter:

> . . . . We watch the fire blazing,
> And feel the roots of the house move, but sit on,
> Seeing the window tremble to come in,
> Hearing the stones cry out under the horizons.

There is a peculiar suspended frenzy to this which is characteristic of Hughes: a stillness in the very centre of atrocity and violence. This held tension is like that of which Gunn speaks in 'To Yvor Winters', in which 'night is always close, complete negation', but the self persists in its stubborn clinging to what it has. What threatens this world is what 'Fragment of an Ancient Tablet' in *Crow* calls 'The ticking bomb of the future', in an image which links a recurrent history with the dark, ferocious powers of sexuality. Just as, in 'Misanthropos', Gunn evokes the end of the universe itself, with the earth falling into the sun, the stars collapsing, to put our human pretensions in place, so Hughes in *Crow* creates a mythic space, in the endless cycles of destruction and renewal, where catastrophe has already happened innumerable times, and will continue to occur. In some peculiar way, this displacement from history to myth takes the terror *out of time,* in order to take the *terror* out of *time.*

Hughes's later poems speak of a world in which the worst has already happened, the apocalypse has occurred, and there is a new and savage ferocity of denial in the poems. The personal experiences that culminated in the suicide of his wife Sylvia Plath in 1963 may provide the harrowing private source of this mood. But what transforms the poems into public, historically representative texts is the extent to which these 'private' catastrophes have coincided with an era in crisis, where the brittle stability of the Cold War has given way to the insecurities of a new and dangerous world, faced by social upheaval throughout eastern and western blocs, by revolution, war and economic disintegration. The nihilism of Crow's vision then corresponds to a larger crisis of confidence in the system which can be traced too in the work of radically different writers, such as Larkin, Enright and Brian Patten.

In Hughes's *Gaudete* (1977) the primordial King Log figure, a dionysian earth-force out of fertility myth, has to be 'cancelled' by the elemental spirits because he 'begins to feel a nostalgia for independent, ordinary human life, free of his peculiar destiny'. Faced by the reality of that explosion it once desired, Hughes's poetry shrinks back into a new nostalgia, for a lost and ordinary innocence, for the arcadian idyll which, it seems, may now be recovered only on the other side of holocaust and outrage. At just the same moment, ironically, many of his contemporaries who started in that familiar world have grasped its untenability, have plunged into the dark dream of catastrophe which haunted Hughes from the start. In a still mythically intensified discourse, Hughes records in the *Moortown* sequence (1979) the movement from rebellious, antithetical spirit to the dream of home, of restoration and reconciliation, which lies behind the elegiac tones of those laureates of the quotidian discussed in the next chapter.

Yet even here, time is confused for Hughes, in a nostalgia, a *recherche du temps perdu* which is as much prospective as retrospective. Moving since the beginning from the realm of history to the timeless sphere of nature and cosmology, Hughes necessarily mystifies the crises which everywhere inform his poetry. 'Nature' becomes a realm ultimately beyond reproach and alteration, not amenable to the 'deliberate human will' of which Gunn speaks in 'On the Move'. Gunn, starting from the assumption that 'Much that is natural to the will must yield', has moved increasingly into a discourse which offers not only reports on emotion and experience but an attempt at rational explanation. The intensity of Hughes's poetry arises from the very refusal to do this. From *The Hawk in the Rain* to *Crow* and beyond, the beasts of his poetry have been scapegoats, ritual sublimations of what is in fact an inner fury. In their blind incomprehension of the energies which infest them, or Crow's sardonic, grim expositions of a world where 'everything goes to hell' ('Apple Tragedy') and God is 'well pleased', these creatures define a reality as absolute and irrefutable as anything envisaged in the darkest of Hardy's fantasies.

'February' – the month of the Roman festival which provided the title, *Lupercal,* to Hughes's second volume in

1960 – is an overt admission of this ritual strategy. At Lupercal, the predatory wolf-god is placated by offering him ritual sacrifices. In Hughes's poem, an unidentified 'he' is haunted by a remembered photograph of 'the hairless, knuckled feet / Of the last wolf killed in Britain'. The convergence, of the superseded and archaic with the modern and mechanised, in the double exposure of the photograph, is a typical moment in Hughes. It is the frozen instant, the opportunities afforded by civilisation itself, which open the door to terror, as in 'Six Young Men'. He is pursued by nightmares of disembodied feet that – in a highly loaded pun –

> Print the moonlit doorstep, or run and run
> Through the hush of parkland, bodiless, headless;
> With small seeming of inconvenience
> By day, too, pursue, siege all thought.

Again, it is the modern technique which has isolated these feet, as a print, to call up archaic terrors. But thought is now besieged by these implacable revenants, which have come simply to reclaim their own, to reappropriate a lost unity, from the world which transformed them into images. To avoid repossession, the man himself sits making substitute heads, wolf-masks, to propitiate these vengeful intruders. But he knows that what they seek is only their right:

> . . . . These feet, deprived,
> Disdaining all that are caged, or storied, or pictured,
> Through and throughout the true world search
> For the vanished head, for the world
>
> Vanished with the head, the teeth, the quick eyes –
> Now, lest they choose his head,
> Under severe moons he sits making
> Wolf-masks, mouths clamped well onto the world.

Beyond the enclosure of the bourgeois self, that fence 'Built by an exercised intelligence', the carnivorous breath waits patiently for its legitimate prey. Hughes's own poems in a sense are wolf-masks, with which he seeks to placate forces robbed of fulfilment in a world which denies their possibility, which preserves their memory only as photographic trophies. These forces are both within the self, in its most archaic recesses, and beyond it, in a future yet to come into its own. The prospect of some sort of collusion between the two opens up 'the neurotic vision, and the vein / Of necromancy' – that same agitated self-abnegation which, in the thirties, led some of its finest poets to surrender their liberal consciences to the necromancy of Stalinism. Ironically Hughes's character, like those earlier poets, first called up such visions in his search for a lost wholeness. His own atavistic nostalgia summoned these greedy revenants. Ultimately, it is a nostalgia for the future, not the past.

8

Margins of Tolerance: Responses to Post-war Decline

Charles Tomlinson's poem 'How Still the Hawk' (in *Seeing is Believing*, 1960) catches a recurring motif of post-war English poetry. It is a minimal meditation, taking the single image of the hawk, hanging 'innocent above / Its native wood' and turning it into a kind of emblem which reflects back upon the stance of the observer:

> Distance, that purifies the act
> Of all intent, has graced
> Intent with beauty.
> Beauty must lie
> As innocence must harm.

For the bird is, of course, hovering above a doomed prey, the unspecified creature that cowers on the map below, and its descent is a 'Plummet of peace' only to one 'who does not share / The nearness and the need'. One can find the same ethics of distance in R. S. Thomas's reflections in 'The Welsh Hill Country', which opens with a self-righteous denunciation of the tourist's lust for the picturesque that also concedes a shameful complicity (*An Acre of land*, 1952):

> Too far for you to see
> The fluke and the foot-rot and the fat maggot
> Gnawing the skin from the small bones,
> The sheep are grazing at Bwlch-y-Fedwen,
> Arranged romantically in the usual manner
> On a bleak background of bald stone.

Whereas, in the poetry of Hardy and of Edward Thomas,

there is a repeated struggle to overcome the distance between the observer and the observed, this poetry takes a kind of guilty delight in it. 'Beauty must lie', and, in the composure of our larger perspective, we can extract an added beauty from the refined luxury of contemplating this moral and aesthetic paradox, or, in the case of R. S. Thomas, a calvinistically self-gratulating anger at the fallenness of our spectatorial detachment. There is no yearning, no desire, no nostalgia even, across this spiritual gulf: the gulf itself is the guarantee of our election, and it is absolute. In being here, rather than there, in all our culpable aloofness, we can celebrate our own insulation from the 'shrivelled circle / Of magnetic fear'.

Eliot speaks of Dante as being the 'most European' and 'least provincial' of poets without ever ceasing to be 'local'. Locality, for Tomlinson, is the taint of being associated with that violent 'native' wood; for R. S. Thomas, in 'Welsh Landscape' (*Song at the Year's Turning,* 1955)

> It is to be aware,
> Above the noisy tractor
> And hum of the machine
> Of strife in the stung woods,
> Vibrant with sped arrows,

of being incorporated in an alien history, the 'spilled blood / That went to the making of the wild sky', the brittle relics and 'sham ghosts' of an 'impotent people, / Sick with inbreeding'.

'Provinciality' perhaps always contains within it the sting of distance. The individual whose centre is always elsewhere, whether in Heaven or in London, inserts his own distance into the landscape, a distance he carries everywhere with him. Yet most of the poetry in the English tradition has had a strong provincial rootedness. In the poetry of the post-war period, however, whether the landscape is native or not, it has usually been at one remove, seen, as so often in Philip Larkin's poetry, through the window of a train, or even of a house in which one is almost equally transient. Coventry, glimpsed from a train in 'I Remember, I Remember', though the poet's birthplace, is not where he has his 'roots', 'only where my childhood was

unspent, . . . just where I started', to be dismissed in a
doggedly negative listing of all the things that didn't happen
there. The poetry of place is, in fact, usually a poetry of
displacements lovingly cultivated.

Distance is a recurring and complex concept in Larkin's
poetry. In 'Arrivals, Departures' it constitutes a reassurance
to the sleepy resident who hears 'Arrivals lowing in a doleful
distance' from the docks, though he is 'nudged from comfort'
by the final stanza. In 'At Grass', it is the very stuff of
nostalgia, as the poem opens with a view of one-time race-
horses reduced to anonymity by retirement. Spatial distance
places the observer in a secure frame: 'The eye can hardly pick
them out'. As the poem develops the image, by recalling a
time when these horses were 'picked out' both by binoculars
and by fame, it compounds spatial and temporal distance with
a further concept, that of a distinguishing excellence:

> Yet fifteen years ago, perhaps
> Two dozen distances sufficed
> To fable them. . . .

'Whatever Happened?' makes distance the very ground of
freedom, as the individual extricates himself from dangerous
and compromising circumstances, leaving 'whatever
happened' transplanted into the ironically significant
perspective where 'All's kodak-distant'. 'Places, Loved Ones'
keeps the same ambivalent composure: the lack of a 'proper
ground', a settled commitment, frees the self from
responsibility. 'Should the town turn dreary, / The girl a
dolt'. The mediations of distance rescue one from the
compromising immediacy of the *instant*, 'that special
one / Who has an instant claim / On everything I own /
Down to my name'. Propriety and property, self-possession,
as for Eliot's early anti-heroes, is at a premium in this poetry.
'Reasons for Attendance' defines the social space of this
distance: the speaker looks in through a lighted window where
dancers, all under twenty-five, dance to the sound of a
trumpet. It is the music which convinces him of his own reality
as an 'individual'. But individuality seems to posit distance as
its *sine qua non,* though it carries with it, too, that omen of

death and dispossession which concludes 'Dry-Point', 'Next, Please' and 'Going'.

'Deceptions', which provides the title for *The Less Deceived* (1955), where all the foregoing poems appeared, makes distance the very ground of our humanity. The poem opens with what seems like a qualification. As it evolves, this is transformed into ultimate consolation: all alike, victim and rapist and pitying poetic voyeur of Mayhew's Victorian anecdote, are equally pitiable, for everything passes. It is a subtle modulation from a time-transcending sympathy –

> Even so distant, I can taste the grief
> Bitter and sharp with stalks, he made you gulp

– with all its touching cumulative detail, through the 'Slums, years, [that] have buried you', the rejection of anything so impertinent as consolation, the somewhat abstract meditation on suffering, to the strangely equivocal separation of violator's and poet's and girl's responses in the last lines –

> For you would hardly care
> That you were less deceived, out on that bed,
> Than he was, stumbling up the breathless stair
> To burst into fulfilment's desolate attic.

But it is perhaps the opening poem of the volume which presents most clearly the function of retrospective distances in Larkin's poetry. The title, 'Lines on a Young Lady's Photograph Album', itself establishes an ironic distance, calling up conventional album verse, many previous poems, by Hardy, MacNeice, Day Lewis on the same theme, and, more naughtily, other famous meditations on the relation between art, time and history. Gaining access to the album is presented as an act of sexual triumph cognate to that implied, negatively, in Keats's description of the Grecian urn as a 'still unravished bride': the two opening lines set up a coy counterpoint:

> At last you yielded up the album, which,
> Once open, sent me distracted. All your ages

Matt and glossy on the thick black pages!
Too much confectionery, too rich:
I choke on such nutritious images.

Far from preserving detachment, the eye here becomes a
predator, 'hunger[ing] from pose to pose' as it scans these
trophies of time and change, photographs of childhood,
adolescence and 'these disquieting chaps who loll / At ease
about your earlier days'. The 'Faithful and disappointing' art
of photography, 'that records / Dull days as dull, and hold-it
smiles as frauds' seems to persuade us overwhelmingly 'That
this is a real girl in a real place, / In every sense empirically
true'. But it is precisely the art as *illusion* which appeals to the
poet. The captured present is in actuality past, and *it always
has been*. The window of the photograph through which we look
here is a window on a time that was *always* out-of-date,
transformed so in the very process of being committed to
print. Distance always involves time for Larkin; but here, the
snapshots enable the past to enter into its true element, as an
immediate fiction. Time, whether personal, or public, is
reduced to unreality by its own passage, as in 'Deceptions'.
And with such illusions, we can never be disillusioned, for all
their candid multiplicity of detail is mere rhetoric, the small
change of artistic 'persuasion':

Or is it just the *past?* Those flowers, that gate,
These misty parks and motors, lacerate
Simply by being over; you
Contract my heart by looking out of date.

Yes, true; but in the end, surely, we cry
Not only at exclusion, but because
It leaves us free to cry. We know *what was*
Won't call on us to justify
Our grief, however hard we yowl across

The gap from eye to page. . . .

This distant instance, or instant distance, gives away the
secret of art's transformations. For though the heart may be

doubly contracted (both shrunken and committed) by this image, it is at the same time set free by its exclusion from event. The yowling across the gap is, then, a mere self-indulgence, another kind of treat, harking back to the gluttonous delight of the opening stanza. These photographs 'condense, / In short, a past that no one now can share, / No matter whose your future', holding her 'like a heaven' where she *lies* (the word picking up all those ambiguities of truth, falsehood and fictionality the whole poem has juggled with) 'Unvariably lovely . . . , / Smaller and clearer as the years go by'. The function of such images, in fact, is not to record the past, and hint at the abandoned futures, but to liberate the *present* from contracts and obligations. Distance, in Larkin's poetry, is a way of renouncing 'responsibility for time'.

Larkin's poetry insists on the specificity of its local colour, but there is a sense in which this provides the same kind of deception. The poem which opens *The Whitsun Weddings* (1964) is ostensibly about Hull, in all its picturesque matter-of-factness. But it is called 'Here', and the town is nowhere mentioned by name. In reality, the poem is about the general condition of 'hereness', that contingency in which a given world forces itself upon our attention in all its provincial otherness. All the details of the poem are in fact pseudo-specificities, generalities listed in their impinging commonplaceness, as in the second stanza, where the cataloguing eye runs the environment, the people and its commodities into one vast shopping-list, consummated in the phrase 'A cut-price crowd, urban yet simple, dwelling / Where only salesmen and relations come'. As the third stanza hints, what we are dealing with here is not a slice of life but a 'pastoral', caught in the 'bluish neutral distance' (stanza four) not of space but of mind. If this landscape is provincial, it is not because it is a place 'where removed lives / Loneliness clarifies'; nor because it is remote from London. Rather, it is provincial because it is far removed from the metropolis of the heart, the true centre of being.

Even when, as in the title poem, the entrained Larkin is homing in on London, this sense of exile persists. On the one hand, he is excluded from the unique particularities of other lives, 'someone running up to bowl', the 'hothouse [which] flashed uniquely'. On the other hand, nostalgia for this empirical immediacy is actually intensified by the recognition that such items are not unique at all, but endlessly repeated, as 'the next town, new and nondescript, / Approached with acres of dismantled cars'. The wedding parties, gathering at each new station, all seem unchallengingly unique for their participants, but the travelling poet sees 'it all again in different terms', terms which he then lovingly catalogues in all their tawdry yet touching generality. That these dozen marriages come to share the poet's itinerant watching of the landscape, in 'this frail / Travelling coincidence', may momentarily include them within the poet's compassion: there is a noticeable opening up of sympathy once they become paid-up fellow-travellers on his journey. Nevertheless, the words 'jewellery substitutes' and the image of the girls 'Marked off unreally from the rest', imply a conviction similar to Eliot's: 'Humankind cannot bear very much reality'. It is as if these particular lives are unreal precisely because they are stereotyped: the general category negates, for Larkin, the value and uniqueness of the individual life. Only the abstracted, distanced observer really preserves his individuality: there is no one else like him on the train.

This condescension, turning to resentment before the actual typicality of what is supposed to be uniquely individual life, pervades the poetry of the post-war period. It expresses the renewed anxiety of a traditional liberal-individualism that has survived into an era of welfare-state social democracy, where mass tastes and values prevail, and the charming yokels of an earlier pastoral have turned into menacingly actual travelling-companions, claiming equal rights with the egregious and refined spectator of their shoddy ordinariness. Larkin usually manages to maintain an equivocal balance in his responses to such a world, poised between annoyance and deference. In more recent work, such as the poems in *High Windows* (1974), this balance has gone, and the mood is a more tight-lipped one, of disdain sharpening to odium. 'Going, Going' is a testimony here, with its lament for an England that he no longer thinks will last out his time – the traditional England of pastoral, where the village louts know their places (climbing 'Such trees as were not cut down'). Though the fifth stanza focusses on the spectacled grins of the Business Pages, which lie behind the commercial despoliations that are turning England into the 'First slum of Europe', such figures are oddly unspecific besides the venomous caricature of the preceding stanza, which seems to finger the real culprits:

> .... The crowd
> Is young in the M1 café;
> Their kids are screaming for more –
> More houses, more parking allowed,
> More caravan sites, more pay.

More for all means less for the privileged sensibility of the threnodist; and the expansion in quantity means a diminution in quality – a quality with which the poetic voice is unmistakably identified. Poets, of course, do not have to be democrats, nor should they be denied the right to indulge middle-aged pique. Larkin's poetry is valuable both in itself and as a symptomatic document of a cultural decline in which it is fundamentally implicated. One can, however, justifiably feel a little uncomfortable with sentiments that refuse to acknowledge their own complicity in that which they lacerate. The 'long perspectives' of which he spoke in 'Reference Back' no longer 'link us to our losses', but enable us to exculpate and extricate ourselves from their compromising contingency. The poet presumably has himself to be in the M1 café, even as a dubious beneficiary of its cuisine, in order to observe all these others. Tourists always complain that the tourists are spoiling the view.

In such situations, a frequent trick of Larkin's is to bridge the gap between refined sensibility and admass culture by a fetchingly idiomatic turn of phrase which reassures that the poet is himself really one of the boys, not a supercilious aesthete. In 'Going, Going' this is effected in the eighth stanza, with the plaintive admission that he feels, for the first time, 'That before I snuff it, the whole / Boiling will be bricked in / Except for the tourist parts'. 'This Be the Verse' justifies its Housmanish world-weariness by its opening bluff colloquialism, as if paying in advance for the mawkishness of what follows: 'They fuck you up, your mum and dad'. But it is perhaps in the magnificent title-poem of *High Windows* that the strategy pays off most impressively.

Here, a translucent nihilism in the concluding lines of the poem is saved from mere afflatus by the careful preparations of its opening. The self-consciously casual and dismissive vulgarity of this opening stanza clears the way for the Dantesque vision of paradisal beauty in the last. The movement from the squalidly tangible world of the opening to the airy lucidities without form or substance in the last enacts, in paradigmatic form, that process of abstraction, of disengagement, which underlies most of Larkin's poems. The careful enjambement at the end of the first stanza, isolating the loose usage of 'paradise' as the last word in a colloquial crescendo, prepares for the two-facedness of that rapid shift to 'everyone young going down the long slide / To happiness, endlessly' and points towards the authentic paradise of the last lines, where 'endless' means not 'perpetually repeated' but 'without bounds':

> When I see a couple of kids
> And guess he's fucking her and she's
> Taking pills or wearing a diaphragm,
> I know this is paradise
>
> Everyone old has dreamed of all their lives.

But before the expansive dénouement can be reached, there has to be a reprise of this movement, in which the poet projects back into the past a response similar to his own, of which an imaginary earlier self was the recipient, not the source. This at once affirms continuity, qualifies the sourness of the present self, and *consoles* him with the possibility that this is no more accurate for the two 'kids' than it was for him. Anyone looking at him, forty years ago, may have thought the same, 'That'll be the life':

> . . . . *He*
> *And his lot will go down the long slide*
> *Like free bloody birds.* And immediately

Rather than words comes the thought of high windows:

The sun-comprehending glass,
And beyond it, the deep blue air, that shows
Nothing, and is nowhere, and is endless.

Such are the consolations of philosophy that the retrojected
words bring express relief, freeing the self from the oppression
of exclusion, and cancelling the coarseness as – in its
gratuitous appearance, as if from nowhere (its proper
home) – it bypasses logic. Such almost tangible negativity is
the heart's true metropolis.

Larkin may find Modernism distasteful, but when he has to
deal with a real, contingent world, his response is Eliot's. In
the rancorous lampoon of a poem such as 'Posterity' he
assumes a Prufrockian, self-deprecating irony which actually
preserves its little lyric secrets from the contempt of others.
'Homage to a Government' calls up echoes of Housman
(particularly his 'Epitaph on an Army of Mercenaries'), but
its occasion is precise and specific: the Wilson government's
decision, in 1969 (the poem provides its own date) to
withdraw its troops from 'East of Suez', for financial reasons.
For Larkin, this is some kind of betrayal, as if, presumably,
the troops had not been stationed out there for what, in the
long term, were financial reasons: to preserve the investments,
raw materials, and cheap labour of an imperialist economy.
The condescension Larkin evinces towards ordinary mortals,
incapable of self-government or self-direction, mere walking
embodiments of some prototype discerned by the generalising
intelligence of the observer / poet, is displayed here as a
possibly disingenuous naivety. This Prufrockian 'naivety'
dissociates the whole question of decolonisation from its
confused and complex history, and presents it as simply one
more venal betrayal in the story of a vulgar and degrading
social democracy. Once again, the true culprit is that
unspeakable *menu peuple* whose motives are gestured at in the
twist of line five into line six:

Next year we are to bring the soldiers home
For lack of money, and it is all right,
Places they guarded, or kept orderly,
Must guard themselves, and keep themselves orderly.

> We want the money for ourselves at home
> Instead of working. And this is all right.

For Larkin, this shabby sell-out by a government intent on placating a restive electorate devalues not only the present but the past and the future. The statues which record an imperial heritage will be standing in the same squares; they will 'look nearly the same'. The subterfuge which, almost unnoticed, erodes a history is skilfully caught in that adverb. But the same poet who in 'This Be the Verse' advises that the only answer to the 'fuck-ups' of life is to 'Get out as early as you can, / And don't have any kids yourself', now evokes posterity as if it were the real and only tribunal before which to judge the perfidies of the present:

> Our children will know it's a different country.
> All we can hope to leave them now is money.

By the same polemic device, children were once cast to ask their fathers (at least on hoardings): 'What did you do in the Great War, daddy?'

Larkin's chosen and self-conscious marginality, in relation to the dominant norms of British culture in the post-war era, is something which can be endlessly debated. D. J. Enright marginalised himself in another way, by becoming a teacher in the University of Singapore, in the period which followed the Emergency (when an insurgent communist movement was violently suppressed), and saw independence as part of a Malaysian Federation, and secession, with the backwash of the race riots of the late sixties. Only on returning home does Enright's work begin to converge with the conventional wisdom of Larkin's vision. Before that, though both poets started from similar biographical and ideological bases, their work diverges markedly in its response to the transformations of the post-war world.

'Goodbye Empire', in Enright's 1972 volume, *Daughters of Earth*, speaks from a periphery worlds away from Larkin's suburb of the spirit. It acknowledges the same base motive for decolonisation but, starting from a different perspective, it doesn't therefore assume that the motive necessarily debases the process. 'Expense' can be reckoned in many currencies:

> It had to go
> So many wounded feelings
> And some killings –
> In a nutshell, too expensive
>
> Though its going
> Scarcely set its subjects free
> For freedom –
> Life still extracts a fee
>
> In wounded feelings
> And also killings
> Slates wiped clean
> Soon attract new chalkings. . . .

The old regime 'Allowed its odd anomalies', such as his 'orphaned Irish dad', an army recruit who 'floundered over India / In the shit and out of it'. Enright's indecorous colloquialism here lacks the self-consciousness of Larkin's: it is totally appropriate both to its context and its user, just as the balanced assessment of the pros and cons of Empire takes in a complex range of experiences (not only the poet's but his father's, not only India but Ireland). Poems such as 'To an Emergent Politician', 'An Underdeveloped Country' and 'More Memories of Underdevelopment' preserve the same dispassionate fairness, allowing the author's transparent liberalism to play over the surface of a situation in which the corruption and oppression is homegrown, and alien to his outsider's eye. But at the same time – feeling sympathy with this world in which, a 'lurching humanist', he tries to teach Hopkins to uncomprehending 'oriental papists' he can respond with outrage, in 'Streets', to the mentality that tries to dissemble the full atrocity of bombing the streets of Hanoi in the name of freedom.

'The Faithful' picks up a theme from Hardy – the insects attracted by a night-light – but gives it a new post-imperial twist. The light also summons lizards who wait within its circle to pounce on the insects; and this becomes the figure of a larger predicament for the western humanist in an Asia where the values he represents are invoked to justify massive American intervention in the Vietnamese civil war:

> It isn't difficult to be a god.
> You hand your lantern out,
> Sink yourself in your own concerns
> And leave the rest to the faithful.

In such poems as this and 'J. T. on his Travels', 'Means Test' and 'Processional', Enright explores the necessary guilt of the affluent, well-meaning westerner in the East without self-indulgence or evasion. In an earlier volume, *Unlawful Assembly* (1968), the Vietnam War at its height had awoken him to incessant self-criticism. In 'Shabby Imperial Dreams' he 'confesses with shame' to such dreams, his 'only plea' being that 'I was sleeping at the time'. 'Go and Wash' speaks of poetry as the not-too-clean water in which the self washes its hands before getting them dirty again. The implication is that the dirt remains in the water, and constitutes poetry's moral awareness. But 'It's an art' is the most comprehensive meditation on the relation between poetry and politics, deliberately enacting the 'massive obliquity' of which it speaks, keeping the name of Vietnam out of the poem until its subterfuge has been tumbled, 'The war being oblique. / Which is to say: / Elsewhere'. It is the 'rabble of / Newspapermen' – 'Venal scribblers of / Purple passages and / Red-streaked reportage' – not the sensitive poets, who tell the truth about this war, for 'Poets are not concerned / With the streaks on the tulips / The small red appearances'. Dr Johnson's prescription becomes an excuse for discriminating ignorance of real blood:

> Vietnam has neither made nor marred a poet.
> The art of poetry is not to say a thing.

The poem concludes with a sideways displacement in which a little girl asks, in school, ' "What is poet?" ' to be told that it is an almost extinct bird of which the BBC still has recordings.

What Enright records here is a recurrent dilemma: the conflict between the apparent disinterestedness of poetry, in the liberal tradition, and the enormities which lie behind it, off the page, atrocities of which newspapermen write in overwritten, badly written, but more urgent prose. Enright feels the relationship between the two intensely, but, locked in his chosen or given identity, he can do little more than gesture obliquely towards the relation. Yet, in poems such as 'After the gods, after the heroes', he can register powerfully the forces which suppress this connection, which enforce the separation of the private individual from a murderous history. Television, radio and newspaper reports quite literally *bring home* to the marginal and privileged individual the real depravity which his culture and his social and economic margins keep at arms' length. He is thrown into the centre of things. And yet, at the same time, he is denied the last foreclosure of distance. The bombs do not rain on him. Enright, however, though still at a remove, lives close enough to know what 'history-making' is really about:

> You can see how easily a man is silenced.
> Merely two or three helpers to twist his arms
> Behind his back, shove him into a conveniently
> Parked vehicle, drive him to a quiet place and
> Beat his teeth in. Eventually he falls silent.
>
> Don't talk about heroism. Its lifetime is a breath.
> Heroes with bullets in their head are just
> Bodies. Their families are put to the expense of
> Burying them. Even the quietest funerals cost money.

His spectatorial position, a Janus on the margins of two cultures, facing both ways, enables him to see with particular sharpness the nature of the historical dilemma here. Remarkably, too, it allows for solidarity between Western liberal individualist and Asian poor which is neither patronising nor romanticising, but which discerns the individual face in that mass which, for Larkin, is simply a collection of stereotypes. The generality of experience and identity does not produce a negative reaction, but affirms a real consanguinity. He, too, after all, is a type, and is not afraid to acknowledge it:

The leaders of the masses seem to have stopped
Leading. Now you are left with the masses.
Their separate preferences and small tenacious ambitions.
Their tendency (being too many to shoot or put in prison)
To survive in private. . . .

In this recognition that we are all simultaneously typecast
and unique, expressed in a language which, while accepting
the necessary generality of utterance, nevertheless manages to
suggest the individual streaks of the tulip, Enright reveals both
the strengths and limitations of the liberal-humanist tradition,
faced by the collective movements of the post-war world. Such
an attitude is summed up in the delicate irony of the title to
one of his best and earliest volumes, *Some Men are Brothers*
(1960), and revealed in many of the poems in the volume. 'A
Polished Performance', for example, works variations upon
the meaning of 'polished', receding from the 'polished capital'
of its opening line, through the 'unpolished innocence' of the
'distant villages', to the final disenchanting revelation of the
feral girl, living in the bush,

> Perfect for the part, perfect,
>   Except for the dropsy
> Which comes from polished rice.

This deliberate recession of perspectives allows him to
subvert the easy metropolitan sentiments which can always
presume upon their centrality in order to enchant the distance
with pastoral vistas. Unlike R. S. Thomas, however, Enright
includes himself as a butt for such reproaches. In 'The Poor
Wake Up Quickly' he sees that he too is an object in the eyes
of others, though he cannot share in their point of view,
wondering 'How do I star in that opium dream?' which afflicts
his trishaw driver. In 'Sightseeing', he uses the receding
images of a temple painting – a demon whose open mouth
contains a roomful of people with, on the wall, a painting of a
demon, whose open mouth, and so on – to acknowledge his
own felt relativity, and also, in a subtle twist, the limits of his
humanist concern. For, at a certain point, 'the artist did not
care' enough to do anything but leave the faces blank in the

room within the room within the room. And the tourist too
has to call a halt:

> Imagination, like the eyes that strain
> Against the wall, is happily too weak
> To number all the jaws there are to slip.

The firm ground of an earlier world has gone. There is not one
centre with innumerable circumferences arranged around it in
ripples, but a dizzying vortex of provisional footholds, in
which every momentary stability contains, also, the menace of
being devoured.

The distinction of Enright's vision, reconciling individual
and collectivity, man and mass, is something which, within
this tradition, was perhaps possible only in the particular
double distance of a post-imperial Asia, with all its
contradictory pulls. Certainly, in a poem such as 'The
Noodle-Vendor's Flute' he achieves a masterly statement of
the dilemma. Like the poem itself, the notes of the flute rise
from a 'real city', are heard in a 'real house', 'Under the noise
of war':

> Yet still the pathos of that double tune
> Defies its provenance, and can warm
> The bitter night.

The tune, issuing from one source, heard by many, catches the
perplexity of an existence which is at once personal and
collective, located in many centres, to each of which the other
centres form part of its periphery. Again, Enright generalises,
but the generalisations embrace rather than dismiss, as the
play on 'common' reveals:

> Sleepless, we turn and sleep.
> Or sickness dwindles to some local limb.
> Bought love for one long moment gives itself.
> Or there a witch assures a frightened child
> She bears no personal grudge.
> And I, like other listeners,
> See my stupid sadness as a common thing.

And being common,
Therefore something rare indeed.

It is in this way that the two notes constitute a 'double tune',
speaking at once of a common sadness and a reassuring
commonalty, as, in the last line, the single city and house
expand to embrace all cities and houses:

> The puffing vendor, surer than a trumpet,
> Tells us we are not alone.
> Each night that same frail midnight tune
> Squeezed from a bogus flute,
> Under the noise of war, after war's noise,
> It mourns the fallen, every night,
> It celebrates survival –
> In real cities, real houses, real time.

Concerned with living in 'real time', Enright in a poem such
as 'Roman Reasons' identifies with the divided loyalties of
Enobarbus in *Antony and Cleopatra* – a man who can see the
Macchiavellian rationale to action, 'finding good
reasons . . . / For the serial assassinations / For the quotidian
killings', who deserts for good reason, but who then dies
'unnoticed', of remorse, 'heart failure in a ditch', torn apart by
the contrary pulls of decency and the instinct for survival in a
world that has other priorities.

There is a poem in Enright's 1975 volume, *Sad Ires,* which
catches the recurrent sadness of such a figure. It is called,
simply and grandiosely, 'History', and it concerns that
separation of history from everyday life which, I have argued,
is a perennial aspect of English poetry:

> All in darkness, a sealed train speeds
> Through Southfields, a village station.
> It is destined for Waterloo,
> It has come from Wimbledon.
>
> What bearded brain does it bear?
> Or what rough beast might it carry?
> A dozen of us, fairly honest workers,
> Are left at the platform's edge looking silly.

The allusions, which form so much of the texture of the poem, are obvious enough, yet continually subverted. The sealed train recalls that train arranged by the German government to carry Lenin across Europe in 1917 to arrive, punctually, at the destiny which had always awaited him: the Russian Revolution. Set against that, is the bucolic ordinariness of the 'village station' through which it passes, and to which, in its self-contained certainty, it is indifferent. Another little man who made the big time as a world-shaker met his destiny at Waterloo, of course; but he didn't come from Wimbledon, and neither did the 'rough beast, its hour come round at last, / Slouch[ing] towards Bethlehem to be born' in Yeats's 'The Second Coming' (a poem which also might have some relation to the October Revolution). The 'sealed' train becomes a figure of a larger closure, that blind absorption in ideology, in the *folie de grandeur* of a historically-appointed mission which animates such revolutionaries, and is sustained, through successive defeats, and amidst all the indifference of a 'history' which is elsewhere, by the mythic example of those few, Lenin or Napoleon, who had the luck to catch the train on time, and get off at the right stop. But this sealed train has another antecedent: the 'little black train' of death of which the blues sing. In this perspective, it is not the dozen 'fairly honest workers' left marginalised on the platform who are silly, but the ideologues, the men of destiny, who despise or simply ignore them.

Sad Ires is, of course, a play on 'satires', and the volume is a highly successful series of exercises in what Enright has come increasingly to make his own line: the subversive affirmation, more in sorrow than in anger, of a stubborn ordinariness, against the pretensions of history's mainliners, in a text which is all surface, which deliberately denies resonant depths, with a dry, clear tone. But 'ires' also contains a mutedly apocalyptic note, with its suggestion of the *dies irae*, the 'day of wrath' which is precisely that 'Second Coming' Yeats envisaged and Lenin enrolled for. In 'Origin of the Haiku' he speaks of a 'conventional lot' who pass the time composing *haiku*. Only when we reach the end of the poem is it clear where precisely this is, in a way which makes apposite the allusions to 'darkness visible' and the mind being 'its own place':

> Such petty projects –
> Yes, but even an epic
> Even *Paradise Lost,*
> Would look puny
> In hell, throughout eternity.
> It's the taking of pains that counts.

But hell, in these poems, is precisely that everyday life in which the self feels at home. 'Just to make you feel at home' is spoken as if by an old inmate welcoming a new soul to hell, a city much like any other. In fact 'This place gets more like the world / Every day', and the poem concludes with the emphatic question: 'Did you notice how I said "every day"?' What sustains life in this perpetual 'cocktail party, minus / The means to get high / Or go home' is conversation about the news from elsewhere, from a world which is felt to be more real exactly because it is not here:

> . . . the world situation,
> The events in Vietnam, Ulster,
> Whatever's going.
> Who do you think invented politics,
> And why? At times I fancy
> That is why the world was created –
> . . . . What else
> To chat about in eternity?

The poetry which has come out of Ulster in recent years illustrates very effectively just how deep this division between poet and history runs in modern poetry. For here, in the renewal of the 'Troubles' since 1968, when the Civil Rights movement began in earnest, through the disintegration into communal violence, the intervention of the British army, and the military campaign of the Provisional IRA, its bombings and assassinations, poetry has come face to face with the realities which are everyday events to a large part of the Third World, but which have been little more than media imaginings to the advanced west. Yet the response is strangely muted. On the one hand, the poetry of such Catholic writers as Seamus Heaney and John Montague explores the sense both of what Heaney calls a 'tribal' complicity and what Montague shrewdly defines as 'wise imperial policy'. On the other hand, a poetry that looks back to the sceptical Protestant tradition of Louis MacNeice takes up a worried, disapproving but finally uncomprehending stance towards an experience with which it feels no sense of affinity. In accents familiar from 'The Movement' such a poetry performs its civic duties equitably, by reflecting, in an abstracted kind of way, on violence, but its hands are indubitably clean. It speaks, at times, with the tone of a shell-shocked Georgianism that could easily be mistaken for indifference before the ugly realities of life, and death, in Ulster.

Its representative moment is Derek Mahon addressing Louis MacNeice in Carrowdore Churchyard, which, he says, 'suits you down to the ground / With its play of shadow, its humane perspective'. Such a poetry seeks to reproduce 'Each fragile, solving ambiguity' of that older poet. 'Neither here nor there', it approaches reality 'at one remove, a substitute / For final answers'. Literariness becomes a recurrent technique for putting a distance between the middle-class self and its panic. This is particularly so in those poems about mutability such as Mahon's witty elegy for Marilyn Monroe, which combines echoes of Villon with those of Monroe's own songs. There is a change of tone when Mahon contemplates, not just personal supersession, but the death of civilisations, as in 'The Golden Bough' which speaks of that which is left after 'The twilight of the cities' – 'the soft / Vegetables where our / Politics were conceived'.

'A Disused Shed in Co. Wexford', is one of those 'places where a thought might grow', as the tourist poet grasps his obligations to the dead. The shed has been empty since civil war days. Its crowding mushrooms become the powerful symbol of all occluded and anonymous lives, abandoned by history:

> They are begging us, you see, in their wordless way,
> To do something, to speak on their behalf

Or at least not to close the door again.
Lost people of Treblinka and Pompeii!
'Save us, save us,' they seem to say,
'Let the god not abandon us
Who have come so far in darkness and in pain.
We too had our lives to live.
You with your light meter and relaxed itinerary,
Let not our naive labours have been in vain!'

In 'Afterlives', such fragile stuff as the flesh is becomes the ground for revelation, for contrition almost, imagining a bomb-torn Belfast:

What middle-class cunts we are
To imagine for one second
That our privileged ideals
Are divine wisdom, and the dim
Forms that kneel at noon
In the city not ourselves.

That deliberate exclamatory lurch into the demotic, as in Larkin's poetry, is an attempt to close the distance between the subject's privileged privacy and the exposure of the 'dim / Forms' of the city. But the almost Platonic abstraction of this last phrase, set against the sudden specificity of class and curse in 'middle-class cunts', perpetuates the division. The 'forms' out there remain objects, and the awkward delaying of the syntax seems to force upon the reader the possibility that it is the city which is 'not ourselves', even as, in its completion, it disowns such spurious detachments.

Mahon's poetry repeatedly returns to this interface, where a guilty but finally secure consciousness abstracts itself from its contingent world even as it concedes its implication in that world. 'The Sea in Winter', which closes his *Poems 1962-1978*, is a major statement of this Anglo-Irish cultural duplicity – what MacNeice called the condition of being 'spiritually-hyphenated without knowing it'. The poet self-reproachfully frets over his ambivalence, asking 'Why am I always staring out / Of windows, preferably from a height . . .?' Nevertheless, he cannot avoid positing a centre which is elsewhere, to which this actual landscape is merely a periphery, feeling 'the curious sense / Of working on the circumference'. Return to Ulster feels like reversion, succumbing to an estranging past which, though it is the self's proper place, nevertheless seems to rob it of all autonomy:

> . . . . knowing I could never cast
> Aside the things that made me what,
> For better or worse, I am. The upshot?
> Chaos and instability,
> The cool gaze of the RUC.

'What . . . I am' is somehow actually alien to the self that judges, internalising that split which Larkin usually manages to keep as a division between subject and object. Here, the self becomes part of that object-world, and an object of its alienating gaze. Yet that adverb 'preferably' above gives away the real scope that this mobile self has. Though he seems to be restored to that shrivelled circle in which Tomlinson's hunted creature cowers, he still has room to have his 'doubts / About this verse-making'. He may speak of being 'trapped . . . / In my own idiom' as much as the drunken midnight passers-by outside. But unlike them he is trapped only in a set of words and the sensibility they define, in something which is, finally, his *own*, chosen property. They, however, are trapped in 'the day each one conceives', and although this implies some subjective role in its creation, it remains inescapably objective and actual: 'Meanwhile the given life goes on'. Each may imagine his own millenial break with the everyday, the final stanzas suggest, but that apocalyptic moment is in fact endlessly deferred, a merely imaginary derailing of 'the given life'. It is through the space opened by that 'meanwhile' that the poetic self makes its escape.

Reality in such poems is sharply polarised into the quotidian and the apocalyptic, and the latter then reduced to mere fantasy; and this ratifies a larger refusal of the concept of history. Even in a society as torn by historic turmoils as Northern Ireland, in which the vendettas and grievances of centuries are daily reproduced in the news bulletins, all that happens is either unassumingly habitual or the fantasies of violent bitter men on which the heart's grown brutal, thrusting their imaginary 'terrible beauty' upon an unwilling 'real' world. In a poem aggressively entitled 'History', Mahon insists that such shabby unchanging ordinariness is the only true dimension in which men and women live; although, noticeably, the landscape he presents is in fact emptied of human presence in a way which recalls Eliot:

> The blinking puddles
> reflected daylong
> Twilight of misery.
>
> Smoke rose in silence
> to the low sky.

'History' is thus refused, in the name of decent ordinariness. For any suggestion that these two planes may actually be one, that historical change proceeds through a process in which the forces latent within the everyday find expression, sometimes violently, sometimes horrifically, within that everyday, can be interpreted as an endorsement of those 'fantasies'. The division of a unitary history into the two categories of 'everyday life' and 'apocalyptic fantasy', with the inevitable downgrading value-judgment on the latter, actually perpetuates that larger separation of the privileged poetic subject from the violations of actual historical change. Hence the repeated note, in these poets, of incredulity, of righteous outrage, the reluctance to believe that it is all actually happening. Walter Benjamin found a similar process at work in Germany in the 1930s, but reached quite different conclusions:

> The tradition of the oppressed teaches us that the 'state of emergency' in which we live is not the exception but the rule. We must attain to a conception of history that is in keeping with this insight. . . . The current amazement that the things we are experiencing are 'still' possible in the twentieth century is *not* philosophical. This amazement is not the beginning of knowledge – unless it is the knowledge that the view of history which gives rise to it is untenable.

Remaining locked in a consumer's view of history, as in his memories of the Home Front in 'Autobiographies', Mahon steadfastly refuses Benjamin's perception. This sequence provides the empirical allegory of such a refusal of history: the newborn child taken home in a taxi 'While the frozen armies trembled / At the gates of Stalingrad', hidden in a cupboard under the stairs while the bombs fall on Belfast, held aloft to see the Victory parade, playing hide-and-seek among the air-raid shelters, recalling the last ration coupons, the return of oranges and bananas to the shops, the forage caps and Lucky Strike packets of American servicemen and, most harrowing of all in its symbolism, watching the films of the Jews released from the concentration camps. The distance of the fortunate beneficiary of victory is here faithfully inscribed.

As Brian Patten admits in *The Irrelevant Song* (1971), the reassurance of 'winning' all the time can wear thin:

> Every time a thing is won,
> Every time a thing is owned,
> Every time a thing is possessed,
> It vanishes.

Such a poem expresses the dissatisfaction which nags at the heart of a society which has renounced history, which, in its triumphant seizing of the spoils of the past, feels still a central lack:

> Only the need is perfect, only the wanting.
> Tranquillity does not suit me;
> I itch for disasters.

But historical change can be conceptualised only as a rotation of 'fashions that infiltrate and cause / What was thought constant to change'. Mutability has always been a preoccupation of solidly enduring ages, as the reduction of history to the enticements of what might be called an apocalyptic whimsy:

> But what future if I admitted to no dream beyond the one
> From which I'm just awoken?

Already in the wood the light grass has darkened.
Like a necklace of deaths the flowers hug the ground. . . .

This is the natural response of the self 'In a smug time, in a
time without astonishment, / in a time that's done away with
wonder', he says in 'Full Circle'. This poem speaks of the
unacceptability in his own time of a prophet who claims
'numerous miracles are about to happen', while 'all about
disasters are occurring', and neither are acknowledged. But in
'The Last Residents' Patten presents the other side of this
attitude, thinking of an earlier poet's response to the failure of
hopes, once revolutionary, redefined by events as utopian fairy
tales:

> Mayakovsky, sitting at your window one afternoon,
> Half-crazy with sorrow, your soul finally shipwrecked,
> What if you had decided to be foolish,
> To be neither cynical nor over-serious,
> In fact, not to care?
>
> Would Russia have changed much?
> The snows melted in Siberia?
> The bright posters propagate a different message?

The real questions are only figuratively addressed to
Mayakovsky, representative of a suicidal disenchanting. The
present poet, years later, sitting in a London window, projects
onto his predecessor some of his own divided being. The
same events occur, 'more subtly now'; and 'the end still seems
the same, / The outcome as inevitable'. The poem doesn't say
what the end might be; instead it cuts to an apocalyptic image
of the last residents of London crumbling among 'plagued
allotments', 'Crying with disbelief and amazement' – an
amazement similar perhaps to that of which Benjamin spoke,
'that the things we are experiencing are "still" possible in the
twentieth century'. The poem contains both a critique of the
myopia which imagines itself insulated from history and a
deeper despair at the impotence of the individual, viewing,
from his ostensibly remote window, a process over which he
has no real control. The myopia and the middle distance, it

suggests unsurely, are in some way integrally related; but the poet wonders whether the private life might have been saved had it ceased to care about what were in any case inevitable 'public' processes. Once again, it is the overview provided by that window which enables him to posit such abstract alternatives, to imagine that, for Mayakovsky, survival was a matter simply of 'deciding' not to care.

In more recent poetry of Patten's the note of apocalyptic elegy has grown stronger. That loss which has always been his theme is now located not in a purely private space but in a realm which seems to be at one and the same time personal and historic. In *Grave Gossip* (1979) its promises seem to have been bought dearly from death and exhaustion itself, as if this new and more dangerous period in European history had brought a new and desperate urgency to his sense of the culture. Patten can cast this in the most improbable terms:

> The Dodo came back.
> It took off its hat.
> It took off its overcoat.
> It took off its dark glasses and
> put them in its pocket.
> It looked exhausted.

Exhaustion, to the point of extinction, is a recurring theme in this volume. And yet, as here, it's often the prelude to an obscure hope. The Dodo is exhausted by all the subterfuge of actually *surviving;* and something new is going to happen. The 'laboratory assistant' who is the speaker here gives the bird a fresh injection of blood, furtively buries in the garden a manuscript containing 'The History of Genetic Possibilities', and sits waiting with 'Genesis' open on his lap as, 'Outside people not from the neighbourhood / were asking questions'.

This exhaustion arises from a general sense of the played-outness of a culture and its forms – forms of experience as of poetry. In 'Hopeful' Patten speaks of being 'exhausted even by what had not yet happened'. The sophisticated party in 'Ghost-culture' is stunned into embarrassed silence when the guest of honour produces from his pocket 'a few crumpled and unexplained petals' and begins to weep from sheer exhaustion. Exhaustion for Patten, in fact, can be a sign of authenticity, of caring enough to wear oneself out, quite different from the numbed indifference of the doctor in 'Song of the Grateful Char', or the psychiatrist professionally immunised to nightmare, murmuring, 'Hush . . . . It is a common dream.'

Patten has lived close to the temptations of mid-life *déjà vu*. In 'A Few Questions About Romeo' he wonders how that adolescent lover, 'miserable and spotty', would have reacted to a death-bed vision of Juliet with 'a frame / common as any girl's'. But he goes on to speak of 'the prison the weary imagine / all living things inhabit' with a tenderness and final solidarity which fends off middle-aged cynicism. Patten is afflicted by a sense of the worn-outness of literary modes. In 'The Right Mask' a poem wanting to be born prescribes to the poet a variety of traditional masks, the troubadour, the rose, the nightingale's song; but even the mask of his own face he has 'lived too long with'. The right mask in the end is one which is 'utterly transparent', in which, ironically, his friends don't recognise him. It is a mark of his readiness to be transparent that he can actually return to these hackneyed masks, and do something new with them. 'A Bird-brained View of Power', for example, admits its derivativeness and conventionality, but in the process makes new links with an antique tradition. The bird, shocked into night-song by car headlights, worries that it keeps important people awake, and may tomorrow be responsible for the kind of tired wrong decisions that unleash war or economic disaster:

> Somewhere in a city, in a city
> Cordoned by fear
> A fistful of feathers believes
> Its song has summoned up demons.
> It listens to the wail of sirens.

'Conversation with a Favourite Enemy' even spells out the analogy of poem and nightingale song. Challenged at a dinner party by his own cynical *alter ego* to make poetry of a napkin folded into bird shape, he is saved by intervenient grace: a nightingale outside 'bursts into fragments' and 'flings a shrapnel of song against the window.' The careful concession of that pun on 'fragments' is then reinforced by the shrewd antithesis of the last lines, which undercuts any easy romantic confidence:

> It is not always like this.
> My enemies are more articulate,
> The nightingale utterly unreliable.

In 'The Critics' Chorus' he speaks of an obscure Grail quest, of

> . . . a need to eat a fruit far off
> from the safe orchard,
> reached by no easy pathway
> or route already mapped.

Lost in the dark wood of middle-life, Patten is also aware that he is following in Dante's footsteps, that generations have trodden here before him. Thus, 'Going Back and Going On' relates not only to Dante but to T. S. Eliot's evocation of him and, nearer still, Theodore Roethke's recapitulation of that relation, seeing, in the slant rays of evening, 'The tiny roots of things just begun' with visionary vividness:

> Just now begun! To think on this halfway through what
> time is left! . . .
> The miracle is obstinate.
> There is no 'going back', no wholly repeatable route,
> No rearranging time or relationships . . .
> Yet no end of celebration need come about.

In 'The Wrong Number' Patten imagines himself as 'The Phantom Connection, / Moving from shadow to shadow', haunting phone-booths, working his way through the London Telephone Directory, seeking the ultimate connection. In 'The Purpose is Ecstasy' he sees rapture, or the hope of making hope actual, as the only way to enter that final place, where the self is freed from habit, and the body from 'its loose desires and ghost-connections'. Patten's 'ghost-connections' in this poetry are extraordinary, and usually long distance. Frequently, he calls up, not one poet alone, but that poet as he is mediated through another. 'A Bird-brained View of Power' most immediately evokes D. J. Enright's 'Noodle Vendor's Flute', but beyond this lies a whole oriental tradition. The 'Brer Rabbit' sequence in its sardonic narrative terseness echoes Hughes's *Crow*, but the very choice of that homely figure of childhood story adds complex ironies. 'Tradition' is reworked by Patten in a way which emphasises its near-terminal condition. In 'I Studied Telephones Constantly' Patten moves through echoes of Spender, Gunn and Sylvia Plath, frantically on the phone to 'Daddy', and many other poets, to a phantom exchange which explains the volume's title, and suggests its larger cultural significance:

> I was listening to the grave gossip.
> Terror leaked from the mouth's pit.
> In telephone exchanges the world over
> The numbers are dying.
> Vast morgues where the operators sleep-walk among the
> > babble,
> Where the ghost phones lament
> For all the calls that went wrong.
> Death owns everyone's telephone number.

Death, the death of friends, of poets, his own death, the imminent death of a culture, haunts these poems, and the telephone is its harbinger. But the phone also represents an ecstasy, innocence and earnestness epitomised by the first teenage call to a girlfriend, 'how it felt to be connected for the first time . . . / I'm sure those wires still cross paradise'.

Poised between these two extremes, Patten's poetry offers the epitome of the larger dilemma examined in this chapter. He defines those margins of tolerance, increasingly narrowing, within which the liberal-humanist tradition of poetry has found itself, in the post-war era. A crucial element in maintaining those margins has been the refusal of history. And yet, at the same time, such a sensibility has been afflicted by a pervasive sense of loss and inadequacy, of contraction and suffocation. The 'hero' of Enright's latest volume is a sadly shrunken Faust (*A Faust Book,* 1979), a man who envisages himself as at the fag-end of an era, waiting for something to turn up that will redeem the shabby present, and, when it doesn't, selling his 'immortal soul' in the hope of gain, on a mass market where 'the going rate for used souls, / Even immortal, was rather low'. Unsated, but without the traditional consolation of a perpetually striving divine discontent, Faust can register only ennui and 'utter loneliness'.

Faust's voracious empty craving; Patten's conviction that 'All's finished here. / In the burrow memory falls away until / There is nothing to cling on to', and the desire, in 'Frogs in the Wood', for the simplicity of being lost again; the suppressed hysteria and obsession with mutability of the Ulster poets; Larkin's aspiration towards the religiose grandeur of the 'sun-comprehending glass' and 'deep blue air' beyond of 'High Windows'; all express a similar mood and urgency, a defeat, and an expectation of something which cannot be defined. Or which can be defined only when those margins of tolerance, those neutral distances, are perilously transgressed.

9

Waist-deep in History: Sylvia Plath

At first sight, Sylvia Plath seems an intensely private poet, 'Clear of voices and history, the staticky / Noise of the new' ('Lesbos'). Yet the opening poem of her first volume, *The Colossus* (1960) is the celebration of 'a different borning' which homes in on the concept of history:

> You move through the era of fishes,
> The smug centuries of the pig –
> Head, toe and finger
> Come clear of the shadow. History
>
> Nourishes these broken flutings. . . .

The poem suggests an analogy between the evolution of the individual and of the species, as the embryo re-enacts, in its brief nine months, the biological changes of millennia. It is a poem about inheritance, in which a self emerges from shadow into individual being in a world where it is late on arrival, where 'Some hard stars / Already yellow the heavens', worms 'Quit their usual habitations', and small birds 'converge, converge'. The 'borning' is much more than a birth. It is a matter of finding defining limits ('bourns') and a destination, a home in the world. This world seems in some way finished before the poem, and the life, start. Its fountains are dry and the roses over, and the incense of death hangs over everything even before 'Your day approaches'. Cryptically, the title suggests, too, a cultural decline, for these half-related events occur within 'The Manor Garden'; the manor, presumably, to which the self is born.

The title poem of *Winter Trees* (1971) likewise places history at the centre of a landscape where the graphic and defined emerges from the indefinite and obscure, and dawn vies with dissolution, growth and propagation with decline and denial:

> On their blotter of fog the trees
> Seem a botanical drawing –
> Memories growing, ring on ring,
> A series of weddings.
>
> Knowing neither abortions nor bitchery,
> Truer than women,
> They seed so effortlessly!
> Tasting the winds, that are footless,
> Waist-deep in history. . . .

Here, too, the poem ends on a downbeat, with the lengthened and almost exhausted line, 'The shadows of ringdoves chanting, but easing nothing'.

Crossing the Water (1971), comprises poems from an earlier phase in Plath's writing, after the publication of *The Colossus* and before the composition of the poems in *Ariel* (1965). In the poem Ted Hughes places first in this volume, 'Wuthering Heights', the horizons ring the speaker like faggots that may catch fire; they are 'always unstable' and 'They only dissolve and dissolve / Like a series of promises, as I step forward'. This is a much more tempestuous world, where when history is translated into the concept of 'destiny' it takes on an intimidating and irresistible violence:

> . . . . the wind
> Pours by like destiny, bending
> Everything in one direction.
> I can feel it trying
> To funnel my heat away.

By comparison, the opening poem of *Ariel* is mild and positive, a 'Morning Song' which welcomes, like those previous aubades, a new life into the world. Yet if 'love set you going like a fat gold watch', the affectionate richness of this opening line is qualified by the chill that falls in the next two stanzas, where entry into history is seen as a dangerously vulnerable transit, a journey into fixity in an exposed and shadowy place. History here has become the musty, hollowly echoing interior of a museum, where the voices of parents are becoming ancestral:

> Our voices echo, magnifying your arrival. New statue.
> In a drafty museum, your nakedness
> Shadows our safety. We stand around blankly as walls.
>
> I'm no more your mother
> Than the cloud that distils a mirror to reflect its own slow
> Effacement at the wind's hand.

The clear air of celebration is sufficiently clouded to add a twinge of obsolescence to the mother stumbling from bed in a Victorian nightgown, and a subliminal menace to that analogy of child's mouth and dawn: 'Your mouth opens clean as a cat's. The window square / Whitens and swallows its dull stars.' Lives emerge to distinction, and are extinguished, with equal facility.

All these poems have a common preoccupation: the relation between the individual self and the process in which it comes to identity, to which it is always irreparably bound, and which, sooner or later, reclaims it. What they embody, as their primary premise, is the *historicity* of the personal life, its status as an historical secretion, the precipitate of an order which precedes and will re-absorb it. In such a perception, Plath's poetry goes beyond the polarised, antithetical image of self and world, of transcendent subject and immanent object, which characterises the poetry of most of her contemporaries. It is precisely because her poetry is intensely private that it records so profoundly and distinctly the experience of living in history. In Plath's poetry, there is no gap between private and public. But it has been closed, not by some wilful choice on the part of the sensitive individual, but by a reality which is itself foreclosing upon the personal life. The acuity of Plath's vision lies in the penetration with which she sees this. It also constitutes its tragedy.

There is a significant difference between the concept of

distance in Plath's verse and in that of the poets discussed in
the previous chapter. For them, distance is a product of the
self's deliberate abstraction from things, a voluntary and
comfortable withdrawal from events which are viewed from a
position of relative security behind reassuring windows. For
Plath, it is quite different, as in 'Totem':

> The engine is killing the track, the track is silver,
> It stretches into the distance. It will be eaten nevertheless.

For Plath, the world withdraws from the individual; and in
this recession, it diminishes radically the self's significance. At
the same time, it still holds the menace of destruction and
engulfment, in a world where

> There is no terminus, only suitcases
> Out of which the same self unfolds like a suit
> Bald and shiny, with pockets of wishes,
>
> Notions and tickets, short circuits and folding mirrors. . . .

Here, as in 'Gulliver', 'those distances / That revolve' are
'untouchable'. In 'Paralytic' the world is a 'starched,
inaccessible breast' where,

> Dead egg, I lie
> Whole
> On a whole world I cannot touch.

This stifling frustration is repeated in 'Poppies in July', for the
world withdraws itself as one tries to grasp it, forever eluding
one's advances:

> Little poppies, little hell flames.
> Do you do no harm?
>
> You flicker. I cannot touch you.
> I put my hand among the flames. Nothing burns.
>
> And it exhausts me to watch you. . . .

If I could bleed, or sleep! –
If my mouth could marry a hurt like that!

Like 'distance', to which it is intimately related, the word 'marry' carries enormous emotional weight in Plath's poetry. For if the distance into which the world withdraws imposes an impoverishing divorce upon the self, the desire to close that lacuna in being leads to a readiness to accept even pain and hurt as the guarantees of authentic contact. But the only final reunion between the self and the world from which it has been ejected lies in that black marriage, and black mass, evoked in 'Tulips'. A patient in a hospital, the self overcomes its deprivation by return to nonentity:

I am nobody; I have nothing to do with explosions.
I have given my name and my day-clothes up to the
                                                nurses
And my history to the anaesthetist and my body to
                                                surgeons. . . .

The water going over her head, she feels the new and original purity of the nun, bride of the void:

How free it is, you have no idea how free –
The peacefulness is so big it dazes you,
And it asks nothing, a name tag, a few trinkets.
It is what the dead close on, finally; I imagine them
Shutting their mouths on it, like a Communion tablet.

Losing the self is a paradoxical process. On the one hand, she sheds her 'baggage' – that extraneous clutch of relationships and commitments that threaten to dredge her up from the congenial depths, like the smiles of husband and children in the family photo, which 'catch onto my skin, little smiling hooks'. On the other hand, the self *is* these possessions, *is* name and dayclothes and history and body, and to lose these is to lose too the residual consciousness they constitute, till she is reduced, by the substantial, living presence of the tulips, to an object of their gaze, 'flat, ridiculous, a cut-paper shadow / Between the eye of the sun and the eye of the tulips'.

Though she has sought effacement, she feels threatened by the vivid tulips which eat her oxygen. Seeking to contain the tulips (they 'should be behind bars like dangerous animals') she recovers a sense of her body not as an imprisoning and alien *donnée* but almost as a nurturing and maternal presence, a benevolent stranger whose sole concern is her care. The poem ends on this dual movement, in which, resenting the impostures of the tulips, she withdraws to that proper distance in which she may grasp her own substantiality, the mystery of her own particular being.

> And I am aware of my heart: it opens and closes
> Its bowl of red blooms out of sheer love of me.
> The water I taste is warm and salt, like the sea,
> And comes from a country far away as health.

Even such a mute affirmation (the remoteness of that far country is significant, as is the identification of her heart with the *alien* vivacity of the flowers) is rare in Plath's poetry. It is almost as if her petty possessiveness alone (The tulips 'eat *my* oxygen') is what overcomes that larger, grander desire to shed possessions: she is not going to be deprived of her proprietorial rights by these parvenus. Indeed, in an earlier stanza she had spoken of the flowers as breathing 'Lightly, through their white swaddlings, like an awful baby', in a reworking of that image of the supplanting child which runs through the poetry. Only by becoming both mother and child herself in the closing lines can she exclude this usurping sibling. That there is consanguinity is undeniable: 'Their redness talks to my wound, it corresponds'. But whether they bring dangerous temptations or a salving grace is unclear, as it usually is when Plath speaks of children. Far from encouraging that lapse into the gulfs of a wound which is not only literal but also metaphysical and – in an archetypal image of female identity – sexual, the tulips seem to provoke her out of surrender, into an aggressively spiteful resistance.

In 'Poem for a Birthday', the seven-part sequence which concludes *The Colossus,* the self speaks sometimes as mother, sometimes as child, and frequently as both at once. The heroine is a Snow-White or Cinderella princess in nightmare exile among incomprehensible and uncomprehending powers. In its unfolding narrative, a psyche struggles towards birth, in the 'city of spare parts' which is the world. The very language of the poem enacts this difficult borning, moving from the riddling indirections of the opening, to the apparently forthright, lucid resolution of the last line: 'I shall be good as new'. Even here, though, the cliché only half conceals troubling indeterminacies: is this a birthday resolution, a promise, or a mere statement? Whichever it is, is it straightforward or ironic? And what, precisely, is the value of that 'as'? For to be as good as one is new is quite different from being as good *as if* one were new. The poem defines its theme in the play between these semantic possibilities.

The opening section title initiates them, calling itself simply 'Who' (without a question-mark) and then proceeding to suggest a self both grotesquely truncated and monotonously obsessive in its reduction: 'I am all mouth'. As in the final line, a cliché takes on complex possibilities: like the newborn baby, this self is obsessed by its own hunger; like the newborn poem, it is nothing but words, endlessly delivering itself.

Though birth is in the air, these opening lines insist upon a withholding, a refusal of motion and change: 'The month of flowering's finished'. This is October, 'the month for storage', and the voice awakes, with a merely rudimentary consciousness, in a shed 'fusty as a mummy's stomach' (with that atrociously apposite pun), among the dead heads, 'Mouldering heads', cabbageheads, eyeless pumpkinheads, where the 'heart is a stopped geranium'. To exist, a tongue, the child has to have a mouth to speak in. But this carries with it the concomitant, of being devoured. The self comes into existence in a world of gulfs which are also entrances and exits, a shadow congealing in doorways. Before it can exist as a subject, it has to make its exit, as an object, from a world of otherness, a 'dull school' in which it learns its own otherness by separating itself from that primary otherness, the Mother:

> Mother, you are the one mouth
> I would be a tongue to. Mother of otherness
> Eat me. Wastebasket gaper, shadow of doorways.
>
> I said: I must remember this, being small . . .

Now they light me up like an electric bulb.
For weeks I can remember nothing at all.

Identity is closely bound up with memory. One grows by accumulating memories. But almost at once, one learns that identity also means being deprived of such powers of recall. Plath here draws on the experience of electro-convulsive therapy described in *The Bell Jar* (1961) for a powerful symbol of the way in which, from its very beginning, the self depends on others for its precarious freedom. 'They' light her up, without reason or explanation; and this gratuitous act is both an illumining of selfhood and a violation of it. Identity is integrally linked with the idea of a wounding, of some painful breach in being which brings the self into separate existence and simultaneously tears away from it that which it knew before: unity with the mother. We become aware of ourselves only in the frustration of needs: our identity is shaped out of the primal experience of *lack,* of absence, of separation and denial. This lack leaves a scar, and that scar, as it heals, is the very mark of our separate and individual being. In the words of Theodor Adorno, 'The specific differences between individuals are equally scars inflicted by society and emblems of human freedom'. The process of wounding lies at the core of all identities, but the precise shape of the cicatrice, of the identity formed, depends upon the always different conditions in which the wound is inflicted.

The second poem in the sequence, 'Dark House', carries us a stage further, to a point at which the child is engaged in the production of her own inner and outer spaces, mapping out a plan of that which belongs and that which is to be excluded. 'This is a dark house, very big. / I made it myself', while 'Thinking of something else' – a 'something else' defined, by the end of this section, as that third who is the male *other,* father and brother and husband. For the child has now learned her own gender identity: from being a rejected owl-pellet, she, too, has become an owl, a mother. She sees by her own light, may any day 'litter puppies / Or mother a horse'. With gender, a different order of otherness has now entered the discourse, that of morality: 'He's to blame' – he being 'All-mouth', the denying rival.

The rest of the poem is an exploration of the complications which arise from these interweaving relations between self, other and third, in which the parties continually change shape and identity, in the kaleidoscopic transformations of an imagery that will not stay still. The image of the mouth recurs: in 'Maenad', she eats 'the fingers of wisdom' beside her father's tree, 'The mother of mouths didn't love me', and

> A red tongue is among us.
> Mother, keep out of my barnyard,
> I am becoming another.
>
> Dog-head, devourer:
> Feed me the berries of dark.
> The lids won't shut. Time
> Unwinds from the great umbilicus of the sun
> Its endless glitter.
>
> I must swallow it all.

To exist, now, the self must assimilate this unwelcoming otherness, which is divided into male and female aspects: it is only then that she can come into full autonomy, with the curt demand: 'Tell me my name'. Though male and female principles struggle, hereafter, throughout the poem, this is not just a conflict *out there,* in the realm of 'Time', but something which is also inside, on the very terrain which constitutes the self. History is internalised by the self at the moment that it acquires these antithetical principles as its moral and emotional baggage. In Plath's poetry, the self is radically double in its sexual identity, only arbitrarily declined into male and female inflexions. In a famous comment on one of her poems, 'Daddy', for the BBC Third Programme, Plath spelt this out in explicitly Freudian terms:

The poem is spoken by a girl with an Electra complex. Her father died while she thought he was God. Her case is complicated by the fact that her father was also a Nazi and her mother very possibly part Jewish. In the daughter the two strains marry and paralyse each other – she has to act out the awful little allegory before she is free of it.

Though the daughter identifies with the 'Jewish' mother, by the end of 'Daddy' she has become a phallic agressor herself, rejoicing as 'the villagers' drive a stake through the 'fat black heart' of the vampire father, cutting the black telephone off 'at the root', in an inescapable image of emasculation, so that 'The voices just can't worm through'. Cutting off the telephone means asserting independence from the voices of the past out of which the self has been shaped.

In that almost unnoticed progression from a single speaker to the collective image of the villagers, Plath gives a further twist to the revolt. She refuses the unitary self imposed by the parental images – a unity always splitting into two opposed principles, of male and female, active and passive, Nazi and Jew, etc. Instead, the self becomes almost what Freud spoke of as the 'brother clan' which overthrows the child-devouring primal father, replacing the single tyrant by a collectivity of equals. Freud never explained how the 'Electra complex', the female equivalent of this Oedipal revolt, lived out its particular rebellions: there is an inadequacy in explaining the specifics of female identity at the heart of his work. But for Plath, the two complexes are remarkably similar. For both Oedipus and Electra, it is the donated sexual identity, within the self, which has to be slain – the internalised image of authority around which the self congeals into separateness and unity.

In 'Daddy' she speaks of herself 'stuck . . . together with glue'. In the title poem of *The Colossus,* which predicts some of the imagery of this later poem, it is the father who is not 'put together entirely' in the daughter's memory, not 'Pieced, glued, and properly jointed', and she goes on to speak of him in terms which reinforce the sense of disintegrated, centreless being, shifting from the various animal noises that issue from his 'great lips', to his silted up throat, the 'weedy acres' of his brow, 'bald, white tumili' of his eyes, the 'cornucopia' of his left ear, across which whole colossal terrain she is engaged in salvage work that will never reclaim the whole, and never be able to see it in its totality.

The poem speaks not just of a particular relationship, with a father who died while Plath was still a child, but of the whole relationship between self and history, mediated through the institutions of a patriarchal society. This is revealed in the fourth stanza, which moves rapidly from the mythic origins of things in the *Oresteia* (where Electra finds herself by sharing in matricide with her brother Orestes) through Rome, to the anarchy of the present:

> A blue sky out of the Oresteia
> Arches above us. O father, all by yourself
> You are pithy and historical as the Roman Forum.
> I open my lunch on a hill of black cypress.
> Your fluted bones and acanthine hair are littered
>
> In their old anarchy to the horizon-line.
> It would take more than a lightning-stroke
> To create such a ruin.

The father as colossus is here both an external and an internalised history, symbolised by those horizons which are simultaneously out there and the internal limits of a consciousness which extends to the skyline. This is a world of *disjecta membra,* to which the self has never been able to give coherence and form because, in losing the paternal model too early, it has failed to reproduce within itself a simulacrum of the father's unitary being, failed to make its own that contradictory welter of relics. Hence: 'I shall never get you put together entirely' is the cry of anguish of a self whose 'hours are married to shadow', for whom the barnyard 'Mule-bray, pig-grunt and bawdy cackles' of the father's discordant voices seems almost 'an oracle, / Mouthpiece of the dead, or of some god or other', mysterious, vatic, but incomprehensible. The struggle to dredge the silt from the throat of the colossus is a struggle to hear clearly the voices of history, to discern what it is trying to say to her – a struggle which in 'Daddy' leads to the final destructive refusal of that past, the tearing-out of the telephone wires, that last rebellion of the historical being against its own historicity, a rebellion soon to issue in the only exit that remained open, an abandonment of the human world altogether, in suicide.

In section four of 'Poem for a Birthday', those voices of history out of which the self is constructed have fallen silent, as

Time itself seems to have come to a dead stop. Identity is seen as the marriage of some indefinable essential being to a residual detritus of language and events. But apocalypse itself is frozen into a perpetual, never completed, continuous present:

> I've married a cupboard of rubbish.
> I bed in a fish puddle.
> Down here the sky is always falling.
> Hogwallow's at the window.
> The star bugs won't leave me this month.
> I housekeep in Time's gut-end
> Among emmets and molluscs,
> Duchess of Nothing,
> Hairtusk's bride.

In the seventh section, this cupboard is no longer merely something external, which the self marries, but a place of return where the speaking self may be extinguished:

> . . . . I entered
> The stomach of indifference, the wordless cupboard.
>
> The mother of pestles diminished me.
> I became a still pebble.

Yet in this return, almost to the source of things, the voice retains its stubborn separate awareness, speaking of its need and displacement. The imagery here draws on that suicide attempt recorded in *The Bell Jar*. Once again, in this prelude to rebirth, she is all mouth; but this time the mouth is unequivocally a voice, piping out locations, before it is a hunger sucking at 'the paps of darkness' – a proclamation of identity found through loss before it is a nuzzling after succour. Right at the core of this struggle for renewal is the fact of language, for it is only in language that deprivation can be defined, only in language that, in the closing lines of the poem, 'The vase, reconstructed, houses / The elusive rose. / Ten fingers shape a bowl for shadows'. From being contained by the womb of language the self becomes in turn a container, gathering its shadow and voices into a provisional coherence.

In 'A Birthday Present' *(Ariel),* this is an ambiguous dowry and christening gift. Separate identity moves only in the perspective of death, for death is what sets limits and definition upon its separateness. The poem opens with a quizzing as to what this 'shimmering', 'unique' indefinable thing is at the edge of vision. But this thing in turn queries the identity of the questioner, whose face is inscribed with all the characteristics of a death's-head, and for whom death is the scar which guarantees its elect being:

> When I am quiet at my cooking I feel it looking, I feel it
> thinking
>
> 'Is this the one I am to appear for,
> Is this the elect one, the one with black eye-pits and a scar?
>
> Measuring the flour, cutting off the surplus,
> Adhering to rules, to rules, to rules.
>
> Is this the one for the annunciation? . . . .'

Self is in reality the union of the two, of the merely defined and the merely potential: its birthday present is the unwrapping of this equivocal union. Once again, it is to the idea of history that the poem turns for the terms of this union, and history immediately calls up the idea of language, as both script and voice:

> It stands at my window, big as the sky.
> It breathes from my sheets, the cold dead centre
>
> Where spilt lives congeal and stiffen to history.
> Let it not come by the mail, finger by finger.
>
> Let it not come by word of mouth. . . .

'History' is both the congealed, oppressive givenness of these 'spilt lives', and the fluid, unrealised possibilities of messages yet to be 'delivered' (in a double sense of the word which harks back to that earlier idea of annunciation). The doubleness is carried through into the final lines of the poem, in which an entry and a closure are simultaneously recorded. To enter is also to foreclose. To be anything at all is necessarily to reject all those other possibilities that gather in the moment of sheer latency. What finally agitates and anguishes the self in Plath's poetry is that greed for otherness that will not be satisfied till it has 'swallow[ed] it all', engulfed objective Time within its subjective and voracious craving.

Again and again in Plath's poetry the transactions between self and history are presented through topographical allegory. At times, as in 'The Colossus', the self is a frantic and diminished worker-ant scuttling about an enormous, anthropomorphised landscape. At others, as in 'Gulliver', it is the self which seems to be the reclining giant, prey to the 'spider-men' and 'inchworms' who have caught it in 'their petty fetters, / Their bribes'. It is they who 'converse in the valley of your fingers', and for them that, in the last line of the poem, 'The shadow of this lip' becomes 'an abyss'. The two allegories are not really contradictory. As for Eliot, so for Plath, the self is at one and the same time the absolute circumference of its experience and history, and a dwarfed and marginalised figure, clinging desperately on to a world that may at any minute abrogate its right to exist at all. From one point of view, then, the whole of history is internalised in the experience of the subject who takes total responsibility for it. From another point of view, the subject is a patient, a victim, a scapegoat even, helplessly transfixed at the receiving end of this history, unable to comprehend the massive forces that overwhelm it. The true ambiguity of the subject lies in the oscillation between the two.

The peculiar power of Plath's poetry lies in its constant shifting of imagistic ground. In 'Elm', for example, the self, ostensibly rooted in a secure, finite, determinate ego, 'break[s] into pieces that fly about like clubs', not only *agitated by* but *becoming* the 'Clouds that pass and disperse'. Fluidity and fixity contend in the imagery, and this contention is the very locus of being. The two penultimate stanzas of 'Elm' break out into a rash of heart-searching questions at the same moment that they affirm 'I am incapable of more knowledge', and the 'faces of love' turn into the petrifying, snake-strangled branches of a Medusa head, in a final image which combines all the poem's contraries of flux and rigidity.

'The Arrival of the Bee Box' analyses some of the contradictions caused by such volatility. It starts with an emphatic assertion of the commanding and disciplining ego: 'I ordered this, this clean wood box'; yet such enclosure and regulation are immediately associated with death, so that the box, in its unnatural, rectangular proportions, seems like 'the coffin of a midget / Or a square baby'. Like Pandora, she is drawn to this windowless mystery, fascinated and repelled; and it is clear that her suzerainty is less than absolute, for the box is not so much 'ordered' as assigned to her: 'I have to live with it overnight'. By the time she returns to the idea of authority, her mood sways mercurially between options:

How can I let them out?
It is the noise that appals me most of all,
It is like a Roman mob,
Small, taken one by one, but my god, together!

I lay my ear to furious Latin.
I am not a Caesar.
I have simply ordered a box of maniacs.
They can be sent back.
They can die, I need feed them nothing, I am the owner.

Yet again, such bravado rapidly fluctuates into an almost prurient solicitude, and then into rash, extravagant over-confidence, culminating in the wisely deferred but still presumptuous promise: 'Tomorrow I will be sweet God, I will set them free. / The box is only temporary'.

She has already conjectured about the consequences of this, in a sequence which moves from inquisitiveness to empathy. In the process, she speculatively reverses the relationship of container and contained:

I wonder how hungry they are.
I wonder if they would forget me

If I just undid the locks and stood back and turned into a
                                                            tree.
There is the laburnum, its blond colonnades,
And the petticoats of the cherry.

They might ignore me immediately
In my moon suit and funeral veil
I am no source of honey
So why should they turn on me?

Turning into a tree, she would retain her natural lines and
organic forms, as the imagery of 'blond colonnades' and
'petticoats' insists on a femininity which, on inspection,
remains vulnerable, its blossoms open to penetration. Turning
into a blossoming tree is the last thing to do if one wishes to
avoid their attention. Thus, a further transformation is
necessary for protection: not into the coquettishly inviting and
available petticoats, but the off-putting, desexualising 'moon
suit' of the bee keeper, fusing the sterile mother with the
inaccessible, hermetically insulated father. This imprisons the
volatile daughter completely within a rigid, cumbersome ego
which cuts her off from the world, placing her in purdah and
in mourning for a lost freedom. By the end of the poem, that
is, despite the final wishful identification with an omnipotent
male God, she has exchanged places, in imagination, with the
grotesque dead baby and the repressed proletarian din of the
opening lines. In this process, she has herself come to deny her
own creativity and freedom, as a 'source of honey'. Yet, if she
is turned on by the bees, it may be precisely because she has
fed them nothing, in her assumed superiority has starved them
of affection and opportunities.

The poem cannot conceal both the yearning and the fear
associated with releasing the bees. Significantly, it had spoken
of their unintelligible syllables and 'furious Latin', where
imperial order is fused with linguistic anarchy, or at least with
an order and meaning denied to the listener (given the
association of Latin with discipline, harmony and empire,
'furious Latin' is almost an oxymoron). The Roman dictator
dictates: his *word* is his command, and his *ordinance* orders
reality. But the poem suggests that the unconscious too is

structured like a language, though it cannot be read in terms of the vocabulary and syntax of the ego. The Latin of the mob is a *repressed* discourse, an argot that turns angry because it is denied expression.

In 'The Swarm'(*Winter Trees*), such a repression is seen to be both political and psychological, a social and a linguistic ordering of reality. The poem opens with an indeterminate image of violence ('Somebody is shooting at something in our town') which is not explained in the first stanza. Indeed that stanza ends with a query, 'Who are they shooting at?' – which places the *target* at the centre of our attention, rather than the *agent* of the shooting. The second stanza is an abrupt and unexplained shift into the dimension of history:

> It is you the knives are out for
> At Waterloo, Waterloo, Napoleon,
> The hump of Elba on your short back,
> And the snow, marshalling its brilliant cutlery
> Mass after mass, saying Shh!

A solitary and commanding individual, set against a threatening multitude: this is the opposition already encountered in the 'Bee Box'. This mass is neither vociferous nor silent, but, 'saying Shh!', is forever at the cross-over from speech to silence, from authority to obedience, commanding as it hushes, hushing as it commands. What the imagery has set up already, then, is a conflict of powers and allegiances.

It is only in the fourth stanza, after the gilded domes of Russia 'melt and float off' that the poem allows the 'swarm' of its title to appear, and repeat the process: 'So the swarm balls and deserts / Seventy feet up, in a black pine tree'. The shots are being fired at the beeswarm, in a traditional way of getting it to return to the hive. But the bees are not simply the swarming unconscious, subject to the cruel imperium of a Napoleonic ego. Insistently, the poem generalises its relevance: a whole political history is focused in the imagery of the bees. The 'honeycomb / Of their dream' is a 'hived station / Where trains, faithful to their steel arcs, / Leave and arrive, and there is no end to the country', calling up not only those later Napoleons, Lenin at the Finland Station and Mussolini who made the trains run on time, but a whole world organised around the norms of a clockwork, mechanically orchestrated production-process. The hive becomes 'Mother France . . . / . . . a new mausoleum, / An ivory palace, a crotch pine', in a shifting series of images which brings together motherhood, death, and a cruel, needling sexuality, all subordinate to 'The smile of a man of business, intensely practical' – the beekeeper Napoleon who has extracted his 'ton of honey' from Europe, from the 'black intractable mind' of the bees.

Language is a recurring metaphor for identity in Plath, and duplicity, doubleness is at the heart of both. Plath's language is always radically *overdetermined,* so that the same image can be charged with quite contradictory associations, conflicting emotional resonances. The bee, for example, stirs complex feelings. It is female, a source of honey and creativity; but it has a male sting ('Stings big as drawing pins!'); it is associated with the father (Otto Plath wrote a treatise called *Bumblebees and Their Ways*), but also with that dark, leonine queen at the core of the hive. In 'The Swarm' and 'The Arrival of the Bee Box' bees are on the one hand the collective 'black, intractable mind' of a genocidal Europe, on the other the 'swarmy' impulsions of the individual unconscious. This unconscious is in turn seen as a threatening and alien proletariat, 'the swarmy feeling of African hands / Minute and shrunk for export, / Black on black, angrily clambering', or 'a Roman mob'. Plath's narratives fork and proliferate in unexpected directions because, in unfolding the implications of a sequence of images, she uncovers the complex and contradictory possibilities condensed in them. This expresses her sense of the self, not as a hierarchically ordered pyramid, but as *an ensemble of possibilities,* a 'swarm' of images, in which none takes precedence for more than a moment, and to which only a provisional coherence can be given. The self is both a rigid, false persona and an amorphous congeries, like the almost fluid bee-swarm, undergoing constant metamorphosis, continually dying and reborn in the mutations of the imagery. The subliminal undertow of the unconscious perpetually draws the conscious self into uncharted depths of feeling, where primitive infantile traumas lie treacherously beneath the surface of articulate speech.

Plath's poems are, first and foremost, carefully constructed *texts*. If their meaning cannot be reduced to the conscious intentions of their author, it equally cannot be reduced to spirit-messages from the unconscious, over which the literary talent has no control. The full meaning of the text lies in the interplay of *all* its levels, *on the terrain of language*. These levels are not only personal (conscious and unconscious) but cultural and social, deriving from both a literary and linguistic tradition and a public and collective history.

Just as the poem, for Plath, derives from its linguistic and poetic antecedents, so the self too is a secretion of its inherited languages. In 'Childless Woman' it emerges at the intersection of many roads:

> My landscape is a hand with no lines,
> The roads bunched to a knot,
> The knot myself,
>
> Myself the rose you achieve. . . .

In 'Lady Lazarus', the rapid shifts of the imagery enact the doubleness of a self which is a solid 'opus', a 'valuable', the 'pure gold baby' of the collective patriarchy, and then, across an enjambement, 'melts to a shriek':

> I turn and burn.
> Do not think I underestimate your great concern.
>
> Ash, ash –
> You poke and stir.
> Flesh, bone, there is nothing there –
>
> A cake of soap,
> A wedding ring,
> A gold filling.

It would be wrong to see Plath's use of the imagery of the concentration camp simply as unacceptable hyperbole, in which a merely private anguish is inflated to the proportions of global atrocity. Rather, concerned that 'personal experience shouldn't be a kind of shut box and mirror-looking narcissistic experience', but 'should be generally relevant, to such things as Hiroshima and Dachau and so on', Plath has seen the deeper correspondences between the personal and the collective tragedies, their common origins in a civilisation founded on repression at the levels both of the body politic and of the carnal body. 'Mary's Song' uses a gruesome analogy to bring home this correspondence, linking, through the image of the 'Sunday lamb', the familiar and the monstrous. For if 'The Sunday lamb cracks in its fat. / Sacrifices its opacity . . .', this heart which renders the opaque translucent, 'A window, holy gold', is a brutal travesty of that 'incandescent' sacrifice in which the Paschal lamb died for man, and the homely domestic oven is transformed rapidly into the gas ovens of Nazi Germany, which in turn becomes a landscape burnt out by fire-bombing:

> The fire makes it precious.
> The same fire
>
> Melting the tallow heretics,
> Ousting the Jews.
> Their thick palls float
>
> Over the cicatrix of Poland, burnt-out
> Germany.
> They do not die.
>
> Grey birds obsess my heart . . .

The heart becomes, by the final lines, the 'holocaust I walk in, / O golden child the world will kill and eat'. The collective deaths have their origins here, in the burnings of the heart, the gall and heartburn of each individual being. The 'golden child' who is held precious will be murdered. The sacrifice, the poem insists, goes on in each heart, and for each heart. The 'cicatrix' that marks a whole people has its sources in those wounds out of which the bourgeois ego has been shaped, those scars which are also emblems of our freedom.

Plath is, in fact, a profoundly political poet, who has seen the generic nature of these private catastrophes, their origin in a civilisation founded on mass manipulation and collective trickery, which recruits its agents by those processes of repression and sublimation, denial and deferment which bring the ego to its belated birth in a family, a class, a gender. The heroine of *The Bell Jar* looks back, after almost a decade, to what is apparently merely a private mental breakdown and attempted suicide. Yet, though the novel never spells out any political significance, what obsesses Esther Greenwood is the event which figures largely and mysteriously in the opening paragraph of the book, and by times thereafter: the electrocution of the atom-spies, the Rosenbergs, and the Cold War revenge hysteria that surrounds it – a killing linked subliminally for Esther with the electric shock therapy she undergoes as treatment for her breakdown, but which she feels as punishment rather than as cure. In both cases, the self is connected to society through an electric, deadly umbilicus.

What Esther fears most of all is being consigned to the charity wards of the hospital, 'with hundreds of people like me, in a big cage in the basement. The more hopeless you were, the further away they hid you'. In a century which has shut away millions, in hospitals, concentration camps and graveyards, in which the self can be 'wiped out . . . like chalk on a blackboard' by administrative diktat, Plath sees a deep correspondence between the paternal concern of the psychiatrist and the authority of the modern state, and between both and the institutions of the family which are the principal agents of that state in creating a new generation of subjects.

Louis Althusser has spoken of that process of 'interpellation', or *calling*, by which the self is constructed as a *subject*, a being not only aware of itself but *subjected to* the authority of the family and the state. The very process in which the subject emerges to self-awareness is one in which, at the same time, it learns that it is the object of the gaze of others, and of that collective Other represented, in its earliest moments, by the mother. Becoming a subject means learning to internalise this other, making the alien gaze one's own, creating an internal distance between the self which acts and the self which judges. This distance is the wound, the gulf, where the subject both loses and finds itself, discovering, in Rimbaud's famous phrase, that 'I is another'. It is this 'difficult borning' that Plath records in 'Poem for a Birthday', whose crucial turning-point is the apparently authoritative command that concludes section three: 'Tell me my name'.

If, here, the self has learnt the imperative voice which endows it with autonomy, at the same time, what it orders reveals the merely secondary nature of this autonomy, restoring it at once to dependency. Though it knows it must have a name, to be free and separate, it knows too that its name is not self-appointed, but an *endowment:* at the very core of its integral being another voice has inserted itself, and holds sway. This 'calling' of the self to be that which it is, to assume its specific social, familial and sexual identity, is what Althusser means by 'interpellation'. In a sense, all Plath's poetry is preoccupied with the process, and with those repeated reinforcements in which the rigorously delimited ego reiterates its commitment to that lineament and lineage, repeats its allegiance to the otherness at its heart.

This is why Plath's poetry has been so powerfully and appropriately co-opted by the Women's Movement. For one of the key moments in interpellation is that point at which the child acquires a sexual identity, a set of 'gender roles', that transforms it into a coherent and sexed being, a boy or girl, and leaves behind the polymorphous narcissism of the baby. Painfully aware of the competing male and female inflexions in her personality, Plath continually returns to this 'mirror phase' in the child's early evolution – the point at which it perceives, in the mirror of the mother's eyes, and then in its own internalised mirror, the sexually specific identity it is expected to assume. Before this point, all is decentred and dispersed, a welter of images and options without a cohering focus. When Plath's poetry returns to the image of the mirror it returns too to the frontier of a realm where images spawn and proliferate and the unitary ego dissolves as, in 'The Couriers', she seeks 'A disturbance in mirrors, / The sea shattering its grey one'.

The Second Voice in the poem 'Three Women' (*Winter Trees*), losing her baby, becomes herself again, and this re-entry into selfhood is associated with images of loss, lack, being bled white, made 'flat and virginal', with 'Nothing that cannot be erased, ripped up and scrapped, begun again'. This re-beginning is something which the self perpetually performs, reinstating in the mirror that self as other we have learned to become, seeing ourselves in the third person:

> This woman who meets me in mirrors – she is neat.
>
> So neat she is transparent, like a spirit.
> How shyly she superimposes her neat self
> On the inferno of African oranges, the heel-hung pigs.
> She is deferring to reality.
> It is I. It is I –
> Tasting the bitterness between my teeth.
> The incalculable malice of the everyday.

Immediately before this, the Third Voice has given her definition of identity:

> I am a wound walking out of hospital.
> I am a wound that they are letting go.
> I leave my health behind. I leave someone
> Who would adhere to me: I undo her fingers like bandages:
> I go.

The three voices of the poem are themselves all inflexions of the one voice, departing into their separatenesses. Identity is a wound, a deferring, a superimposing (with all its resonances of authority and repression). It is, crucially, an *abandoning:* at its heart is the central experience of lack, a void that cannot be filled. As for the 'Insomniac' *(Crossing the Water):*

> His head is a little interior of grey mirrors.
> Each gesture flees immediately down an alley
> Of diminishing perspectives, and its significance
> Drains like water out the hole at the far end.
> He lives without privacy in a lidless room.

To live in the self is to live in history, to take responsibility for these 'Cold folds of ego' ('The Night Dances'). 'Letter in November' (*Ariel*) seems to come to terms with such a subjected historical being, patrolling an estate that becomes an emblem of the soul:

> This is my property.
> Two times a day
> I pace it, sniffing
> The barbarous holly with its viridian
> Scallops, pure iron,
>
> And the wall of old corpses.
> I love them.
> I love them like history.
> The apples are golden,
> Imagine it.

In 'Gerontion', Eliot had proclaimed his secession from history, delighting that:

> I was neither at the hot gates
> Nor fought in the warm rain
> Nor knee deep in the salt marsh, heaving a cutlass,
> Bitten by flies, fought.

'Letter in November' (the opposite of Eliot's 'dry month'), refuses such a renunciation, in words which unmistakably recollect Eliot's poem:

> O love, O celibate.
> Nobody but me
> Walks the waist-high wet.
> The irreplaceable
> Golds bleed and deepen, the mouths of Thermopylae.

Thermopylae ('the hot gates'), a battle in which a wall of Greek corpses held back the invading Persians for long enough to allow organised resistance, becomes an image of a resilient selfhood prepared to accept its historicity, its merely partial freedom. The 'waist-high wet' is the appropriate figure of such a world. It is a world that cannot be renounced except by that unpeeling, foaming to wheat, and suicidal melting 'Into the red / Eye, the cauldron of morning' which the title poem of *Ariel* contemplates. Whether one sees Plath's own suicide as a final surrender to history, or a revolt against it, is beside the point. The power of her poetry lies in its stubborn witness to the duplicitous nature and the ambiguous victories of such a war.

All survival is founded on innumerable deaths. What Plath records, not just with honesty but with a vivid and rare authenticity of language, is the price paid for such victories. That gulf in being which for Hardy, at the beginning of this century, had seemed to be a 'dark space' between self and other, has in her poetry been redefined as an internal gulf, where the self may easily drown in its own darkness. Her poetry reveals, that is, the coming to crisis of a dilemma that western culture has endlessly deferred. In the thirties, in the dual movement of Pound and the marxist poets, the bourgeois self had sought deliverance from its own historicity in submission to alien gods. In *After Strange Gods* (1934), as in his poetry, Eliot had called the tradition back to authentic self-abasement, before the one true God. But the end was the same: an escape from the unfreedom of particular being. In the post-war period, the tradition re-assembled and regrouped its forces, settling into a political and literary conventionality amidst which, in the writings of Gunn and Hughes in particular, the old disturbances still prowled unplacated.

As so often in the line I have tried to trace in this book, it is the outsider, the American expatriate half-assimilated to the English tradition, who registers its strains most forcefully. Even the vehemence with which, in *After Strange Gods,* the neophyte Eliot summons Hardy, Lawrence, Joyce and Yeats back to the fold of an invented 'orthodoxy' reveals this strain. Faced by the factitiousness of identity, Eliot reacts by assuming an almost parodic Englishness. Pound, in contrast, wrestles with the given self, as do Plath and Robert Lowell. The stubborn Americanness of their poetic personae, the edginess, the emotional brinkmanship, makes them particularly sensitive to the stresses within that tradition, which its homegrown products sought to avoid, shrinking back from the full challenge of Modernism. When Pound, in *Guide to Kulchur,* responds to something in Hardy which his English acolytes miss, when Plath turns to Hardy, or the Brontes, or even to Ted Hughes himself, for an imagery which speaks to her own extremity, when Robert Lowell in *History* (1973) casts a cold eye on a century of English culture, repeating, in the process, the critique Pound conducted in *Hugh Selwyn Mauberley,* they speak not as outsiders but as intimates, wickedly familiar with the tradition they survey, winkling out its flaws and weaknesses. At the centre of it is that divorce of the self from its history which, in the end, merely deepens its complicity. In different ways, in their struggle to overcome this distance, they reveal its origins in the very structure of the self. The self of Plath's poem 'Winter Trees' is 'Full of wings, otherworldliness'. But it knows, too, that it is rooted in a particular and compromised history. Its memories have grown, ring on ring, in a 'series of weddings' between inner and outer in which its particular identity was confirmed. In the end, there is no alternative to being 'Waist-deep in history', and no ease from this burden.

10

A Moment of Danger

'History', says Robert Lowell, in the title poem of his last, major sequence, 'has to live with what was here':

> clutching and close to fumbling what we had –
> it is so dull and gruesome how we die,
> unlike writing, life never finishes.

History itself was a reworking of 'what was here', of the poems and experiences recorded in that earlier sequence, *Notebook* (1969, 1970). There, he had spoken of a more elusive, intangible concept:

> . . . . I am learning to live in history.
> What is history? What you cannot touch.

What has closed the gap for this patrician soul, in those few years, is the nightmare of Vietnam, which haunts all of these poems, casting its shadow over even the most innocent of personal reminiscences. For the speaker of these poems has realised both his incompetence, morally and socially, and his responsibility. He has taken up the burden of the mystery. Past complacencies are here reworded in the discovery of old obsessions, new significances, as Lowell relives in these last poems, with a new and bitter irony, not just lines, motifs and episodes from his earlier work, but key moments in the whole past history of western culture, back to its beginnings, beyond Rome and Greece and Israel. 'Plotted', in *The Dolphin* (1973), takes up the time-worn figure of Hamlet, not like Prufrock, in mock-modest disclaimer, but as a representative actor-victim of history's plots:

I too manoeuvred on a guiding string
as I execute my written plot.
I feel how Hamlet, stuck with the Revenge Play
his father wrote him . . .
. . . declaimed the words his prompter fed him,
knowing convention called him forth to murder,
loss of free will and license of the stage,
Death's not an event in life, it's not lived through.

The plot is written already: it simply needs to be 'executed', and the chilling *double entendre* of that word catches the irony of Hamlet's unwanted vocation, called to administer 'justice' by the whole outmoded convention of the Revenge Play within which he comes to separate identity. He has been donated, by the past, a part which he does not feel is really his. This is not what he meant at all, yet he has no option but to follow through the absurd logic of the situation. He is already a posthumous man. And all the time there is the 'real' life he imagines for himself, the life he could have led if he had not been placed here, in this superannuated farce.

Rewriting an already written-off and rewritten 'history' in *History*, Lowell demonstrates just how much we too, as readers of the past, are at the mercy of *writing*. For the 'history' we assume as a given is merely that which has been recorded, preserved, transmitted. 'What was here', like the secretive events of Lowell's previous poems, is sifted and re-sifted, arranged and re-arranged in new sequences by the backward-looking mind, in a process which can never be complete because 'unlike writing, life never finishes'. Overlaying personal life, Greek, Roman and Hebrew history, the history and prehistory of the planet, and contemporary events in modern America, Asia, Europe, as if they were all synchronous in the 'history' of the poem, Lowell takes a quite different line from Eliot in 'Tradition and the Individual Talent'. Plotted together, these interwoven stories indicate just how much our sense of the past, and therefore our present, is a matter of jumbled and discordant discourses, counterpointed, condensed, excerpted, fused, juxtaposed or dispersed in the chronicles of time. 'Abel was finished; death is not remote', he tells us in the title poem, and then adds, 'As in our Bibles . . . / the . . . hunter's moon ascends – a child could give it a face'. The interpretative act, making all these connections, is like the child's invention of the man in the moon. But this invented face then takes on a horrifying personal dimension. The face is the poet's, a death's head staring out from the text which will outlive the unfinished life:

> . . . two holes, two holes,
> my eyes, my mouth, between them a skull's no-nose –
> O there's a terrifying innocence in my face
> drenched with the silver salvage of the mornfrost.

A later sonnet, 'Sheep', calling on us to remember the anonymous generations stretching back to the origin of things, like us 'afraid of violence, / afraid of anything, timid as sheep', reverts to this grinning *memento mori,* in the image of the Sphinx. As numberless as the sands of the desert, their collective labours survive only as the Sphinx – monolithic testimony to the multitude of vanished acts from which 'history', the surviving record, is an abstraction:

> what were once identities simplified
> to a single, indignant, collusive grin.

The collusion of which Lowell speaks here and throughout the volume is not just that of the artist but of every individual with the past that made him or her, which he or she chooses to accept. Walter Benjamin, writing at a moment of danger in his own life, described it in his *Theses on the Philosophy of History* as a recurring choice, present in every life, and in every work of art:

To articulate the past historically does not mean to recognise it 'the way it really was' (Ranke). It means to seize hold of a memory as it flashes up at a moment of danger. Historical materialism wishes to retain that image of the past which unexpectedly appears to a man singled out by history at a moment of danger. The danger affects both the content of the tradition and its receivers. The same threat hangs over both: that of becoming a tool of the ruling classes. In every era the attempt must be made to wrest tradition away from a conformism that is about to overpower it. . . . Only that historian will have the gift of fanning the spark of hope in the past who is firmly convinced that *even the dead* will not be safe from the enemy if he wins. . . .

This is not a specifically 'marxist' task, though 'historical materialism', as Benjamin defines it, is a powerful weapon in such a struggle. Indeed, in a recent interview in the *New Statesman* ('Under Judgment', 8 February 1980), Geoffrey Hill, a poet whose work is unequivocally committed to the recovery of history, identified his own case with what he called the tradition of 'Radical Toryism'. Hill denied suggestions that his poetry plays off the present against a richer past, and indulges in 'nostalgia' and 'melancholy'. Instead, he says, he is concerned with 'those processes of the past which were the original betrayals either in "the governance of England" or in the governance of Empire, the consequences of which we are reaping'. Any loss, nostalgia or melancholy in the poems arises from 'an attempt to depict lyrically the consequences of old betrayals'. He continues:

I am moved to anger by the notorious statement 'History is bunk', and I am moved to agreement by a slightly less well-known statement which suggests that those who do not understand history are condemned to re-live it. I think that it is a tragedy for a nation or a people to lose the sense of history, not because I think that the people is thereby necessarily losing some mystical private possession, but because I think that it is losing some vital dimension of intelligence. I'm entirely in sympathy with those who would argue that in order to control the present one needs to be steeped in the past. I think my sense of history is in itself anything but nostalgic, but I accept nostalgia as part of the *psychological* experience of a society and of an ancient and troubled nation.

A struggle of sorts is being waged across these very protestations, disclosed, for example, in that language of betrayal which calls up Pound, and in that insistence upon an ancient and troubled nationhood, with its echoes of Hardy,

Edward Thomas and Eliot, set against the 'progressive' rhetoric of controlling the present, with its echoes of the thirties.

Hill's terms are almost those of Eliot, yet they are subtly and substantially different in their account of tradition. For Hill speaks of a two-way transaction, in which our senses both of poetry and history are extended, as part of a larger struggle for self-comprehension. 'The poet's gift', says Hill, 'is to make history and politics and religion speak for themselves through the strata of language'. In his *Mercian Hymns* (1971), the obscurer regions of Anglo-Saxon history are probed by investigating that subsoil where past and present coexist, where the Saxon King Offa points in the direction both of myth ('King of the perennial holly-groves') and past and present history, 'architect of the historic rampart and ditch' but also 'overlord of the M5'. For the past is everywhere present in its effects, shaping the culture as it shapes the landscape. These poems, like Thomas's 'Digging', like the *Cantos,* use the archaeological motif to suggest 'Not strangeness, but strange likeness' between our 'Obstinate, outclassed forefathers' and their 'staggeringly-gifted' children (XXIX).

In *King Log* (1968) he had attempted the same thing for some of the casualties of the Wars of the Roses, barely-remembered victims of obscure defeats, whose deaths, nevertheless, were part of the compost of a unitary English nation. The last poem of the sequence, 'Funeral Music', speaks of these obscure dead 'Not as we are but as we must appear, / Contractual ghosts of pity' in the memory of the present, 'bear[ing] witness, / Despite ourselves, to what is beyond us'. Yet the poem ends on a decidedly modern note, speaking of that *interruption* of life, that breaking short of the plot of a personal history, which is the characteristic encounter, in a moment of danger, between the private self and its public realm:

> . . . . Then tell me, love,
> How that should comfort us – or anyone
> Dragged half-unnerved out of this worldly place,
> Crying to the end 'I have not finished'.

What Hill's individuals recurrently discover is the knowledge that — in another overlay of historical moments – comes to 'Ovid in the Third Reich':

>   . . . . God
> Is distant, difficult. Things happen.
> Too near the ancient troughs of blood
> Innocence is no earthly weapon.
>
> I have learned one thing: not to look down
> So much upon the damned. . . .

Christopher Middleton has spoken of this 'historical sense' as arising from a recognition of the ubiquity and seamlessness of the historical process – 'history as something happening in me and you and all around us all the time'. The poet must be sensitive to 'the pulse of an existence which is lived consciously in a state not only of personal crisis but also a sense of being involved in a social crisis'. Many of his poems are concerned with those larger moments of danger in which the ostensibly private self is ripped out of its dream of security, restored to its fragile mortality in the real nightmare of history. The figures of his poetry are repeatedly caught unawares, at some moment of vulnerability and unpreparedness, by a history that will not be kept waiting. 'Five Psalms of Common Man' (*Torse 3*) speaks of an order in which the 'ordinary' is repeatedly interrupted, and 'The nights of past time never slept to the end / re-enact themselves in the existing order of fear'. History is a succession of catastrophes, announced by 'the stranger at the door, who did not knock' ('The King of the Chaldees'). In 'The Arrest of Pastor Paul Schneider' (*Our Flowers*) the holy plotter against the Nazis is dragged from a dream of arrest to its actuality. In 'January 1919' (*Nonsequences*) the German socialist Liebknecht, dreamer of revolution, is woken to its actuality – death – his 'holed head' torn out of context to be displayed 'bleeding across a heap of progressive magazines'. 'Pavlovic Variations' (*Our Flowers*) turns Stalin's camps, without glibness, into a universal symbol of twentieth-century history, uprooting men and women from their own proper lives to a dream of deportation and massacre, 'figures torn from a fog'.

But for Middleton, the 'moment of danger' is not confined to such extreme situations. It is there in every minute of ordinary, everyday life. In 'Idiocy of Rural Life (Variant 2)', *(Lonely Suppers)* he considers the gas ovens at Treblinka as possible repositories of his own 'eclipsed / Future', in an attempt to think himself back into the experience of their actual victims. To be alive and merely reading about such atrocities is to expose the self to danger, to the corruptions of an apparently innocent act, reading when so many are dead; so that, placing the book down on the table, 'in terror', he has to 'fight now / For the thought: bush, table, / Oblong, what can they mean?' Such an experience calls into question the language and terms of everyday life itself. Nothing has an absolute meaning; everything has to be re-assessed in the light of history. Much of Middleton's poetry is in fact a sombre meditation on the commodities which constitute our daily life, which we take so much for granted, as isolated objects, things we possess. But like Hardy, in 'During Wind and Rain', he grasps the long labour that has gone into making, winning and holding them. In 'Mérindol Interior 1970' *(Lonely Suppers)* the 'bringer of news', bursting from beyond the cosy domesticity of personal life with news of the Vietnam war,

> Darkens all that is done for us – on crusts of blood
> Torn from the back of the world we spread our butter.

These domestic interiors are sustained by the violations that go on, ostensibly 'out there', in that external world, where the real price has to be paid, by other people, for our life-styles. In his interrogation of commodities, and of works of art which have the status of commodities, Middleton exposes the larger contradictions of that cultural tradition which Benjamin urged us in 1940 to contemplate with horror, for 'There is no document of civilisation which is not at the same time a document of barbarism.'

In different ways, all the poets considered here have attempted this difficult act, have cross-examined the culture of which they are bearers, not just as artists, but in the very foundations of their identity. They have reached different conclusions: have given up, defeated, or gone on to denunciations by turn hysterical, plaintive or self-justifying, or to celebrations more damning than any critique. At the core of this confrontation with history lies a crucial recognition, at times only half guessed-at, at times exposed with all the ferocity of an outraged innocence: the fact of *complicity*. The inviolable voice of the poet is stung into song by the very violations history imposes upon it. It is itself the trace, the scar left by that violation, as Philomel's song can do no more than name the aggressor who made such song necessary.

Yet one must stress, too, the positive side of this. For to acknowledge complicity is the beginning of grace. The English tradition has been one in which, again and again, guilt has struggled with complacency, a strenuous conscience with the casual distractions of a self-satisfied indolence. If it has not been in the forefront of the struggle, English poetry in this century has nevertheless returned to that moment of danger where it is weighed in the balance. In this trepidation, as well as in its unsureness, it has repeatedly found itself at that moment of choice of which Middleton speaks in his prose-poem in *Our Flowers*, 'The Historian'.

Procopius, the 'hero' of this poem, is the official historian of the reign of Justinian (Pound's law-giving Byzantine emperor). For Procopius, however, Justinian is merely another tyrant, whom he has 'served' so that he can truly serve a higher master, historical truth. All the time that he has been writing his 'official' *Histories* he has been buying time to write his *Secret History* of the age, which reveals its true, vicious contours. 'Things might not be so bad if I did not always have to write in a hurry', he remarks, fantasising on the ideal conditions in which a historian should work. But of course he is not an abstract observer and recorder of events; he is also a participant, an accomplice, by his canny silence, in the atrocities he records, in which 'They uproot entire populations, weeping children, the tenderness of old women, . . . and march them at planting-time from their villages into faraway camps of special huts where there is nothing to do but die. . . . In the name of the laws. For the acquisition and storage of riches. For the few and no questions'.

Procopius in a sense recognises this, noting 'How two-faced

one is, especially when facing oneself'. Yet, locked in the conviction that, somehow, his *Secret History* can redeem the public histories he has had to accede in and falsify, that by telling the truth he can rescue the past – his present – from total abandonment, he persists in his task. The poem leaves him forever caught in the act, interrupted in the writing of his 'secret history' by the agents of that larger, external history, who will not wait for him to put the full-stop to his period. The poem enacts the whole dilemma of art in our times. History itself cuts short the historian: arrested (in both senses) in mid-sentence, Procopius is seized at the very moment he grasps the truth of Marx's famous thesis on Feuerbach: that interpreting the world is less important than changing it, and that the witness is always potentially the victim. This is the moment in which we all live, as writers and readers, but also as participants in a history whose voice will not be stilled, whose urgency bears down like the sea on our own lives – here, in the luminous instant, the everyday moment of danger:

> It is still mysterious here, still real, here in this room of mine. They are still clattering about down there in the street. Tomorrow the blue dust will go on rising, the new towers along the sea-shore too, built there to shove back the sea which licks at their palaces. The thought still bothers me, that, instead of writing, I might have changed the

Bibliography

This is not a comprehensive bibliography, but cites only those works substantially considered in the text. Where possible, I have cited the most inclusive or available edition of the works involved, rather than separate first editions (the dates of which are indicated in the text). For a more comprehensive bibliography of the poets discussed here, readers should consult my volume in the Macmillan Great Writers Student Library, *Twentieth-Century Poetry* (1981), or James Vinson (ed.), *Contemporary Poets,* Macmillan 1980.

Auden, W. H., *The Ascent of F6 and On the Frontier* (with C. Isherwood), London: Faber and Faber 1958

Auden, W. H., *Collected Poems,* ed. Edward Mendelson, London: Faber and Faber 1976 (contains the final texts of short and longer poems, and forewords)

Auden, W. H., *The Dog Beneath the Skin* (with C. Isherwood), London: Faber and Faber 1968

Auden, W. H., *The Dyer's Hand and Other Essays,* London: Faber and Faber 1975

Auden, W. H., *The English Auden: Poems, Essays and Dramatic Writings 1927-39,* ed. Edward Mendelson, London: Faber and Faber 1977 (contains the earlier versions and suppressed texts of poems from the thirties)

Auden, W. H., *Letters from Iceland* (with Louis MacNeice), London: Faber and Faber 1937

Benjamin, Walter, *Illuminations,* ed. Hannah Arendt, London: Fontana Books 1973

Cornford, John, *Understand the Weapon, Understand the Wound,* ed. John Galassi, Manchester: Carcanet New Press 1976

Davie, Donald, *Collected Poems 1950-70,* London: Routledge and Kegan Paul 1972

Day Lewis, C., *A Time to Dance, Noah and the Waters and Other Poems,* London: Hogarth Press 1936

Eliot, T. S., *After Strange Gods,* London: Faber and Faber 1934

Eliot, T. S., *Collected Poems: 1909-1962.* London: Faber and Faber 1963

Eliot, T. S., *The Complete Plays,* London: Faber and Faber 1969

Eliot, T. S., *For Lancelot Andrewes: Essays on Style and Order,* London: Faber 1928

Eliot, T. S., *The Idea of a Christian Society,* London: Faber and Faber 1939

Eliot, T. S., *Knowledge and Experience in the Philosophy of F. H. Bradley,* London: Faber and Faber 1964

Eliot, T. S., *On Poetry and Poets,* London: Faber and Faber 1957

Eliot, T. S., *The Sacred Wood: Essays on Poetry and Criticism,* London: Methuen 1960

Eliot, T. S., *Selected Essays,* London: Faber and Faber 1972

Eliot, T. S., *To Criticise the Critic and Other Writings,* London: Faber and Faber 1965

Eliot, T. S., *The Use of Poetry and the Use of Criticism,* London: Faber and Faber 1964

Eliot, T. S., *The Waste Land: A Facsimile and Transcript of the Original Drafts,* ed. Valerie Eliot, London: Faber and Faber 1971

Enright, D. J., *Daughters of Earth.* London: Chatto and Windus 1972

Enright, D. J., *A Faust Book,* London: Oxford University Press 1979

Enright, D. J., *Sad Ires and others,* London: Chatto and Windus 1975

Enright, D. J., *Some Men are Brothers,* London: Chatto and Windus 1960

Enright, D. J., *Unlawful Assembly,* London: Chatto and Windus 1968

Gunn, Thom, *Moly,* London: Faber and Faber 1971

Gunn, Thom, *My Sad Captains,* London: Faber and Faber 1961

Gunn, Thom, *The Sense of Movement,* London: Faber and Faber 1957

Gunn, Thom, *Touch,* London: Faber and Faber 1967

Hardy, Thomas, *The Complete Poems,* ed. James Gibson, London: Macmillan 1978

Hardy, Thomas, *The Dynasts: An Epic-Drama of the War with Napoleon,* London: Macmillan 1924

Hardy, Florence Emily, *The Life of Thomas Hardy, 1840-1928,* London: Macmillan 1962 (this incorporates in one volume *The Early Life* and *The Later Years.*)

Heaney, Seamus, *Death of a Naturalist,* London, Faber and Faber 1966

Heaney, Seamus, *North,* London: Faber and Faber 1975

Hill, Geoffrey, *King Log,* London: Andre Deutsch 1968

Hill, Geoffrey, *Mercian Hymns,* London: Andre Deutsch 1971

Housman, A. E., *Collected Poems,* ed. John Carter, London: Jonathan Cape 1939

Hughes, Ted, *Crow: From the Life and Songs of the Crow,* London: Faber and Faber 1972

Hughes, Ted, *Gaudete,* London: Faber and Faber 1977

Hughes, Ted, *The Hawk in the Rain,* London: Faber and Faber 1957

Hughes, Ted, *Lupercal,* London: Faber and Faber 1960

Hughes, Ted, *Moortown,* London: Faber and Faber 1979

Hughes, Ted, *Wodwo,* London: Faber and Faber 1967

Larkin, Philip, *High Windows,* London: Faber and Faber 1974

Larkin, Philip, *The Less Deceived,* Hessle, Yorks.: Marvell Press 1955

Larkin, Philip, *The Whitsun Weddings,* London: Faber and Faber 1964

Lowell, Robert, *The Dolphin,* London: Faber and Faber 1973

Lowell, Robert, *History,* London: Faber and Faber 1973

Lowell, Robert, *Notebook,* London: Faber and Faber 1970

Lukács, Georg, *History and Class Consciousness,* London: Merlin Press 1971

Mahon, Derek, *Poems 1962-78,* London: Oxford University Press 1979

Marcuse, Herbert, *One Dimensional Man,* London: Sphere Books 1968

Middleton, Christopher, *The Lonely Suppers of W. V. Balloon,* Cheadle: Carcanet 1975

Middleton, Christopher, interviewed by Ian Hamilton *London Magazine,* IV, 6 (November 1964)

Middleton, Christopher, *Nonsequences: Selfpoems,* London: Longman 1965

Middleton, Christopher, *Our Flowers and Nice Bones,* London: Fulcrum Press 1969

Middleton, Christopher, *Torse 3: Poems 1949-61,* London: Longman 1962

Patten, Brian, *Grave Gossip,* London: Allen and Unwin 1979

Patten, Brian, *The Irrelevant Song,* London: Allen and Unwin 1971

Plath, Sylvia, *Ariel,* London: Faber and Faber 1965

Plath, Sylvia, *The Bell Jar,* London: Faber and Faber 1966

Plath, Sylvia, *The Colossus,* London: Faber and Faber 1972

Plath, Sylvia, *Crossing the Water,* London: Faber and Faber 1975

Plath, Sylvia, *Winter Trees,* London: Faber and Faber 1975

Pound, Ezra, *The Cantos,* London: Faber and Faber 1975

Pound, Ezra, *Collected Shorter Poems,* London: Faber and Faber 1968

Pound, Ezra, *Gaudier-Brzeska: A Memoir,* New York: New Directions 1974

Pound, Ezra, *Guide to Kulchur,* London: Peter Owen 1952

Pound, Ezra, *Jefferson and/or Mussolini,* London: Stanley Nott 1935

Pound, Ezra, *Literary Essays of Ezra Pound,* ed. and introduced by T. S. Eliot, London: Faber and Faber 1960

Pound, Ezra, *Selected Prose, 1909-1965,* ed. and introduced by William Cookson, London: Faber and Faber 1978

Roberts, Michael, *Selected Poems and Prose,* ed. and introduced by Frederick Grubb, Manchester: Carcanet New Press 1980

Spender, Stephen, *The Destructive Element: A Study of Modern Writers and Beliefs,* London: Cape 1935

Spender, Stephen, *Poems,* London: Faber and Faber 1933

Spender, Stephen, *The Still Centre,* London: Faber and Faber 1939

Spender, Stephen, *The Thirties and After: Poetry, Politics, People (1933-75),* London: Macmillan 1978

Spender, Stephen, *Trial of a Judge,* London: Faber and Faber 1938

Spender, Stephen, *World Within World: The Autobiography of Stephen Spender,* London: Hamish Hamilton 1961

Tate, Allen (ed.), *T. S. Eliot: The Man and His Work,* London: Chatto and Windus 1967

Thomas, Edward, *The Collected Poems,* ed. and introduced by R. George Thomas, Oxford: The Clarendon Press 1978

Thomas, Edward, *The Happy-Go-Lucky Morgans,* London: Duckworth 1913

Thomas, Edward, *The Heart of England,* London: J. M. Dent 1906

Thomas, Edward, *Lafcadio Hearn,* London: Constable 1912

Thomas, Edward, *Rose Acre Papers,* London: S. C. Brown, Langham and Co. 1904

Thomas, Edward, *The South Country,* London: J. M. Dent 1909

Thomas, R. S., *An Acre of Land,* Newtown: Montgomeryshire Printing Co. 1952

Thomas, R. S., *Song at the Year's Turning: Poems 1942-54,* London: Hart Davis 1955

Tomlinson, Charles, *Selected Poems 1951-74,* London: Oxford University Press 1978

Warren, Robert Penn, *Brother to Dragons: A Tale in Verse and Voices,* London: Eyre and Spottiswoode 1954

Index